The Black Carib Wars

The Black Carib Wars

Freedom, Survival and the Making of the Garifuna

Christopher Taylor

Signal

Signal Books, Oxford

First Published in 2012 by
Signal Books Ltd
36 Minster Road
Oxford
OX4 1LY
www.signalbooks.co.uk

A catalogue record for this book is available from the British Library.

ISBN 978-1-908493-04-0 Paper

Production: Samantha Halstead
Cover Design: Daisy Leitch, Barry Ainslie
Cover Illustrations: from Bryan Edwards, *The History, Civil and Commercial, of the British Colonies in the West Indies*, courtesy of The British Museum
Illustrations: courtesy The British Museum
Maps: Paul Taylor
Printed in India

Contents

For my mother, Kathleen Taylor

Acknowledgements

First and foremost I would like to thank all the members of the delegation, organized by the Garifuna Coalition Inc and led by its president, José Francisco Avila, who visited St. Vincent in July 2009 and who so generously allowed me to share the experience of their return to Youroumaÿn. In particular, I'm grateful to Carlos Gamboa and Angel Guity Fernández for several illuminating and thought-provoking conversations about Garifuna life and history.

Also in St. Vincent I would like to thank Vanessa Demircyan, for sharing her interest in contemporary Caribs there and for pointing me towards some French sources, to David Fergusson for steering me in the direction of some interesting items in the Vincentian archives, and to Edwin Johnson, a champion of St. Vincent's Carib heritage, for his views on the history of Greiggs and for accompanying me to the summit of the Soufrière.

I am very grateful to Professor Peter Hulme of the University of Essex for kindly agreeing to read an earlier draft of this manuscript. His comments and suggestions for further research were much appreciated. Any errors of fact or follies of interpretation are, of course, my own.

Thanks to James Ferguson of Signal Books for all his work in getting this book into print and for lending me his copy of Sir William Young's An Account of the Black Caribs of St Vincent—I may be in a position to return it soon.

Finally, I would like to thank my wife, Deena, for everything, and for introducing me to Andy Palacio's Wátina.

Introduction

THE SUN PEEKED timidly through the clouds above Dorsetshire Hill as the last flourish of the Vincentian national anthem lingered on the steel pan. The schoolchildren fidgeted through the brief speeches which the eye of the television camera dutifully recorded. Then came a sound, a tune vaguely familiar, but sung in a language few present could understand. It had been heard in St. Vincent the previous day in Kingstown's Catholic cathedral and now the sixteen-strong delegation, returning from exile, were once again singing the Lord's Prayer in Garifuna, a language known on this island long before people speaking English, French or Spanish cast covetous eyes upon it. As they sang the Garifuna women rocked back and forth, bending low in unison in a simple dance that had the force of generations behind it, recalling both an African and an Amerindian past. A wreath was laid at the foot of the simple obelisk commemorating the Black Carib resistance leader Chatoyer—officially the Right Excellent Joseph Chatoyer, First National Hero of St. Vincent—and, as the hand drummers beat the retreat, the rain swept in once again to bring the ceremony to a hurried end.

The members of the Garifuna delegation—men and women, young and old—were completing an emotional return to a long-lost homeland more than 200 years after their ancestors were forced into exile. They had come from New York, scene of a second, voluntary, displacement; all were originally from Honduras or elsewhere along the Caribbean coast of Central America. Brimming with emotion, they had burst into song on arrival at the airport terminal building. For some of the Vincentians they met, the veneration the exiles felt for this small island towards the bottom of the Windward chain was fascinating, inspiring but also slightly puzzling, like being informed that they were already actually living in the promised land. For most people in the West Indies their idea of an ancestral homeland is usually somewhere else.

My interest in the story of the Garifuna people began about twenty years ago in Nicaragua. In the village of Orinoco on Nicaragua's remote (from Managua) Atlantic Coast I watched a baseball match and heard in outline the story of the people's origin in a shipwreck and a war on the island of St. Vincent. I visited the north coast of Honduras and, on a voyage from the village of Nueva Armenia, experienced first-hand the fabled excellence of Garifuna seamanship. It was only years later, on hearing an album by a Garifuna musician from Belize, with its lyrics in the Garifuna language and evident pride in Garifuna culture, that I began to wonder what the real history behind the music was.

The Garifuna story is unique. While the history of all but the most recently arrived black populations of the Americas passes through the experience of slavery, Garifuna people take pride in their past as a free people living for generations according to their own customs on St. Vincent. Their language, passed down from the Amerindian side of their heritage, bears living witness to their radically different history. In colonial times they were known to antagonists and allies alike as Black Caribs, a name which encapsulates their mixed African/Amerindian heritage, and their story—from their traditional origin in a shipwreck, to their battles against the French and British, to their final, cataclysmic struggle to retain their independence at the end of the eighteenth century—is the subject of this book.

The Black Caribs lived on the island of St. Vincent in the seventeenth and eighteenth centuries. They resisted the designs of European colonizers for generations after the native people of other Caribbean islands had succumbed to white conquerors. After Britain was awarded St. Vincent by treaty (with the French, not the Caribs) in 1763 the struggle to maintain their independence intensified. The Black Caribs fought the British army to a standstill in a gruelling six-month war in the early 1770s, rose again at the end of the decade to help the French oust the British, and, after the island had again been returned to their antagonists by treaty between the two European powers, waged one final struggle to kick the British out. Led by Chatoyer they came within an ace of succeeding, but at the decisive moment their leader fell in battle and the tide of the war turned. The Black Caribs fought on for another year before, abandoned by their French allies, they were starved into submission.

Countless Caribs were killed in the struggle, after which the desperate and famished survivors of the war were interned on a waterless islet where half their number died. Finally, in March 1797 the remnants of the Black Carib nation—barely two thousand men, women and children—were transported in British ships 1,700 miles away to the northwest where they were deposited on the Spanish-controlled island of Roatán off the coast of Honduras.

The defeat and deportation of the Black Caribs marked the effective end not just of their presence on St. Vincent but of an entire way of life in the islands of the Caribbean. By the time of their climactic struggle against the British Empire the native populations of Cuba, Jamaica and the rest of the Greater Antilles were long since dead, the victims of warfare and disease. Elsewhere in the Caribbean only a few families held on at the margins of the new colonial societies. St. Vincent was the site of the last battle of people living a traditional lifestyle against the European colonialists anywhere in the islands. It was here that the Caribbean saw its Little Big Horn and its Wounded Knee.

The mountains and the wind shaped the stage upon which the tragedy was played out. The centre of St. Vincent is a volcanic massif through which even today no roads pass. The Caribs were the only ones who knew the secrets of the mountain passes and the tracks through their densely wooded slopes. Settlement, whether Carib or European, was and is concentrated around the coast where the few tracts of relatively flat land lie. The key division of the island is between windward and leeward—essentially east and west. The trade winds blow steadily from the east and send the waves crashing against the rocky headlands of the exposed coast. It was on the sheltered, leeward shore that the sailing ships of the Europeans could find anchorages and where they gained their first footholds on the island. It was to the rugged windward where Africans fleeing slavery on the island of Barbados could drift on the current towards freedom. It was here that the Black Caribs made their home, raised their families and where they made their last stand, because it was also the place which British planters believed was best-suited to growing sugar for export and which they were determined to possess.

St. Vincent's rainy season runs roughly from June to December but the clouds that form around the lowering four-thousand-foot Soufriere volcano which dominates the topography of the island mean rain is common even during the dry season. Temperatures are high year-round. The white colonizers frequently complained of the unhealthiness of the climate but the Black Caribs found it ideal. Fishing in the streams and the sea, as well as hunting in the woods and the provisions they grew in little garden plots furnished them with an abundance of food. "The spontaneous productions of the Earth, in this Country, are so many, and so adapted to the subsistence of Man, that the Wants of Nature are easily supplied; and a Charaib is easily satisfied, with respect to his food," wrote one British governor of the island, with a hint of disapproval.[1] They lived life at their own pace, in harmony with their environment, and enjoyed nothing better than sharing a drink or several in each other's company.

The Black Caribs left next to no written records. Apart from a letter signed by various Carib chiefs to the French governor of Martinique and a proclamation in Chatoyer's name, no documents in the Caribs' own words exist and absolutely none in their own tongue, which was not a written language at the time. So their history in St. Vincent must be pieced together from English and French sources, often openly hostile to the Black Caribs.

Even the name Carib is something bestowed on them by outsiders. According to the first European to extensively document their culture and language, a French missionary called Raymond Breton, the Caribs called themselves Kalliponam in the form of their speech used by women and Kallinago in the men's speech (compare Garinagu, the plural form of Garifuna in the modern language). The name Carib (caribe) was first recorded by Christopher Columbus and this word, or variants of it (caniba, caraïbe, charaib, kalina, etc), was adopted by other European languages. One suggested derivation of Carib is that it means brave warrior and this would suggest that Caribs were essentially defined by their armed opposition to European expansion in their region.[2] When Daniel Defoe came to write *Robinson Crusoe* it was bloodthirsty Caribs who struck fear into the castaway on his Caribbean island (although even in Defoe's story it is the Caribs who do most of the dying).

Things become more confusing when Europeans attempt to describe the presence of an African-descended population on St. Vincent. Many eighteenth-century accounts in English speak of Black Caribs and Yellow or Red Caribs, representing two populations with a similar culture but differentiated by their colour. But other sources refer to Negroes and Indians or simply to Caribs. All of these terms contain an element of ambiguity. One of the first accounts of an encounter with the Caribs of St. Vincent was recorded by an English seaman, Lawrence Keymis, in 1596.[3] He refers to the "Indians" and "one of their slaves". If the slave was black, which in the context seems likely, it would probably be the earliest written reference to Africans in St. Vincent.

The Black Caribs themselves embodied the characteristics of both natives and newcomers. As a people they were the product of the mixing of the indigenous Caribs and the Africans who were forcibly brought to the region by European colonists to serve as slaves. They said their African forebears had been survivors of a shipwrecked slave ship who had combined with the resident Amerindians of St. Vincent and adopted their way of life. The result was a people whose features tended predominantly to reflect their African ancestry but who spoke the language of the islands. Later there was conflict between the two groups and the more unmixed Yellow Caribs were largely displaced by the Black Caribs.

From ancestral Carib culture they inherited a spirit of independence: no man commanded beyond his immediate family-based village except in time of war. From their African forebears, who only found themselves in the western hemisphere because of slavery, they inherited a determination never to submit to bondage. It is perhaps because of this that they fought on, until they were literally starving, to remain in the only country they had ever called home.

The drama of the Black Caribs—from their first coming into being as a people, through their struggles to maintain their independence to their eventual defeat and exile—all this took place on an island barely bigger than the Isle of Wight (or less than a tenth the size of Long Island). In the end they suffered a terrible, crushing defeat. But it was not quite the end. Dumped on a distant shore, the few hardy survivors did not die out. A gentleman of St. Vincent, shortly after the deportation, wrote that this "singular tribe of mankind… are now nearly extinct and

[it] will soon be forgot that such a race ever existed".[4] Instead, they lived, grew and prospered. Within weeks the Black Caribs—the Garifuna—moved from Roatán to Honduras and from there spread along the Caribbean coast of Central America to Belize, Guatemala and Nicaragua where their descendants can still be found today. Their survival, with their unique culture intact, is the ultimate testament to their forebears' tenacious spirit.

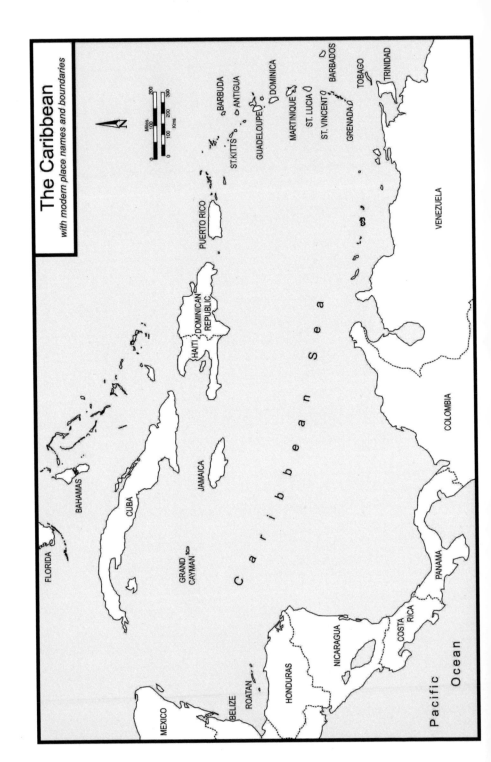

The Caribbean
with modern place names and boundaries

1. Youroumaÿn

"The first view of St Vincent's is magnificent: its noble mountains rise in masses, each higher than the one before it; until the mountains of the centre, crowned with mists, seem to look down with majesty upon the subject hills around, which gradually decrease in height, until they approach the Caribbean Sea, whose deep blue waves fling their snowy foam, conch-shells, sponges, marine eggs, and white coral, at their feet. The fertile plains and vales are hidden by these mountains, which have perpetual verdure: yet, owing to the cultivation of their bases, sides, and even summits, and the ever-varying kaleidoscope of light and shade caused by the shifting clouds, the surface of this island has a singularly part-coloured appearance; and, when the traveller looks from its elevations, his eye is gratified with the sight of the Grenadines, which, although no longer fertile, are so beautifully placed and so fantastically formed, that they heighten in an eminent degree the beauty of the sea-view ..." [1]

EL Joseph, *Warner Arundell, the Adventures of a Creole*, 1838

YOUROUMAŸN. That was the name the Caribs gave to the island Europeans knew as St. Vincent—or at least that was how it was recorded by Adrien Le Breton, a Jesuit missionary who spent ten years living there at the end of the seventeenth century.[2] No more than twenty-two miles from north to south and fourteen to sixteen miles wide, with fertile land to grow crops, woods to hunt game and a surrounding sea abundant with fish, Youroumaÿn had everything that the Caribs needed. The mountain at its centre is a volcano, responsible in the geological past for the island's very existence, and from its flanks ridges extend down towards the sea dividing the land into a series of wooded valleys. Alongside the streams that flow down to the rugged coast the Caribs made their homes.

"The Island of St. Vincent is the most populous of any possess'd by the *Caribbians,*" asserted Charles de Rochefort, a Protestant pastor who visited the West Indies in the mid-seventeenth century. "The *Caribbians* have many fair Villages, where they live pleasantly, and without

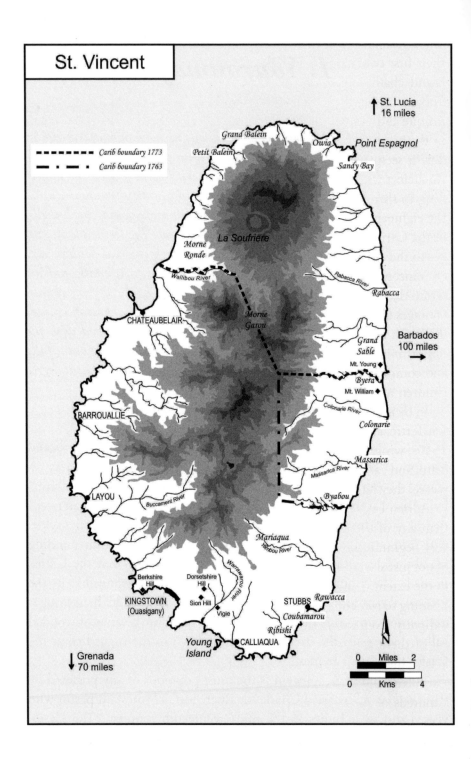

St. Vincent

St. Lucia
16 miles

- - - - - - Carib boundary 1773
- · - · - · - Carib boundary 1763

Grand Balein

Petit Balein

Owia

Point Espagnol

Sandy Bay

*Morne
Ronde*

La Soufrière

Wallibou River

Rabacca River

Rabacca

CHATEAUBELAIR

*Morne
Garou*

*Grand
Sable*

Barbados
100 miles

Mt. Young ◆

Byera

Mt. William ◆

Colonarie River

Colonarie

BARROUALLIE

Massarica

Massarica River

LAYOU

Byabou

Buccament River

Mariaqua

Yambou River

Berkshire
Hill

Dorsetshire
Hill ◆

Warrawarrou River

STUBBS

Rawacca

KINGSTOWN
(Ouasigany)

Sion Hill

Vigie

Coubamarou

Ribishi

*Young
Island*

CALLIAQUA

N

Grenada
70 miles

0   Miles   2

0   Kms   4

any disturbance."[3] Other lands were also home to Caribs at the time of their first contact with Europeans. The Caribs ranged over the whole island chain, stretching some five hundred miles from Grenada and Tobago in the south, through St. Vincent, St. Lucia, Dominica, Martinique and Guadeloupe, up to Antigua and St. Christopher (St. Kitts) in the north. Trinidad was largely the province of Arawaks and Barbados, it seems, was no longer permanently occupied. By the time that Rochefort was writing, though, the Caribs' territory was already beginning to shrink in the face of European encroachment. At the turn of the eighteenth century St. Vincent was described as "the head-quarters of the Caribs".[4]

To the outsider's eye it seemed as if the topography of Youroumaÿn/ St. Vincent was uniquely conducive to the Carib way of life. Le Breton wrote that "the fortunate complicity of the country astonishingly encourages the people's frenzy for total independence... the island... is riddled with bays and hollows... [and]... offers each father of a family the opportunity to choose... his ideal site, far from any foreign constraint and completely safe... to lead his life exactly as he pleases with his wife, children and dear ones."[5] This spirit of independence was remarked upon by nearly all early European accounts of the Caribs. Jean Baptiste Du Tertre, a French soldier-turned-missionary in the West Indies in the 1640s, wrote: "No polity is seen among them; they all live in freedom, drink and eat when they are hungry or thirsty, work and rest when they please; they have no worries..."[6]

Adrien Le Breton spent more time among the Caribs of St. Vincent than any of these writers but he told the same story. "Even from the very beginning of their communal living, they were filled with hatred of not just slavery, but any form of injunction, authority or submission, to the extent that these very words themselves are unbearable to them. Yielding to someone else and obeying an order is for them the ultimate indignity. Even today, this explains the virulence of their total freedom. All of them are perfectly equal, and they recognise absolutely no official, chief or magistrate."[7] So although people speaking the Island Carib language and sharing the same culture lived on islands spanning hundreds of miles, there was no Carib state in the West Indies. No man, no chief, commanded beyond his immediate district, except in time of war.

Early descriptions tend to remark upon the Caribs' health and vigour. Raymond Breton, a missionary of the Dominican order who was sent to the region by Cardinal Richelieu and who lived on the island of Dominica from 1641 to 1651, wrote, "they are of good stature and well proportioned, strong, robust, ordinarily fleshy, and healthy... Their natural colour is sallow, strongly tanned... Their hair is completely black..."[8] Rochefort thought them a "handsome well-shape'd people, well proportion'd in all parts of their bodies... of a smiling countenance, middle stature, having broad shoulders, and large buttocks", adding that "their complexion is naturally of an Olive-colour."[9] They appeared to enjoy great longevity; various accounts suggested that Caribs frequently lived beyond a hundred years of age and that these venerable figures showed little of the stooped posture and wrinkled skin of old age. Rochefort claimed that it was common for Caribs to reach 150, although how he verified such a marvel is unclear (indeed, the Island Carib language had no words for numbers above twenty[10]). According to Raymond Breton, "Their long life must be attributed to their lack of care."[11]

A Carib man might take as many wives as he could provide for and a profusion of wives and children was an indicator of status. The man would build each new spouse a house (which might even be on a different island) and little friction was reported among the various wives. Villages were typically based upon a single extended family headed by a male "chief" or "captain"[12] and tended to be sited on rising ground to avoid still air and attendant mosquitoes. They also needed to be near rivers or brooks since the Caribs liked to bathe first thing every morning. The main building was called by the French a *carbet,* originally an oval structure that might measure sixty to eighty feet long by twenty feet and was thatched with *roseaux* (reeds) or *latanier* (palm fronds). It was here that the men ate, that guests were received and that feasts were held. The women and children would generally eat in separate, smaller houses. The main furniture was in the form of wooden stools or tables with a woven top called a *matoutou.* All slept in hammocks (a Carib word).

Following their morning ablutions, the men would sit on a small stool while the women painted them with *roucou,* a red pigment derived from the seeds of the annatto tree, which as well as serving as an adornment helped to protect the skin from the sun and from insects.

The women would then paint their own bodies. Facial piercings and feathers in the hair completed the look. Men might play on the flute while the women made breakfast. Ready to face the day, the men occupied themselves with fishing and hunting or, when necessary, felling trees. Land crabs and other shellfish were important elements of their diet but birds and small mammals such as the agouti might also be brought in. Their activities were not so intense that they did not allow time for them to "spend entire half-days sitting on top of a rock, or on the riverbank, their eyes fixed on land or sea, without saying a single word".[13] Although women were frequently described as slaves to their menfolk by Europeans, Raymond Breton observed sardonically that neither men nor women killed themselves through overwork. One of the Caribs' preferred activities was visiting other communities near and far, occasions that were always marked by elaborate hospitality and celebration.

Women were busy near constantly, not just looking after the home and children but growing crops, preparing food and spinning cotton. It was noted that mothers cared for their offspring with great tenderness,[14] even if one aspect of this seemed remarkable to outsiders: mothers would press their baby's head between boards to create the characteristic Carib look of a backwards-sloping forehead. In clearings in the woods the women raised cassava (the root crop also known as manioc or yuca) in small gardens among the stumps of trees felled by the men. These provision grounds were moved from time to time as the soil became exhausted. Other vegetables, including beans, yams and other tubers, plus plantains and bananas were also grown. Fruit trees were often cultivated near the houses, with the pineapple particularly prized. Cassava was the Caribs' indispensable staple but preparing it was a complex process, involving grating the tubers and straining the product through a tall sieve. "Their cassava press is a rather short wide pipe made of basket-work. After the manioc has been grated, the wet cassava meal is put into this pipe, which is then hung to a branch of a tree with a heavy stone tied to the bottom. This weight gradually pulls out the pipe till it is long and narrow and thus squeezes the water out of the meal."[15] Women made and cooked cassava bread (*areba*) fresh every day and juice from the plant was used with the addition of peppers and lime juice to make a hot, spicy sauce or broth called *tumallen*

—Caribs loved spicy food. This versatile plant was also the basis for an alcoholic drink known as *ouïcou*, for which the women often masticated the cassava to speed the fermentation process (*ouïcou* prepared in this way was said to be "incomparably better"[16]). This drink was an important part of Carib feasts; indeed these events were known as *ouïcous* or later, after trade with the French, *vins*.

These carousals were frequent and drinking was at the centre of Carib culture. Rochefort lists seven motives for a *ouïcou*: as a council of war; on a return from an expedition; on the birth of a male child; when a child's hair is first cut; when a boy comes of age to go to war; when trees are cut to build a new house or make a garden; and at the launching of a new vessel. Men, women and children might be present at such a feast. First the men, then the women, would dance, the latter shuffling their feet with one hand on their head and the other on their hip amid singing and flute playing. Most songs were about warfare; others dealt with birds, fish, and women.[17] After much drinking, and smoking, the evening would often end in raised emotions and, as old grievances were recalled, violence. With no government, revenge was the principal instrument of justice and a *ouïcou*, with an antagonist's guard perhaps lowered, was the perfect place to exact vengeance for some previous offence. If warfare was being contemplated it was up to the chief or "captain" hosting the *ouïcou* to persuade his guests to fight. Caribs always listened patiently to each other without interruption. After much drinking an old woman present might harangue those present, reminding them of past injustices suffered at the hands of their enemies and previous acts of bravery. She might also brandish a body part, such as an arm, of a slain enemy from a previous war, smoked—*boucaned*—to preserve it. The captain hosting the *ouïcou* would then reiterate her arguments. A date a few days thence, ideally coinciding with the full moon, would be set for the war party to assemble. The man proposing the action was in command but only for the duration of the raid.

The Caribs had a reputation as fearsome warriors. Trained from boyhood, they were deadly with a bow in hand. "Not only do the Indians shoot straight, but they shoot so quickly that they can loose ten or a dozen arrows in the time it takes to load a gun."[18] It was claimed they could regularly hit a half-crown piece at a hundred paces. The Caribs sometimes poisoned their arrows with the sap of the manchineel tree.[19] In time, following trade with the Europeans, they transferred their marksmanship to firearms. For close-quarters fighting Caribs wielded the *boutou*, a heavy, three-foot-long wooden club, often elaborately carved and decorated.

Before setting off, warriors donned war-paint, overlaying black pigment around the eyes and mouth, or in stripes all over the body. The raiding party travelled in large canoes, or pirogues, which might carry fifty or more men and were fitted with sails for travel between the islands (Caribs also used canoes—another Carib word—less than twenty feet long for fishing); a few women would be taken along to prepare food. The ideal mode of attack was by the light of the full moon or at daybreak, surprising the enemy in their hammocks. One tactic was to shoot flaming arrows into the dry palm leaf roofs of houses and then kill the fleeing inhabitants. Surprise was a key element of Carib tactics and if this was compromised the attack would often be abandoned. Battles rarely lasted beyond midday and determined resistance quickly disheartened attackers. The Caribs always took great pains to carry their wounded and dead from the field.

The Caribs told the early French missionaries who lived among them that their ancestors originally came from the mainland of South America. According to Adrien Le Breton, "It is absolutely certain" that the Caribs, or Karaÿbes, "originated among the people living not far off on the coast of the continent,"[20] and it was a belief reported on other islands where Caribs spoke to European chroniclers. The Caribs referred to their kin on the mainland as Galibis.

Anthropologists suggest their ancestors originated in the continent's Amazonian interior and migrated to the islands from the region of the Guianas. Archaeological evidence supports the idea that Caribs arrived in St. Vincent from the Guianas about 1200AD, displacing the Arawaks[21], who are presumed to have been responsible for the enigmatic rock carvings still visible on the island, and that they lived there in large numbers.[22]

The Caribs said that they had killed the original Arawak inhabitants of the islands.[23] Not all the Arawaks, though. The men were put to death but the women were spared and taken as slaves or wives or both. Male Arawak prisoners, it was said, would be elaborately tortured and the Caribs greatly admired the captive who could endure this stoically, although this practice appeared to be dying out even at the time it was recorded.

The Caribs' style of conquest left its mark on their language. Father Raymond Breton, who compiled the first Carib dictionary, found that the men and women spoke a completely different language "and among them it would be ridiculous to employ the men's language in speaking to women and vice versa". The women, it is believed, retained the language of the Arawaks, while the men spoke a version of the language they brought from the mainland, perhaps modified into a pidgin to be understood throughout the islands.[24] Just a few vestiges of these differences between men's and women's speech are preserved in the Garifuna language today. Linguists, incidentally, classify the Island Carib tongue and modern Garifuna, its direct descendant, as belonging to the Arawak rather than the Carib language group, perhaps indicating that through the womenfolk the Arawak tongue prevailed.[25]

On St. Vincent a new element would be pitched into this demographic mix.

Like Robinson Crusoe's Caribbean adventure, the story of the Black Caribs of St. Vincent begins with a shipwreck. At some point a European ship carrying enslaved Africans foundered in the area of St. Vincent and the Grenadines and some or all of its human cargo made it to shore and were taken in by the native inhabitants. Various versions of this tale have been recorded but the details of what actually happened are very hard to pin down.

Looking back from 1789 the British governor of the island, James Seton, said the ship was wrecked "on the windward part of the island of St. Vincent, in the year 1734".[26] An earlier governor, writing in 1777, put the date of the shipwreck 65 years earlier, that is, in 1712.[27] But Sir William Young, writing in the 1790s, says the ship was sailing from the Bight of Benin in West Africa to Barbados and was wrecked "about the year 1675"[28] on the coast of Bequia, the largest of the Grenadines and the closest to St. Vincent itself. A hurricane did in fact strike Barbados in that year. Young's account is one of the most detailed, but it is also written many years after the events it purports to describe. If

Young's date were correct it must have been a very big ship because a report to the English government dating from 1676, just one year after the supposed date of the shipwreck, stated that St. Vincent was home to "about 3,000 negro inhabitants"[29] even if that figure may have been an exaggeration. In fact, as early as 1667 English government records note that the population of St. Vincent is "all Indians, and some negroes from the loss of two Spanish ships in 1635". In 1719 a certain Thomas Weir reported to Britain's Commissioners for Trade and Plantations that St. Vincent's black population derived from "two ships from Guinea, that happened formerly to be successively shipwrecked there".[30] In the eighteenth century it was said that it was a Dutch vessel, the *Palmyra*, that had been wrecked and conversely that it had been a British ship whose owners were still trying to reclaim their lost cargo. In 1748 the French governor of Martinique reported to Tourouya, or Touriac, a Black Carib chief from St. Vincent, that the British and Dutch maintained that his people were descendants of the wreck of a Dutch slave ship off one of the Grenadines. Tourouya replied that it was a lie: the ship had been Spanish.[31]

Troublingly, the versions tend to become more detailed the further in time they are from the events they describe, right up to the present day. Nevertheless, the persistence of the shipwreck story through so many relatively early accounts means it is likely that these European writers were recording a genuine oral tradition and that at least one shipwreck of a slaving vessel did occur. In the hazardous seafaring conditions of the age of sail and in the region which gave the world the hurricane (another Carib word) shipwrecks were not uncommon. In 1666 Lord Francis Willoughby, the governor of Barbados, was lost in a storm off Guadeloupe along with fifteen ships.

Details such as the nationality of the vessel, the location of the wreck and the origin of its cargo, however, must be treated with circumspection. Young, for example, confidently asserts that the Africans aboard were from "a warlike Moco tribe" from the Bight of Benin. Unfortunately there is no evidence to support this and good reason to doubt it. If Mocos did arrive in St. Vincent they left no particular trace in the culture. Slave traders typically collected their cargo from a large number of different slave-trading forts on the African coast spanning thousands of miles. Each of these forts might collect slaves from a vast hinterland and a slave ship might visit several of these ports before setting off for the Caribbean on the Middle Passage.

To the objection that Africans on a slave ship would be held in chains and therefore unlikely to survive a wreck, one eighteenth-century account suggests an answer. Emmanuel-François, Marquis de Lambertye, a French colonial official who had extensive contacts with Vincentian Caribs, wrote: "In the early days of European settlement in the Antilles, on a ship coming from Guinea full of Blacks for the cultivation of the colonies, the slaves revolted and threw all the whites into the sea after killing them; but as they didn't know how to navigate they were forced to let the ship drift in the currents. The trade winds, which are prevalently easterly throughout the year between the tropics, quite naturally led the slave vessel to the first land in the most windward part of northern America: the island of St Vincent was the first that the Blacks saw. Naturally, wherever the ship ended up, they would run it aground so as not to drown. As might be imagined, they all hurried ashore to look for signs of life. The Red Caribs—American natives who occupied the island—received them with the usual humaneness and showed them a side of the island previously uninhabited where they could establish themselves."[32]

A French report from 1700 asserts that both men and women had survived the shipwreck. "There were negroes and negresses, they had children, and several of the negroes married daughters of the Caribs, thereby their numbers have increased."[33] In lyrical mood, Sir William Young (father of the historian and the man in charge of carving up St. Vincent's land among colonists) imagined the scene after the shipwreck. "Thus from apparent evils, do sometimes flow, the greatest blessings. Recovered from their fears, and refreshed with such sustenance as could be found, it is natural to suppose they soon solaced themselves with their female friends of the party; and as a state of nature is no enemy to propagation, they of course gave birth to a free people."[34] This was written in 1764 as Young was trying to entice colonists to the island. His tone was to change dramatically later.

Whoever struggled ashore from the shipwreck they were not the only Africans on St. Vincent. Almost from the start of European settlement in the Caribbean, Africans were present. Faced with the precipitous decline of the native population, from disease, warfare or

10

"pining away" under the exactions of the first Spanish colonists, a new sort of workforce was sought. Bartolomé de las Casas, the Spanish priest[35] and defender of the Indians of the Americas, was one of the first to advocate the importation of African slaves to ease the burden of forced work on the native population (he later changed his mind). Within ten years of Christopher Columbus' arrival in the West Indies in 1492 African slaves were being imported to the region.

Carib raids on Spanish settlements in the Greater Antilles soon began to bring home Africans among the captives. One, Luisa de Navarrete, testified to her experience in 1580 following her escape. She had been seized in a raid on Puerto Rico in 1576 and carried off to Dominica. During her captivity she witnessed annual expeditions to raid the Spanish colonies to leeward. According to Navarrete, a freed African slave married to a Spaniard, "they have carried away a great quantity of negroes and left some in Dominica and distributed the rest among the Indians of these islands, which they take to their lands in order to serve them."[36] Many, she said, had adopted the native way of life and "do as the Indians do".[37]

Most accounts suggest that even if the newcomers were put to work by the Caribs, the character of this servitude was less harsh than that experienced at the hands of the Europeans and that they might end up being considered members of the family. According to one account, "they pardoned the Negro-slaves they met with, and having brought them ashore put them to work in their Habitations; thence came the Negroes which they have at present in St Vincents and some other islands."[38]

Intriguingly, Rochefort, writing in the 1650s, states that the Caribs had attacked the English colonies at Antigua and Montserrat and carried off men, women and children to Dominica and St. Vincent. While these were later released through French intercession, Rochefort also claimed: "They have at this present in the Island of St Vincents some young Boys and Girls of the *English* nation, who being carried away very young, have clearly forgot their Parents, and would hardly return with them, so well are they pleased with the humour of the *Caribbians,* who for their part treat them as mildly as if they were of their own Nation." The same writer adds that some of the Caribs' black slaves were from English plantations and others were from Spanish ships cast away on their coasts.

Carib raids continued over many decades and numerous captives were taken. Already in the sixteenth century it was estimated that 300 European and African captives were held on the island of Dominica. As the Lesser Antilles were progressively occupied by other European powers, principally the French and English, from 1625 Africans were imported in ever greater numbers to work on the new, labour-intensive plantations growing tobacco, cotton and sugar. From the start, enslaved Africans tried to escape. Analyzing the fugitives' motives, Du Tertre maintained that new arrivals, fresh from their homeland, rebelled against the unaccustomed hard work and tried to get home; those who had been in the islands longer reacted against bad treatment. But the friar also conceded that one of the predominant reasons for Africans running away was simply "*le desir de la liberté*".

The planters of Barbados, one of the earliest English colonies in the Caribbean, had particular cause for concern. Runaway slaves escaping from Barbados[39] could commandeer a boat or make a raft in the knowledge that the prevailing current would take them directly to St. Vincent, a hundred miles downwind. According to a tradition on the island, many of the runaways would wash up at Byabou Bay on the windward coast. Throughout the many treaties signed with the Caribs of St. Vincent the invariable demand from the Europeans was for the return of runaway slaves, although the number actually handed back appears to have been limited. The presence of a large black population on St. Vincent free of European control acted as a magnet for runaways who for the European slave owners represented a significant economic drain. It was also alleged that some escaped slaves were illicitly resold by the Caribs to Europeans on other West Indian islands.

An issue of the *St. Vincent Gazette* from Saturday 23 May 1778 is instructive. When two African slaves and a canoe went missing from Barbados it was natural for the owners to advertize in St. Vincent. "An African Canoe, with two new Negroe Men, was driven out to sea from Barbados. A reward of ten Joes for each slave in the canoe, and two Joes for the canoe, is offered for their return in good condition." The same issue also carried notices seeking the return of three runaways from St. Vincent.

Jean-Baptiste Labat, a Jesuit priest who lived in the Caribbean at the turn of the eighteenth century and visited St. Vincent briefly, believed that most of those of African descent on St. Vincent came from Barbados, which might help to explain why no population comparable to the Black Caribs developed on other islands of the Lesser Antilles. "In former times the Caribs brought the runaway slaves back to their masters," he observed, "or sold them to the French and Spaniards. For some reason, that I am not aware of, the Indians stopped doing this, and regarded these runaways as an addition to their nation." One reason for the change may have been to counter the population decline among the Amerindian Caribs which had been the most pronounced effect of contact with Europeans.

However they arrived, those of African ancestry soon began to assert themselves. Although there is no detailed contemporary account of what happened, according to Young, writing more than a century later, the Africans proved to be unruly servants and their new Amerindian masters, fearing the consequences should their number increase, resolved to kill all the male children. In response to this Herodian policy, it is asserted, the Africans revolted, killing what Caribs they could and decamping with their wives and children to the wooded slopes of the windward coast. There they thrived. Although their lifestyles were very similar, Labat was struck by "the antipathy which exists between the Carib and the African. The Caribs imagine they are far superior to the Blacks, while the latter, who are not a whit behind the former in conceit, despise the Indians and call them savages."[40] It should, though, be noted that Labat spent very little time in St. Vincent and Young was reconstructing events from long before he was born. The concentration of the Black Caribs on the windward coast may well have been a more gradual, less conflictive process. The British in the eighteenth century sought to delegitimize the Black Caribs as mere runaway slaves, who had no right to freedom let alone the land they lived on. Conversely, the Black Caribs stressed their Indian-ness, that they were heirs to a culture that predated the Europeans' arrival, and the shipwreck story, which placed their history outside the prison of the plantation, was an important bolster to that identity.

Given that English and French sources speak of two distinct populations on St. Vincent from the 1660s it is likely that the Black Caribs began living separately before this date and certainly by the end of the century. Their former hosts or masters, hereafter referred to as Yellow or

Red Caribs in English and French sources, now found themselves subject to raids in which their women were carried off by the Black Caribs. Labat wrote that "what annoys the Indians more than the loss of half their island is that the negroes continually steal their women and girls. It is not possible for the Caribs to rescue them, as the negroes, who are a much braver race and in far superior numbers, only laugh at them, illtreat them, and possibly will one day make them work as their slaves."

Conflict continued for many years. In 1700 the French governor of Martinique was asked to intercede between the two groups and responded by designating a line of demarcation between the two populations known as the *"barre de l'isle"* which divided the island in two. The Black Caribs claimed the wild windward coast while the Yellow Caribs remained to leeward. Although the windward territory was later to be much coveted for the fertility of its soil, it is likely that its inaccessibility, particularly to European ships seeking an anchorage on its rocky shore, was a key attraction for the Black Caribs. Despite French mediation, antagonism between the two groups simmered. Following an English naval expedition to St. Vincent, the governor of Barbados reported in 1707 that "The Blacks and Indieans have been for some time att warr there."[41] However, at the end of that same year a French colonial official visited the island and met a combined assembly of Yellow and Black Caribs. One of the Black Carib captains promised that in the event of a British intervention his people would come to the aid of the Yellow Caribs.[42] It was, though, an uneasy alliance, since the official, Monsieur Coullet, noted: "they greatly fear the Negroes of this island, of whom there are 12 to 15 for every Carib."

Estimates of total Carib numbers at this period and of the relative numbers of Black and Yellow Caribs vary considerably. In the 1670s the governor of Barbados estimated that the islands of Dominica, St. Lucia and St. Vincent were inhabited by 1,500 bowmen (plus, presumably, their families), of whom 600 were "negroes" of St. Vincent.[43] The Carib population was already in decline at this point as their range was progressively reduced. Yellow Carib numbers on St. Vincent continued to fall through the eighteenth century. In 1777 the governor of St.Vincent estimated that only forty Yellow Caribs remained on the island. By the 1720s the total Black Carib population was estimated at four thousand, although the zeal with which they guarded their territory from prying eyes meant such figures were largely guesswork. Later Garifuna communities in Central America acquired a reputation for fertility[44] and, with a large family adding to a man's prestige, the rate of natural increase among the Black Caribs of St. Vincent seems to have been impressively high.

While the conflict between the Yellow and Black Caribs would certainly have produced casualties, there is little evidence of the sort of wholesale slaughter that would have been necessary to bring about such a dramatic demographic collapse of the former in relation to the latter. Disease, though, could have played an important part. Following contact in 1492, the Amerindian populations of the Caribbean were subjected to a range of Old World infections to which they had little or no resistance, including influenza, smallpox, measles, anthrax, chicken pox, diphtheria, plague, scarlet fever and typhus. Diseases let loose on a "virgin" population can have devastating consequences: when smallpox reached isolated Iceland in 1777, 36 per cent of the population died. In the Caribbean, the Spanish chronicler Gonzalo Fernández de Oviedo estimated that of one million native inhabitants of Hispaniola in 1492 only five hundred men, women and children remained fifty years later. The scale of the demographic collapse is astounding and for many years scholars believed that the chroniclers' estimates of the pre-Columbian population of the Caribbean must have been exaggerated. Latterly, however, many academics have revised upwards their estimates of initial population levels—and therefore of the scale of the die-off.

The Caribs, with their dispersed social structure and geographical spread over numerous small islands, may have suffered comparatively less than their Arawak counterparts in the Greater Antilles as most of the diseases brought by Europeans were spread through direct human contact and so tended to thrive among large concentrations of people. This may have allowed populations to recover somewhat between epidemics. However, the advent of plantation agriculture and the mass importation of African slaves brought diseases from that continent in their wake to which both Caribs and Europeans were vulnerable, in particular falciparum malaria and yellow fever, both of which are carried by mosquitoes. West Africans typically possess a number of genetic modifications which offer some protection against malaria and Africans proved so resistant to yellow fever in the Caribbean that it was a long time before whites realized that Africans could be susceptible to the disease at all.

Yellow fever's first recorded outbreak in the Caribbean was in Barbados in 1647, its relatively late appearance perhaps due to the difficulty of the virus surviving the Atlantic crossing because of the peculiarities of its life cycle. The virus would probably need to pass through three generations of mosquitoes successively finding new hosts to infect among the ship's crew or human cargo on the crossing from Africa. Yellow fever is not recorded in St. Vincent until 1793 but, as numerous outbreaks were experienced in nearby islands such as Barbados, Guadeloupe, Martinique, St Kitts and St. Lucia from the mid-seventeenth century onwards, it is likely that it was only the lack of Europeans on hand to record them that prevented earlier epidemics being noted. Among the population of St. Vincent those of West African descent would have had a much greater ability to resist the ravages of yellow fever than the Amerindian Yellow Caribs.[45] A British observer of the Black Caribs in the 1760s commented on "the activity and Hardiness of their disposition which they Deriv'd from their African ancestors", noting that it was "not as yet lost by the Intermixture with the Red or original Caribs in these climates".[46]

Although Europeans could draw a clear distinction in the late seventeenth century between "Indians" and "Negroes" on St. Vincent, both populations were the products of racial mixing, albeit to varying degrees. Among the Black Caribs it is evident that aspects of African physiognomy prevailed. It is difficult at this distance to judge the proportions of the different elements of the Black Carib bloodline but some genetic studies have been carried out on modern-day Garifuna populations in Central America and on surviving Carib populations in St. Vincent. According to one comparative study, "the St. Vincent Black Caribs' gene pool contains the highest proportion of Amerindian genes (approximately 50%), while the coastal [Central American] communities exhibit a more African ancestry (up to 80%)."[47] This discrepancy is explained either by admixture of more African blood since the exile in Central America, the selective deportation in 1797 of Caribs with more African characteristics or natural selection in a malarial environment of those with greater African-derived resistance to the disease. The second explanation certainly has the support of the historical evidence. The British did selectively deport Black Caribs and even released from captivity some Yellow Caribs. Land was given, for example at Sandy Bay, to Yellow Caribs remaining on St. Vincent after the Second Carib War. Indeed, despite the study's reference to "St. Vincent Black Caribs" it is among the descendants of these Yellow Caribs, incorporating considerable mixing with non-Caribs over the subsequent two centuries, that the St. Vincent sample is based. Also, it is worth noting that even taking into account the genetic mixing of the last two hundred or so years, the Central American Garifuna sample still shows a proportion of at least twenty per cent Amerindian genes, suggesting that the original exiled Black Carib population, although with a preponderant African biological heritage, was the product of significant mixture with the St. Vincent Carib population.[48] By the late eighteenth century disease, warfare and emigration had reduced the Yellow Carib population to "two or three families only" by one estimate[49], by which time the terms Carib and Black Carib are all but synonymous in colonial accounts.

What was abundantly clear to writers in the eighteenth century was that the darker-skinned group had taken on the culture of the Amerindian Caribs (indicating that at one point at least the two groups must have lived in close proximity). Most importantly, the Black Caribs adopted the Island Carib language. Slaves from Africa spoke a wide variety of different tongues so the Caribs' language would have provided a ready lingua franca as well as being a way to communicate with their Amerindian masters or neighbours. African slaves were no strangers to overcoming differences of background when flung together on the other side of the Atlantic. As one seventeenth-century observer noted: "They are passionate Lovers of one another; and though they are born in different Countries, and sometimes, when at home, Enemies one to another, yet when occasion requires they mutually support and assist one another, as if they were all Brethren."[50]

The African arrivals in St. Vincent would have been familiar with tropical agriculture of a type similar to that practised by the Caribs—indeed it would have been much more attractive to them than the forced backbreaking toil of the Europeans' plantation cultivation. The Black Caribs were quickly indistinguishable from the Yellow Caribs in terms of dress, diet, language and lifestyle—everything, in fact, except pigmentation and similar racial characteristics. They even adopted the Carib practice of head deformation. This also served to distinguish them from enslaved or free blacks which, given European demands for the return of runaways, was of signal importance.

What the Africans brought to Black Carib culture is harder to say. The Middle Passage involved a violent severance and an enforced oblivion which make it difficult to establish direct links between life in Africa and the New World. The slaves brought virtually no physical objects with them. African musical influences can certainly be heard in Garifuna music today but references to music among the Black Caribs of St. Vincent in the eighteenth century are too scanty to draw any conclusions. One African contribution may have been spiritual. Communication with dead ancestors is an important part of modern Garifuna spiritual life and this may in part be a legacy of the transplanted souls of Africa.[51] Contemporary writers certainly noticed similarities between the religious practices of African slaves and Black Caribs.[52]

One characteristic united the Amerindian and the African parts of the Black Carib heritage more than any other: a spirit of independence. For the dark-skinned Black Caribs the very real possibility of being seized and pressed into slavery by white men can have only stiffened their resolve to live their own lives in their own homeland, a sentiment already embedded deep in Carib culture. "There are no people in the world so jealous of their liberty, or who resent more the smallest check to their freedom," wrote Labat. "They laugh at us for obeying and respecting our rulers, and say that we must be their slaves, and that since we allow them to give us orders we must be also cowards."[53]

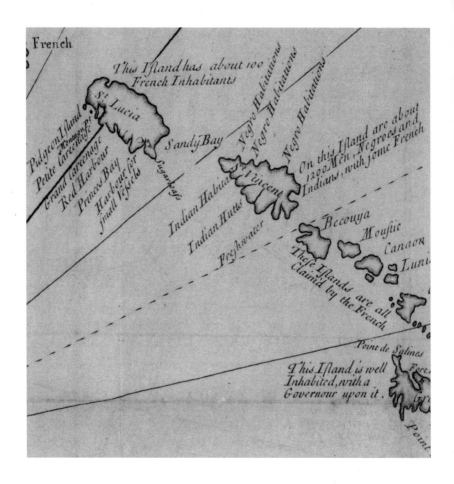

Detail of map taken from John Montagu's 1725 book, *A Relation of the late intended settlement of the islands of St. Lucia and St. Vincent, in America,* which includes an account of Nathaniel Braithwaite's expedition. In its references to "Indian Hutts" on the leeward side of St. Vincent and "Negro Habitations" to windward the map clearly indicates the presence of two populations on the island, elsewhere referred to as Yellow and Black Caribs. Also apparent is the presence of a number of French people who had been settling on St. Vincent in the early eighteenth century.

2. Good Friends, Cruel Enemies

"Thou hast driven me, says this poor people, out of St Christophers, Mevis, Montserrat, St Martins, Antego, Gardeloupe, Barbouthos, St Eustace's, etc, neither of which places belong to thee, and whereto thou couldest not make any lawful pretence: And thou threatnest me every day to take away that little which is left me: What shall become of the poor miserable Caribbian? Must he go and live in the Sea with the fishes? Thy Country must needs be a wretched one, since thou leavest it to come and take away mine: Or thou must needs be full of malice, thus to persecute me out of a frolick." [1]
Charles de Rochefort, *The History of the Caribby-Islands*, 1666

IN JANUARY 1723 two British ships called at St. Vincent on a special mission. The commander of the expedition, John Braithwaite, was under orders to inform the island's inhabitants that they should consider themselves "natural born subjects of Great-Britain" and to sound them out about admitting British settlers.

Braithwaite's expedition began inauspiciously. The "Indian chief" he lavished with presents turned out to be nothing of the sort but an impostor sent to test the extent of British largesse. When he was surrounded by an armed group and taken inland to meet the natives' "General"—who, alarmingly, appeared to be advised by a Frenchman—he was met frostily and denied the customary wood and water for his vessels. Taking his leave, Braithwaite had to push his way back to his boat through threatening crowds of Indians, who now included a number of gun-toting black men ("Negroes, all armed with fusees [flintlock rifles]"). Undeterred, Braithwaite sent gifts of rum, beef, bread and some cutlasses and tried again. On this occasion he "found the brother of the chief of the Negroes was arrived with five hundred Negroes, most armed with fuzees". He again found them suspicious—with reason—that his little force represented the advance guard of a pretended British colonial enterprise but, keeping his counsel for the time being, was otherwise well received.

The "Indian General" and "chief of the Negroes" were eventually persuaded to come on board ship where Braithwaite gave them gifts and plied them with wine—for they disdained to drink the rum he offered. Finally he plucked up the courage to reveal the true nature of his mission. At this point, the mood changed abruptly.

"They told me it was well I had not mentioned it a-shore, for their power could not have protected me; that it was impossible; the Dutch had before attempted it but were forced to retire. They likewise told me... they would trust no Europeans; that they owned themselves under the protection of the French, but would as soon oppose to their settling amongst 'em or any act of force from 'em, as us; as they had lately given an example, by killing several... They advised me to think what they said was an act of friendship."[2]

On that menacing note the meeting broke up. In the face of this defiant statement of independence, Braithwaite sailed off to report back to his commander, Nathaniel Uring, who was having his own problems at the nearby island of St. Lucia. Having received Captain Braithwaite's report, Uring "judged there was like to be little good done at St. Vincent"[3] and sailed back to England. And that, for the time being at least, was the end of that.

The names of the "Indian General" and the "chief of the Negroes" are unrecorded but this episode is revealing in a number of other ways. First, it shows that by this time the island of St. Vincent was inhabited by two distinct groups: one Amerindian, the other of African descent. Second, the British coveted the island and wished to add it to their Caribbean possessions. Third, the French had already established close relations with the natives and a small number were living alongside them. Fourth, that the native inhabitants had recently fought off the aggressive colonial ambitions of the French, and by their account the Dutch before them. In fact, a French attack had been repulsed with heavy loss of life just four years earlier and "it was by very large presents that the French had ever got their favour again".[4] Most important of all, it shows the determination of St. Vincent's inhabitants to preserve their freedom and their way of life. And as the presence of large quantities of firearms, many of them delivered days earlier by French ships, shows, they were prepared to form tactical alliances with anyone who might help them in that objective. This time the British had been rebuffed, but they would return.

By the time of this encounter the inhabitants of St. Vincent had more than two hundred years' experience of Europeans--and of keeping them at arm's length. Since the arrival of Christopher Columbus in the Caribbean in 1492, the once-thriving native population of the big islands of the Greater Antilles where the Spanish had concentrated their colonizing efforts—Cuba, Hispaniola, Puerto Rico and Jamaica—had effectively ceased to exist, the victims of disease, war and enslavement. Other European invaders, particularly the French and English, had made inroads in the smaller islands of the eastern Caribbean.

Relations between the Caribs and the Christian interlopers from Europe had got off to a bad start. The day after Columbus made his historic first contact with the people of the Caribbean he wrote to Ferdinand and Isabella, his royal Spanish patrons, that "should your Highnesses command it all the inhabitants could be taken away to Castile or held as slaves on the island, for with fifty men we could subjugate them all and make them do whatever we wish."[5] On that first voyage he was told by the inhabitants of Hispaniola about a warlike people living to windward called Caribs.

The Caribs were not just doughty warriors, they also, according to Columbus, ate the flesh of their victims. Carib and cannibal were variants of the same word and were synonymous for Europeans. On his second voyage, which took him through the Lesser Antilles, Columbus recovered human arm and leg bones from deserted Carib houses.

Tales of cannibalism certainly excited European audiences and a number of accounts were published of the Caribs' supposed predilection for human meat. One fancifully had a Carib informant comparing in the manner of a restaurant critic the relative culinary appeal of a cooked Frenchman, as opposed to a Spaniard or Englishman. Daniel Defoe's *Robinson Crusoe* was still evoking the horror of Carib cannibals killing humans for the pot in 1719. However, hard evidence of cannibalism was less readily available and some modern authors have suggested that Carib anthropophagy was really a myth.[6]

One of the most vivid early accounts describes how the body parts of slain enemies would be ritually cooked at the Caribs' *ouïcou* feasts. "The Women lick the very sticks whereon the fat dropped, not so much from the deliciousness they find in that kind of sustenance as from the excessive pleasure they conceive in being revenged in that manner of their chiefest enemies, and to heighten this rage and hatred against the Arovages they save the fat that comes from it; and keep it carefully in little Gourds to pour some few drops thereof into their sauces at their solemn entertainments, so to perpetuate as much as lies in their power, the motive of revenge."[7]

Others agreed that human flesh was used in rituals relating to warfare but not as a regular part of the Caribs' diet. "They rather eat out of Mallice, chewing only one Mouthfull and spitting it out againe, and animating one another thereby to be feirce and cruell to the Enemies, as a thing pleaseing to the Gods, and it hath been a great mistake in those that have reported the Southerne Indians eat one another as food, for it's performed rather as a Religious Injunction, although the Custome be Barberous."[8]

Labat, writing at the turn of the eighteenth century, was unconvinced by the image of Caribs as man-eaters. His view was that "though the Caribs do *boucan* the limbs of enemies they have slain, it is only done to preserve the memory of the fight and rouse them to future vengeance, and not with any idea of eating them."[9] He made the simple point that "if they were cannibals in those days [i.e. in the early days of European contact], why are they not cannibals now?"[10] It was certainly striking that numerous missionaries had actually spent years living among the Caribs without being consigned to the pot.

The Spanish crown's response to the tales of bloodthirsty Caribs was a decree in 1503 making it legal for them to be enslaved, unlike the supposedly peaceful Arawaks. The natives of St. Vincent were specifically included in its provisions in 1512. Royal protection did little for the Arawak inhabitants of the Spanish-occupied islands: within a generation they were all but extinct.

The Caribs were perhaps lucky that, with their eyes dazzled by the riches of Mexico and later Peru, the Spanish saw little attraction in trying to settle the smaller islands of the Lesser Antilles. That did not prevent Spanish-Carib relations in the islands in the sixteenth century from being characterized by cycles of raids, massacres and reprisals that left the Caribs with an abiding hatred of the Spanish (Raymond Breton records that Spaniards twice massacred the Caribs of St. Christopher and once those of Guadeloupe).[11] The sixteenth-century English privateer Sir John Hawkins recorded the enmity between the two groups.

"The Cannibals of that Island [Dominica] and also other adjacent are the most desperate warriors that are in the Indies by the Spaniards' report, who are never able to conquer them, and they are molested by them not a little, when they are driven to water there in any of those Islands."[12]

Caribs found other Europeans taking an interest in their territory. Dutch, French and English ships visited their islands and, from the early seventeenth century, gave disturbing signs of wanting to settle permanently. These islands appealed as they were conveniently close to Spanish possessions to serve as raiding bases and for their potential for growing tobacco and other cash crops. European ships frequently stopped at the Windward Islands which were often the first landfall after the Atlantic crossing and were normally allowed to take on wood and water by the resident Caribs. The Caribs also welcomed opportunities to trade for European products, particularly liquor, firearms and metal items such as fish hooks. But any sign of attempts to establish a permanent settlement produced a reaction of suspicion, hostility and often violent reprisal.

The Caribs tended to be concentrated on the larger, more mountainous islands of the Lesser Antilles while on the lower-lying, more arid islands they maintained gardens which might supply them with provisions on their travels. The European invaders had little understanding of Carib agriculture and it is doubtful they would have acted differently even if they did but it does explain why Caribs fought so tenaciously to keep Europeans from settling even apparently uninhabited islands. What made such a lifestyle possible was the Caribs' extraordinary seamanship, which turned the waters up and down the island chain into a highway.

When Sir Thomas Warner arrived on the island of St. Christopher in January 1624 to establish an English colony, the resident Caribs brought food in the form of cassava bread, potatoes, plantains, pineapples, turtles, iguanas and fish. Warner developed good relations initially with the local chief, Tegreman (or Tigreman). But as the French under Belain d'Esnambuc planted their own settlers on the island tensions between the Caribs and the Europeans grew. In 1625 the island's Caribs attacked the English settlement. The following year the English and French united to surprise the Caribs and massacre them as they slept.

They claimed that they were pre-empting a Carib plot to exterminate them. It sounds like a convenient pretext but it may have been true. All sides recognized physical annihilation of the enemy as a key tactic in the struggle for territory and the English and French had given every indication that they planned to take over the whole island. As the family chronicler of Sir Thomas Warner wrote, it was "the universal judgment of historians" that the Caribs were "a formidable obstacle to the early settlers and the ultimate solution of the problem was provided only by a war of extermination".[13] The Europeans boasted of killing Tegreman and 120 Caribs on St. Christopher. Caribs from other islands rallied to take revenge but many— 2,000 by one account[14]—died when their reprisal raid was repulsed. By the end of the decade only a few women and mixed-race children remained of the Caribs of St. Christopher.

The defeat at St. Christopher marked the start of a northern European invasion that within 35 years would see the Caribs' once great range effectively confined to the islands of Dominica and St. Vincent, to which refugees from other islands repaired. The English overcame fierce Carib resistance to occupy nearby Nevis in 1628; Antigua and Montserrat followed in 1632. The 1630s saw the French extend their dominion to Martinique and Guadeloupe, and Caribs fought tenaciously to frustrate fledgling colonization efforts in islands such as Tobago, Grenada and St. Lucia. In 1649 the Carib chief Kaierouane tried to accommodate French expansionism by "selling" the island of Grenada in exchange for some liquor and metal goods. Kaierouane had imposed stipulations on the size and position of the French settlement but these were ignored by the rapidly growing community of colonists. Conflict was inevitable and Caribs from St. Vincent, enraged that the French had destroyed some of their villages, joined forces with their brothers in Grenada. French reinforcements from Martinique surprised the Caribs in the midst of a *ouïcou*. Eighty or so were massacred but about forty survivors threw themselves off a cliff at the northern end of the island rather than be captured. The promontory was later known as Morne des Sauteurs ("Leapers' Hill").[15]

Jean-Charles de Baas-Castelmore, France's first governor general of the West Indies in the mid-1670s, recognized the Caribs as formidable adversaries: "The war we have against the Dutch, against the Emperor and against the Spanish gives the people of the isles much sorrow, but they fear these three powers less than war against the Caribs, because it is of a nature and a conduct so difficult that it is almost impossible to resist."[16] It was a view echoed among the English colonists. Sir William Stapleton, governor of the English Leeward Islands, wrote in 1674: "the islanders dread them [the Caribs] more than any other, because they can come with 30 or 40 periagoes [pirogues or large canoes] to windward, whilst they are at leeward in the trenches or opposing a landing Christian enemy, and so destroy men, women, and children, and burn all, as the people of Antigua and Montserrat have felt in the last war".[17]

But despite this fierce indigenous resistance, the Caribs were progressively losing ground to European settlers. No matter how many of the intruders were killed or expelled, there were always more ships to bring a seemingly inexhaustible supply of replacements. Casualties from warfare were harder for the Caribs to replace and disease, though largely unrecorded among native populations, must have taken a heavy toll following the unwitting introduction of Old World diseases to which they had no natural resistance. They especially feared smallpox because "not knowing a cure for it, it often does as much destruction among them as the plague does in Europe".[18] Raymond Breton claimed "nearly all" had been affected by venereal disease.[19] Reliable estimates of the Carib population are hard to come by[20] but it is clear that along with the reduction in their territorial range their numbers plummeted after contact with Europeans.

Settlers and sailors were not the only white people coming to Carib territory. In most cases the first Europeans to live among Caribs and record their impressions were missionaries such as Raymond Breton, part of the Dominican order's mission on the islands of Guadeloupe and Dominica. It was not until the 1650s that another order, the Jesuits, decided to try their luck on St. Vincent. The project began inauspiciously in 1652 when the first priest sent there, Father André Déian, had to be recalled almost immediately to replace a colleague who had been bitten by a snake. The mission was refounded at the start of the following year with the dispatch of Father Pierre Aubergeon, who had learnt the Caribs' language.

Father Aubergeon's arrival was eased by an incident which the French capitalized upon to increase their influence. A French sailor captured two Caribs from St. Vincent and sold them on the island of Tortuga. The father of one of the pair was known as Baba,[21] "one of the most important Caribs of St. Vincent",[22] and he petitioned Philippe de Long-villiers de Poincy, the leading French official in the West Indies, to have them returned. The two freed Caribs went to St. Christopher to give thanks for their liberation and called for Father Aubergeon to be sent to their home island, although whether the Caribs viewed him as an evangelist or a hostage is open to debate. He arrived in March 1653 and his missionary work was enthusiastically supported by Baba.

The new mission soon ran into trouble when a hurricane struck the island on 13 July. But following Baba's example, many Caribs asked to be instructed in the Catholic faith. Father Aubergeon found himself the centre of attention, with Caribs coming to his quarters to invite him to visit their own *carbet*. The priest set up a little school for the children, teaching them how to make the sign of the cross and how to say their prayers, as well as the main points of the catechism. People of all ages besieged him with requests to be baptized. Father Pierre Pelleprat, another Jesuit who visited Aubergeon at St. Vincent, reported that he had witnessed the priest being pestered by a troop of children saying "Baptize me too, Father, baptize me!"[23]

However, an enthusiasm for baptism was not necessarily the same as an enthusiasm for Christianity. The Caribs had their own tradition of swapping names with respected guests much as a person being baptized would typically take the name of his godfather or godmother. Furthermore, "their Godfathers and Godmothers gave them new Cloathes, and made them some other little Presents on the day of their Baptism, and treated them very sumptuously, within eight days after they had received that Sacrament they desired to receive it again, that there might be other Presents and good cheer."[24] Also, religion was only a part of the story. The Jesuit mission was funded by the French West India company (Compagnie des Isles de l'Amérique), which was in charge of the French colonial project in the Caribbean at the time, and aside from their spiritual role missionaries were also a potentially valuable resident link with the Caribs, a form of soft diplomacy. An official French government report of 1699 noted that "this mission allows some links to be established between the French and the Caribs of St. Vincent and that by this channel one can be alerted to many things which happen among them of which it is always good to be informed…"[25] Over time, this was certainly a factor in the better relations the French enjoyed with the Caribs in contrast to those of the English. On the Carib side, too, politics played their part. Baba was an "*homme d'autorité*",[26] and may have hoped to boost his own power with this link to the French, but the decentralized nature of Carib society meant he did not and could not speak for everybody, a fact that would have tragic consequences for the missionaries.

In the short term, the Jesuits felt the situation was promising enough to send a second priest, Father François Gueimu, to bolster the effort on St. Vincent. The priests' house was probably sited at either Barrouallie or Chateaubelair on the leeward side of the island, and they were joined there by two young French lay helpers. But they were not immune from broader French-Carib tensions. First the Caribs of Dominica massacred the French on the island of Marie-Galante and sought to enlist the Caribs of St. Vincent as allies. Baba was opposed but an atmosphere of French-Carib conflict was growing. Then a French sea captain seized and tortured a Carib from St. Vincent who was sailing with him, alleging he had had some part in the murder of one of his crew by the natives on the mainland. Returning to St. Vincent the Carib reported his mistreatment at the hands of the Frenchman and vowed revenge. Then a French trader got involved in a drunken quarrel with one of the main men of the island and would have killed him but for a faulty pistol. A friend of the intended victim vowed revenge and killed the inebriated Frenchman in his bed. Fearing retribution, he resolved to do away with all the Frenchmen on the island and went from house to house recruiting allies.

At 7 o'clock on the morning of 23 January 1654, an hour after sunrise, the Jesuits were celebrating mass in the chapel of their house. The Caribs burst in and killed the two priests and a young French helper. The other ran off into the woods but was pursued and he too was killed. The Caribs threw their bodies into the sea.

The Jesuits' calvary was the start of a more general outbreak of hostilities between the Caribs and the French.[27] A force of Caribs sailed to Grenada where they massacred between sixty and eighty French people and a number of their slaves, burning houses, pillaging, and carrying off women. The French responded by sending three men-o'-war to St.

Vincent and spending a week killing any Caribs—men, women or children—they came across and destroying coastal villages. It was merely the prelude to several years of conflict in which the Caribs suffered heavy casualties, particularly among warriors.

Despite the evident dangers on St. Vincent the Jesuits did return to the island in 1670. Twelve Jesuits successively took the word of the Christian God to St. Vincent's Caribs. The last of these was Father Adrien Le Breton, who lived on the island between 1693 and 1702 and recorded his impressions of Carib life. Ultimately, though, the Jesuit mission did not outlast Le Breton's time on the island. For nearly fifty years off and on the Jesuits had worked diligently to win Carib souls for Jesus. But by any measure it was one of the most spectacularly unsuccessful efforts in history.[28] When the Jesuits abandoned the island they left behind no churches and no practising native Christians. Their experience mirrored that of the Dominican missionaries in Dominica: "Everything done up to the present to educate and convert the Caribs has failed. For more than thirty years our Order has maintained missionaries who have studied their language and lived among them. The missionaries have taught them the catechism and prayers, and have neglected nothing to win them to Christianity, but all their work has been fruitless. Fathers Raymond, a Breton priest, and Phillipe de Beaumont... lived in Dominica for five-and-twenty years without doing more than baptize a few children as they were dying, and a few adults morally certain to die within a few moments."[29] A gloomy report on the Jesuit mission to St. Vincent in 1688 had reported that the Caribs of the island had "a strong loathing for Christianity",[30] Adrien Le Breton spent his years on St. Vincent in fruitless toil living in fear of another massacre—"a sad life", thought Labat.[31]

The Caribs' own religious ideas were recorded with some interest by the missionaries, and by their account revolved around bad spirits (*maboyas* or *mapoyas*) and good spirits (*ichéiri*) who needed to be placated, often through the intercession of *boyés*,[32] variously described by the missionary-chroniclers as sorcerers, magicians or shamans. As well as treating with *maboyas*, using offerings of cassava or *ouïcou*, *boyés* could be called upon to help with questions of revenge, with illness and to predict the outcome of war. One reason why Caribs allowed the Christian holy men to live among them may have been that they believed they offered some protection from the *maboyas*.

The Caribs were happy to hear the priests out but found Christian theology eminently resistible. "They will listen to a discourse about God, etc and finally say: 'Friend, thou art very Eloquent and Subtle, I wish I could talk as well as thee'." But eloquence was not enough. The Caribs stated frankly "That if they should be persuaded by such discourses, their Neighbours would laugh at them."[33] The priests ascribed the Caribs' failure to embrace the Gospel to the negative example of the Christians who were increasingly encroaching on their territory. Du Tertre blamed "the poor impression the Savages have formed of the bad lives of the Christians; because they have seen men come to take possession of their lands, & those of their neighbours, with unheard of cruelty, who sought only gold, and whose way of life was somewhat more barbarous than their own". He added: "privately the very name Christian makes their heart pound and their teeth grind".[34] Perhaps it was always going to be a tall order to persuade a people who lived healthy, relaxed lives on beautiful islands which provided abundant food and who obeyed no authority but their own that paradise was a state that could only be achieved after death and under the stern guidance of the Church.

The conflict that followed the Jesuit massacre was formally ended on 31 March 1660 when fifteen Carib captains including representatives from St. Vincent came to the chateau in Basse Terre, St. Christopher, to put their mark to a peace treaty with the French and English. The deal legitimized the French and English presence in the islands they had settled but crucially recognized the Caribs' rights to Dominica and St. Vincent, their last remaining strongholds. These islands were declared neutral, that is, not claimed by either European power, and effectively a reservation for the Caribs. At the signing Baba requested that "in consideration of his services" the inhabitants of Martinique should release his nephews whom they had taken prisoner.[35] For France and England it offered the prospect of developing their colonies, and in particular plantation agriculture, without the constant fear of Indian attack. For the Caribs it was a sad recognition of the ground that had been lost—the vast majority of their range—but at the same time it offered the chance to preserve their independence in a reduced territory. It also highlighted the triangular relationship that had grown up between

Caribs, French and English—sometimes allies, sometimes enemies—and that would determine St. Vincent's fate until the end of the eighteenth century. The treaty, though, did not mark the end of European interest in St. Vincent (nor of fighting between French, English and Caribs).

Unbeknown to the Caribs of St. Vincent, their island had been granted by King Charles II of England to the Earl of Carlisle in 1627 together with all "the Caribbees", essentially the Lesser Antilles. Along with a yearly rent of £100, the colony, which was to be known as "the Carlisle or the islands of Carlisle province", was to provide the king, his heirs and successors with a white horse whenever they visited. For all its ambition, this grant had no practical effect and the king subsequently bought back the grant from Carlisle's heir before granting Lord Francis Willoughby of Parham similar rights.

In practice, Lord Willoughby's domain was Barbados; no Englishmen settled St. Vincent. However, he was not blind to the island's strategic importance. He had been given authority to treat with the natives or "in case you shall find them injurious or contumacious, you have free leave and Power to prosecute them with Fire and Sword, and all such ways as in War are usual, both by Sea and Land".[36] He noted that "The Indians are turbulent and active" and, in a foretaste of what would become an abiding preoccupation, advocated maintaining an English presence to counteract the French who "are frequently among them and ready to invite them to breach and blood".[37] After the Caribs sided with the Dutch and French in the Anglo-Dutch War of 1665-7 Willoughby sent a military expedition to St. Vincent.

Details of the venture are few but on 23 March 1668 the English force succeeded in rounding up a number of Carib "captains" on a warship anchored off St. Vincent to sign a treaty. In it, they acknowledged themselves as subject to the King of England and "agreed to be friends to all in amity with the English and enemies to their enemies". As was to be a feature of all subsequent treaties between the two sides, the Caribs agreed to return any runaway slaves from Barbados. The treaty was signed by Nicholas, Aloons, Rebura, Suroe, Nay and Wappya as well as "the Grand Brabba and 14 more of the chiefest captains".[38]

At first glance there appears to be little in the treaty for the Caribs, beyond the dubious benefits of English friendship. But what was important to them was to keep the foreigners out and retain control of their land. This treaty did just that; protestations of submission to an English monarch thousands of miles away were an essentially empty gesture on their part. It is not clear if the "chiefest captains" of St. Vincent included Black Caribs, among whom runaways from Barbados would most likely be sheltered, but it is certain that the island by this time had supported a significant African-descended population for over a generation.

The English colonial authorities in Barbados had a different approach to St. Vincent and the Caribs from those of the English colonies in the Leeward Islands. Barbados lay to windward and, having had its own forests cut down, settlers there valued St. Vincent as a source of wood for building, especially for sugar mills. The colonists in Barbados, England's oldest-established West Indian colony, saw the Leeward Islands as competitors whose interests they were far from keen to advance; hence, according to the governor, Sir Richard Dutton, they saw subduing the Caribs as "no concern of theirs".[39] The main objective of the governor of Barbados was to limit the French influence on the island. Like the Barbadian planters, those of the French islands of Martinique and Guadeloupe coveted St. Vincent's wood. The Caribs had not inhabited Barbados within living memory (and perhaps never) and showed no interest in attacking English possessions there. Islands such as St. Christopher, Antigua and Montserrat had until recently been integral parts of the Caribs' territory and lay on the traditional route of their raiding parties. Also, they were territories of interest to the French, the Caribs' intermittent allies.

In 1674 Caribs from St. Vincent and Dominica, in alliance with the French, attacked English possessions on Antigua and Montserrat. A number of women and children were carried off. The inhabitants of St. Christopher and Nevis called for the "destruction" of the Caribs citing "outrages on his Majesty's subjects who have been inhumanly butchered, miserably mangled, dismembered, and other villanies not to be mentioned by a Christian".[40] The response, as ever, was another bloody raid, with Governor Stapleton sending Philip Warner to St. Vincent and other islands to punish the Caribs.

This expedition marked the end of the remarkable career of Philip Warner's half-brother, Thomas "Indian" Warner. The latter was born in

Antigua, the son of Sir Thomas Warner, governor of St. Christopher, and a Carib woman. After his father's death his English stepmother sent him to work in the fields with the slaves and generally treated him badly. Humiliated, he ran away to live among his mother's people on the island of Dominica.

However, the governor of Barbados, Lord Francis Willoughby, took an interest in him, seeing in him a way to increase English influence among the Caribs. He took Warner to England and presented him at court. Indian Warner adopted European dress but on his return to his people reverted to Carib ways. Willoughby saw Warner as a means of getting around the treaty of neutrality and appointed him governor of Dominica on 16 April 1664, investing him with "full powers". France and England were at this time at war. After Willoughby's death at sea in 1666 Warner's commission was renewed by Willoughby's brother and successor as governor, William. He was captured by the French in the same year.

Throughout his meteoric career as an English colonial governor and Carib war chief, Indian Warner's loyalties were continually called into question, particularly by the English of Antigua, the island from which he had fled. In 1665 a French report suggested that Indian Warner was turning the Caribs of St. Vincent against a nascent English settlement on St. Lucia by claiming that is was the prelude to an English plan to enslave them.

Indian Warner was recognized as a key figure by the planters of Barbados and of the Leeward Islands and by the French. In 1674 the dispirited Jesuit mission on St. Vincent asked to be evacuated but the French ship sent to do so became involved in an altercation with the Caribs which ended in the latter killing the crew. The Caribs then proceeded to Grenada where they massacred another fourteen French people. Already embroiled in a war with the Dutch and Spanish, the local French governor sought the help of Dominican Caribs to mount a punitive expedition against those of St. Vincent. Indian Warner set off with seven pirogues but the result was a disappointment for the French. The hoped-for military campaign fizzled out in a series of feasts at *carbets* around St. Vincent involving the Caribs of both islands.

When Colonel Philip Warner arrived in Dominica on Christmas Day 1674 seeking revenge for the Carib attacks on St. Christopher and

Nevis his 300-strong Antiguan force was joined by Indian Warner and thirty leeward coast Caribs, and together they attacked the pro-French windward Caribs. Four of these were killed and a further thirty were massacred after being lured aboard an English ship.

According to the ship's captain, William Hamlin, Indian Warner and his followers joined in an alcohol-fuelled victory celebration on deck but were then treacherously slain by the English when their guard was down. The killing of Indian Warner—a royal official—by his half-brother provoked an outraged reaction in London. The king ordered the arrest of Philip Warner, citing "the barbarous murder or massacre, committed by Col. P. Warner and his confederates", and he was imprisoned in the Tower of London. By the time he came to trial Philip Warner had mobilized a strong lobbying effort on his behalf. He was judged not in London but in Barbados by a jury of 25 fellow planters and found not guilty.

The royal order for Warner's arrest had noted that "there is reason to believe that the Windward Indians may have been much alienated from the English by this action" and suggested "sending them some heads" to reassure them of English justice. His subsequent acquittal can only have further alienated them. Indian Warner, a formidable leader and a bridge between two cultures, had had the potential to strengthen ties between the English and the Caribs but the enduring legacy of the "Indian Warner affair" was to deepen Carib distrust of the English, the beneficiaries of which were the French.

Having themselves been in the forefront of the European onslaught in the West Indies, notably in their bloody conquests of Guadeloupe and Martinique, the French now increasingly sought to secure the Caribs as allies. They signed a treaty in 1678 with "Pierre Moigna and Jonana, two Caribs from the island of St. Vincent acting on behalf of their entire nation" in which their chief concern appears to have been to keep the Caribs away from Grenada where the French were establishing themselves, a development which the Vincentian Caribs saw as a threat to their communication with the mainland. The treaty also states that "They shall bear arms against enemies of the state when they shall be alerted by us."[41] The fact that the French had been such formidable foes appears to have won them a measure of respect from the Caribs which never attached itself to the English.

Barbuda was subject to a Carib attack on 4 July 1681 when 2,000 warriors descended on the island in fifty pirogues. Eight colonists were killed. Governor Stapleton lobbied Barbados to join a concerted attack against the Carib heartlands and succeeded in getting the king to order the governor Sir Richard Dutton to offer his assistance in "driving the Indians to the Main".[42] Dutton declined, saying he was limited by instructions not to make war. But Dutton was no dove. "In my opinion this war should be undertaken, provided that we are so prepared as to carry it on vigorously even to the extirpation of these savages," he wrote.[43]

Stapleton was not deterred and set about organizing his own raid. In June 1683 Stapleton reported to the Lords of Trade and Plantations on "my Indian hunting".[44] He conceded that the expedition had been brought to a premature halt, blaming the rains and a lack of provisions. The Caribs' fighting tactics on their own ground were clearly a major concern. Stapleton feared the consequences of his troops marching in the woods with their powder wet leaving them vulnerable to ambush by the Caribs, whose bowstrings were made of silk grass and were unaffected by the damp. The Caribs were also believed to have 45 firearms supplied by the French. He claimed to have killed at least eleven Caribs, including "Captain Tabary" who had led the attacks on Barbuda and Montserrat, but said the Caribs' practice of carrying away their casualties made an accurate body count impossible. The English suffered five wounded, of whom one died later from a poisoned arrow. They burnt down more than three hundred houses on St. Vincent and Dominica and destroyed 46 large pirogues and canoes at St. Vincent, as well as "a prodigious quantity of provisions".

Despite the destruction the Caribs were unbowed. In August 1686 Captain John Temple sailed in the *Mary Rose* to St. Vincent from Barbados to assert the English claim to the island and order foreigners (the French) to leave or swear fealty, but "found the Indians and negroes very insolent".[45] In a tense encounter he took the ship's boat to within hailing distance of the shore where Caribs were massed with bows and arrows. Despite assurances that the English force meant no harm, the Caribs let fly at the sloop "using very base language". The English fired back, drove them off and then went ashore to burn their houses. The *Mary Rose* sailed on to leeward but received an identical response. The English left having burnt more houses and destroyed provision grounds. The lieutenant governor of Barbados reported that: "I have caused the King's arms to be fitly and decently carved in wood and to be affixed in the most notable place [in St. Vincent]." (He added: "I hope that the French will not presume to shoot them down and break them in pieces in an insolent and scornful manner, as they formerly did, as soon as the frigate had left them.")[46] The whole incident produced a formal protest from the French that the English actions were a violation of the treaty of neutrality. Its effect on Carib attitudes to the English can only be imagined.

While the English mounted sporadic expeditions to try to impose their will on St. Vincent the French could sit back and watch as their countrymen insinuated themselves on the leeward coast of the island as woodcutters, farmers and traders. Agents for the colony of Barbados claimed to the Lords of Trade and Plantations that the English had several times made settlements upon St Lucia and St. Vincent "though by reason of sundry accidents those settlements had no continuance".[47] If so, these abortive attempts left no trace on the latter island. By 1719, except for the occasional pirate,[48] there were no English people on St. Vincent.

Belatedly a subsequent governor of Barbados, Mitford Crowe, tried a more subtle diplomacy. He had brought to him in 1707 "some of the cheafe Indians" of the islands of St. Vincent and Dominica "who I have cloath'd and been kinde to".[49] They assured him of their loyalty to the King of England but Crowe noticed that they understood more French than English. Captain Clarke, who had brought the Caribs to Barbados aboard HMS *Crown*, observed that "it appears plainly they are very hearty to ye French interests".[50] In October Governor Crowe induced seven Carib captains to sign an agreement aboard HMS *Lynn* in which they promised to assist any English ships arriving there and to return any runaway slaves from Barbados.[51]

But while the British were sending gunboats to persuade the Caribs the French were wooing them on their own terms. A month later, no doubt in response to the British initiative, a French official, Monsieur Coullet, was dispatched from Martinique to negotiate with the Caribs. Coullet, who was well-known to the Caribs, stayed in the *carbet* of Chief Abel Piaie from where he sent out an invitation to all the island's other chiefs to come and receive presents from the King of France.[52]

Abel Piaie is almost certainly the "Capt. Abell" who signed Governor Crowe's treaty and given that he came from "Rebeco Bay" (Rabacca), in the heart of the windward territory, he was almost certainly a Black Carib. A total of 57 chiefs, "Caribs as well as negroes", gathered in an assembly to hear out their French visitor. Showing respect for native custom, Coullet stripped naked and embraced each of the chiefs one after the other. Then he chided them for supplying wood to the British and for sending their children to Barbados. He accused Abel Piaie of leading the British to valuable trees and ordered him to burn them so the Barbados planters could not benefit from them. The whole assembly agreed and 10,000 francs worth of timber went up in smoke. He asked them to kill one or two Englishmen, cut off their hands, *boucan* them and bring them to Martinique as a token of their friendship.

With this satisfactory outcome he opened a barrel of eau-de-vie which was enthusiastically consumed by those present. The evening ended in traditional fashion, with quarrels, fights and bloodshed. Many were wounded, including Chief Inada who received an arrow wound between the legs, but none of this marred the diplomatic coup. Coullet's approach was based on his long experience which meant that he knew "better than anyone how to win their hearts" and was surely a factor in France's relative success in maintaining Carib friendship. There is no record of any British official removing his trousers in pursuit of good relations with the Caribs.

The French tactics bore fruit over the subsequent decades. In 1728 John Bennet, a Barbados merchant, warned that Frenchmen were subtly making inroads among the Caribs of the neutral islands. The French, he wrote, "are making themselves master of St. Vincents by the only advisable method. Were they to do it openly and by force, the negroes and Indians would obstruct them, as they have formerly done, but by the preaching and insinuation of their Fryers, and gratuities of rum[,] sugar, and other little commodities, they insensibly insinuate themselves into the affections of those people, and begin to make themselves not only acceptable, but usefull and necessary amongst them."[53] With the help of the missionaries' soft diplomacy and of independent traders, hunters and fishermen, French settlers were able to grow a variety of crops on the island and even export corn to Barbados, while engaging in trade with the Caribs.

Despite the lack of resident Englishmen on the scene, word filtered back to London of a remarkable event at St. Vincent in 1718. Daniel Defoe, in his role as a journalist for *Myst's Journal,* reported that he had received accounts "from so many several hands, and several places" that in the night of 27 March "a dreadful Flash of Lightning" was seen, accompanied by "innumerable Clashes of Thunder". The following morning there was a "deep impenetrable darkness; but below, all round the edge of the horizon, it look'd as if the Heavens were all on Fire". A mysterious substance "as thick as smoke, but fine as dust, and yet solid as sand" fell for two or three days and night and lay inches thick at Martinique. These ominous developments culminated in an earth-shattering explosion. Defoe wrote: "That the Terror was inexpressible, and cannot be represented by Words; that the noise of the bursting of the Earth at first, is not possible to be described; that the force of the Blow or Blast was such, and the whole body of the Island was rais'd so furiously, that the Earth was entirely separated into small particles like Dust; and as it rose to an immense Height, so it spread itself to an incredible Distance, and fell light and gradually, like a small but thick Mist."[54] Nothing remained, Defoe wrote, "except three little Rocks".

Clearly, St. Vincent had not disappeared into thin air, as some readers of *Myst's Journal* evidently pointed out. The following month Defoe wrote: "They pretend to tell us a strange Story, viz., that the Island of St. Vincent is found again, and is turn'd into a Volcano, or burning Mountain; but we must acknowledge we do not believe one word of it." Defoe may have been guilty of overstatement but his remains the first written account of an eruption of St. Vincent's Soufriere volcano.

An eruption on anything like the scale reported by Defoe—and the traveller Alexander von Humboldt also referred to the eruption of 1718[55]—would have had a huge impact on the Caribs. The volcano was right in the middle of Carib territory and when the same volcano erupted in 1902 nearly 1,700 people died. In the wake of the immediate impact, though, the Caribs would have adapted, shifting their provision grounds, and perhaps their homes, that had been blighted by volcanic ash.

In the early eighteenth century settlers on surrounding islands were looking to St. Vincent as a source of more than just wood and water. Another potentially saleable commodity was an apparent abundance of black people living on the windward coast. To many European eyes these represented the chance of a profit in the slave markets. By the turn of the eighteenth century leading inhabitants of the French-ruled islands had for some time been agitating for an expedition to St. Vincent to capture black people living on the windward who might be sold into slavery in the French or Spanish colonies. They claimed that St. Vincent's black population were largely runaways from Martinique— in reality the distance between the islands and the prevailing currents made this very unlikely. A report into the feasibility of such an expedition warned that it would be a "very difficult" undertaking.[56] Since landing on the rugged windward coast where the Black Caribs lived would be too perilous it would be necessary to disembark on the leeward shore and seek the support of the Yellow Caribs to find or cut paths through the woods into the windward territory. The author of the report said that (Yellow) Caribs who had visited Martinique had suggested they would support such a French attack because they feared that local Black Caribs would increase in number and mistreat them. But he warned that many Black Caribs were allied with the Yellow Caribs and "*vivent ensemble en bonne intelligence*" (live together on good terms). He warned that not too much credence should be placed on Carib declarations of their intentions since "they talk little, take a long time to explain themselves, and judge very adroitly what one wants them to say, [and] often speak to please what they believe one wants of them". The report added that: "It is very certain that they would prefer to see 2,000 negroes established in their island than to see just 50 armed Frenchmen disembark."

Nothing came of this in the short term but the idea of a slaving expedition to St. Vincent (on the spurious grounds of hunting runaways from Martinique) did not go away. Labat reported: "I have often heard this matter discussed and many plans have been made to capture these negroes and sell them to the Spaniards for their mines."[57] Yellow Caribs entertained on a French ship off St. Vincent in 1705 indicated they were eager for help in their ongoing struggle against the Black Caribs. Father Adrien Le Breton, who had been brought back to the island to mediate in the case of the murder of a French settler by a Carib, learned that "there had been a considerable massacre on both sides and that there was real war between them and the negroes".[58]

In 1719 the military commander of Martinique, the Marquis de Feuquières, revived the idea of a slaving raid on St. Vincent. Two military officials, Messrs Poulain de Guerville and Du Bucq, were to lead the expedition. The project was ill-starred from the start. The plan was to take a force of 1,000 to 1,200 men but in the event it was a much reduced party of some three hundred who set out from Fort Royal and St. Pierre in July. The active cooperation of the Yellow Caribs was a key part of the plan but the organizers of the expedition would have done well to have studied the report from 1700. Yellow Carib support was generally unforthcoming although a few did accompany the French as guides.[59] The Black Caribs, though, were even more familiar with the lie of the land. Carib warfare relied on surprise and the Black Caribs would have seen the French force coming for miles. Also, numbers and terrain were not to the invaders' advantage. The French estimated there were some 2,000 *nègres marrons* in the windward part of St. Vincent (plus 3-4,000 women and children). A British observer watching the preparations in Martinique was dubious about the expedition's chances: "I believe their success against the Negroes will be small, all of them being acquainted with the Use of a Musket."[60] What the French found as they picked their way into Black Carib territory were the smoking ruins of houses. Their quarry had destroyed their own homes and slipped away into the thickly wooded interior.

Poulain led a detachment of 150 men into the bush to try to locate the Black Caribs. They marched for about an hour without catching sight of the enemy but then, hearing a noise from the forest, Poulain decided to divide his force still further, leading a party of thirty. It was the prelude to disaster. A force of Black Caribs was lying in wait to ambush them. Poulain was killed on the spot with five or six others. Then they fell upon the rest of the troop, sending most of them running pell-mell back to their boats. Word was sent back to Martinique for reinforcements but none were forthcoming. The Black Caribs could surely have pressed home their advantage against the beleaguered force but evidently were already looking ahead to a negotiated solution. With the troops on St. Vincent now suffering from dysentery, the acting commander, Du Bucq, had no option but to pull out.

41

According to French accounts, eight or ten of the French force were killed and fifteen or sixteen wounded (the British put French losses at thirty to forty dead)[61] but the slaving expedition was an abject failure—not a single Black Carib was captured—and the French never again sent a military force against the Black Caribs. Paradoxically it had the effect of strengthening Yellow Carib attachment to the French, who were already established as settlers on the leeward coast. On 3 December chiefs of the principal Yellow Carib families, "after long deliberation and enjoying all the liberty with which we are born", signed a treaty with the French at the "*grand carbet de Cariacoua*" (Calliaqua), in which they sought the "powerful protection" of the French to prevent them "falling under the domination of perfidious negroes who we have allowed to establish themselves in our island to our great misfortune".[62] The agreement also allowed for property sales and left open the possibility of the Yellow Caribs leaving the island altogether. The Yellow Caribs had formally accepted French sovereignty and opened the door to a growing French presence on the leeward territory of the island. Their fortunes, however, did not improve. More than fifty years later four Black Carib chiefs recalled their victory over Poulain and Du Bucq and noted that: "After the departure of the French we defeated the red Caribs. The island of St. Vincent remained with us."[63]

However, the Poulain debacle also resulted in a swift rapprochement with the Black Caribs. A delegation of Black Caribs sailed by pirogue to Martinique to protest to the French authorities about what they saw as an unjustified outbreak of hostilities. They brought with them the Cross of St. Louis taken from Poulain's corpse along with the personal effects of other French officers. In return they received "very large presents". To remove any justification for further action they swore friendship to the French and promised not to molest the Yellow Caribs and to return any runaway slaves. Although these promises were no more than had been made before and would be made many times again, both to the French and the British, the Black Caribs were clearly alarmed at having had to fight a defensive war on their own territory. An English account of the conflict claims the Black Caribs "had kil'd many of their wives and children to prevent their falling into the Fr. hands, and declared themselves under the English subjection and fought under their colours."[64] Ultimately they calculated that good relations with the

French, who now had a permanent presence on the island, were their best tactic.

The planters of Martinique reasoned that despite the military failure in St. Vincent the expedition had had some benefits. It had bound the Yellow Caribs closer to the French (the treaty would be renewed in 1727) and led them to encourage more French settlement on the leeward part of the island. It had also allowed them to familiarize themselves with the wealth and fertility of the island. The Black Caribs' formal submission to the Martinique authorities was likewise a welcome development. The key consideration was the strategic balance with Great Britain which already enjoyed an advantage in the form of the Royal Navy. If the Caribs did not ally themselves with the French they might well do so with the British, as highlighted by the claim that they had raised a British flag in fighting off Poulain's adventure. The price the French paid in lavish gift-giving was well worth paying. "The savages are good friends, but cruel enemies; their warfare is that much more to be feared because it is without quarter and they never attack their enemies except by surprise," they noted.[65] For the Black Caribs, the memory of their victory over the French was still very fresh more than fifty years later when they drew on it for inspiration in their conflict with the British in what became known as the First Carib War.

So it was that when Captain Braithwaite arrived at St. Vincent less than four years after the bloody clash between the French and the Black Caribs, he found a united front of antipathy towards any British pretensions on the island. In 1722 King George I granted the Duke of Montagu the islands of St Lucia and St. Vincent "with ye same powers, privilidges and benefits, which petitioner is possess'd of in his Manor of Bewley".[66] The government had been urged to settle the islands and Montagu saw an opportunity to grow rich on the back of his own Caribbean empire. He solicited settlers, declaring that the "Islands are very rich in soyle and productive of sugar, indigo, cotton, piemento, ginger, cocoa, anotto etc. and having not as yet been broken up will yield very great increase to the settlers."[67] They would be entitled to grants of ten acres for themselves and ten acres for every white person in their family, plus five acres for every slave. Grants were to be limited to five hundred acres and planters from Barbados and other West Indian islands were to be excluded. The Royal Navy ships *Winchelsea, Feversham, Hector* and *Lynn* were assigned to support the expedition and Nathaniel Uring was named as deputy governor of St. Vincent.

The expedition encountered problems from the start. Landing at St Lucia on 16 December 1722, Uring and his hundred-odd settlers were dismayed to be confronted by a French force bearing a proclamation ordering them to leave the island within fifteen days. While the two European groups traded proofs of authority with each other, Uring dispatched a party to St. Vincent to "get together the Cheifest of the… Negroes, Indians and Mulattoes" and read them Montagu's declaration that if they registered within three months they would "be treated in the same Manner as natural born Subjects of his Majesty within these Islands".[68]

The first impression of St. Vincent encouraged the view that this would be a good site for a colony. In particular the windward coast, where the Black Caribs were based and which would be fought over so bitterly for the rest of the century, seemed perfect from a planter's point of view. "[T]he eastward of St. Vincent, was a Pleasant Prospect; there seem'd to be a large Quantity of good Land planted, and fit to plant from the South West to the North East. In some Places along Shore there were Heads of Rocks not very high; but in many Places there seem'd to be good landing with pleasant Descents down to the Waterside in fine green Patches, and a great deal of Upper Land lay unmanur'd fit for Plantations," wrote the captain of one of the vessels, Robert Egerton.[69]

Braithwaite's reception at St. Vincent, though, was little better than Uring's at St. Lucia. Again the influence of Britain's colonial rivals reared its head. French agents had told the Caribs "that the English came now only as spy's to view their Island, and that their design was in the end only to trick them and destroy them; and further, that if they enter'd into any Articles with the English, or accepted of any presents from them, the French would come, and carry them all away captives to Martineco".[70] Furthermore, two French sloops had the day before delivered arms and ammunition to the island along with news of the failure of the British settlement attempt at St. Lucia. All the men carried cutlasses, some also muskets, pistols, bows and arrows. Captain Orme, who commanded the warship on which the "Indian general" and the "chief of the negroes" were entertained, reported that "they are so intimate and well acquainted with the French, that most of them speak that language, and a great many of them have been baptized in the Catholick Faith." He felt that settlement of the island could only be achieved by making friends with the inhabitants, but suspected that the French had already beaten them to it.

The British St. Vincent enterprise ended almost before it had begun. With the Caribs resolute in their opposition, Captain Braithwaite left the island firing off a cannon in salute and being answered by a disciplined fusillade from the Black Caribs on the shore. Meanwhile in the face of a French show of force Uring had no option but to withdraw from St. Lucia. Five years later the Duke of Montagu asked to be allowed to swap his grant in the two islands for one in the less contested territory of Tobago.

Following the abject failure of their colonizing project, the British watched with impotent concern as the French presence on St. Vincent grew. Sieur de Laborde, writing just after the turn of the eighteenth century, thought the European presence on the island very limited: "there are even some at St. Vincent who have never seen Christians."[71] But within a few years French people from Martinique and Guadeloupe were settling there, particularly after the failure of Poulain's slaving expedition pushed the leeward Yellow Caribs further into the arms of the French. John Ridley, master and owner of the sloop *Endeavour,* reported that while on a woodcutting expedition at the St. Vincent bay of Corbaco he had found six or seven French families settled there and a further fourteen or fifteen at another bay a league further north. There they raised "provisions and a very great quantity of tobacco". The French settlers said that more of their countrymen were daily coming over to settle from Martinique and demanded to know by what authority the English presumed to cut timber there.[72] In 1729 the master of a schooner complained to a Royal Navy captain that he too had been prevented from cutting wood on the island and that the French inhabitants, who were by now estimated to number three hundred, had "fired at him all night and encouraged the negroes and Indians to set fire to his vessel".[73] In 1735 the British calculated that there were 117 Frenchmen capable of bearing arms on St. Vincent[74] and were receiving troubling reports that they had established a civil government there. The following year the Council of Trade and Plantations fretted that the French "are daily encreasing in numbers" in both St. Vincent and Dominica.[75]

In 1748 the Treaty of Aix-la-Chapelle, which ended the War of the Austrian Succession, reiterated the neutral status of St. Vincent but the French paid only lip service to its terms while quietly establishing facts on the ground. That same year the French governor of Martinique, Charles de Tubières, Marquis of Caylus, could report with satisfaction that many French people had settled on St. Vincent and lived in harmony with the Black and Red (Yellow) Caribs and that he had received no complaints from either side. The French were well established on the leeward coast at places such as Layou and Ouasigany (later renamed Kingstown by the British). They had established formal structures of government in eight leeward districts, ranging from Chateaubelair in the north round to Calliaqua in the south. A British writer reported that at this time "the *Negroes* inhabited the Shore to the *North East*, their Hutts near the Water-side".[76] Caylus said that he had given passports to all the *capitaines de pirogue* who had come to call on him and had not "skimped on taffia [low-grade rum] nor the other presents which keep them attached to the French".[77] Perhaps because of this the Caribs had attacked the English on the sea and in the Grenadines where they came to collect wood "and committed cruelties which I would have hoped to prevent".

When Longvilliers de Poincy, the governor of Grenada, visited St. Vincent in early 1750 he was impressed by how the French settlers were flourishing. The main crops were coffee and tobacco, although some cotton and food crops were grown. The Caribs, though, would not allow sugar mills to be built, nor stone buildings. Poincy landed at Layou and visited various communities. He found Buccament, adjacent to Layou, to be the most considerable of them, the town even boasting a "fairly fine church", while he was "astonished" by the wealth of the inhabitants of Ouasigany.[78]

French settlements were confined to bays on the leeward coast and the river valleys extending inland. The mountainous interior and the whole of the windward coast were in the hands of the Black Caribs. The man the French recognized as the "General" of the Black Caribs was called Tourouya and it is even conceivable that it was he who delivered that dusty response to Captain Braithwaite 25 or so years earlier.[79] Relations between the two sides were cordial and Tourouya was particularly close to a senior Martinique-based administrative official, the Marquis de Lambertye. An important military figure, Lambertye detected in Tourouya "signs of great probity, justice, and integrity as much in his observations as in the wisdom of his administration", adding that the Carib chief was "the least brutal of his nation" and had attempted to change his people's "dissolute customs". He was curious about French ways and discussed subjects such as religion and medicine with Lambertye. Most remarkably of all, Lambertye reported that Tourouya "wrote me several letters when I was in Martinique, which—although in quite bizarre style, quite unlike the European—demonstrate his virtue and his morals: I have carefully preserved them".[80] Sadly none of these documents appears to have survived.[81]

Whatever the strangely styled musings of these lost letters, surviving documents reveal that Tourouya's principal concern in his dealings with the French was land, and in particular preventing European encroachment on Carib territory. In 1749 Tourouya had spent half a day in a meeting with a local French official complaining about settlers seeking to build roads into Carib territory. Plans for the road had created *"une grande tumulte"*[82] among the Caribs, the most distracted of whom had threatened to kill their wives and children and attack the French in Martinique.

Tourouya then visited the Marquis de Caylus in person in Martinique, accompanied by a Red Carib who had a grievance against a Frenchman who wanted to acquire his land against his will. Caylus received Tourouya cordially and gave him presents, as was standard practice. The governor sought to pacify Tourouya by issuing orders to officials in St. Vincent not to build roads into Carib territory and exhorting them to show "strong friendship and good neighbourliness", satisfied that the visit signified a recognition of French sovereignty. Tourouya asked for and was granted permission to build some houses at Ouasigany, where the French had laid out the three streets parallel to the sea which still form the heart of Kingstown. The houses, in which Tourouya, his family and friends were to reside, were to be made of "reeds" in the Carib style and positioned along fifty feet of the seafront.

When Poincy visited St. Vincent the following year he had a face-to-face meeting lasting two hours with Tourouya. Poincy described

Tourouya as being established in "Mornagarou on the border of Ouasigany", territory which was already believed to include the island's best agricultural land and was jealously guarded against European penetration (Mornagarou or Morne Garou at this time usually refers to a mountainous area in the centre of the island but in this case it appears to be used more generally). Tourouya seemed eager to please and Poincy reassured him of protection against encroachment by French settlers. In response to Poincy's complaints about Black Caribs troubling the French, in particular the conduct of Petit Louis, a Carib leader of some 15-20 people, Tourouya volunteered that Petit Louis would not live long.[83] Poincy deduced that Tourouya was calculating that killing Petit Louis would both please the French and strengthen his own authority among the Black Caribs.

Such was Tourouya's desire to ingratiate himself that he volunteered for baptism and even offered to send his male children to live in the house of the leading French official on St. Vincent, actions that recall those of Baba in the previous century. One son was indeed taken on by Lambertye as a valet, a position in which he acquitted himself rather poorly, largely because of his drinking. Lambertye described Tourouya as the "sovereign cacique" (chief) of the Black Caribs[84] and claimed that this was a hereditary position since their first arrival in St. Vincent (although there is little evidence to back up this assertion). He added that Tourouya owned a hundred black slaves "which he bought in our colonies".

However, any idea that Tourouya spoke for all the island's Black Caribs was quickly dispelled. On 24 July 1752 the Marquis Maximin de Bompar wrote to his successor as governor of Martinique, Alexandre Rouillé de Rocourt (Bompar remained governor general of the French West Indies), about an alarming incident that had occurred the previous evening. Just as he was sitting down to dinner in company with other French officials a deputation of Black Caribs burst in upon them to complain about a piece of land at a place called Manacro in Carib country that Rouillé's secretary, a Monsieur Perain, claimed to have purchased. Manacro was described as a bay in the north of the island "which is absolutely essential to them for fishing"[85] and has been identified as Owia.[86] (Sir William Young described the disputed land as being "on the extreme territory of the Red Charaibs".)[87] The leader of the deputation, called Bigot, was agitated, insisting that he and his people would never allow anyone to settle in their lands. Attempting to defuse the situation, Bompar suggested that perhaps the land had been sold by Red Caribs. Bigot replied that there were only a handful of these left on the island, and those only on the Black Caribs' sufferance, and that they had no power to dispose of anything. Bompar then ventured that perhaps Tourouya had given his approval. Bigot was equally dismissive. Tourouya, he said, had no power to dispose of land either, and in any case he only had authority within his own territory, just as Bigot had authority in his (Bigot was based at Point Espagnol, adjacent to Owia). Finally, in threatening tones he warned that he and his people would rather die than allow Frenchmen to settle in the Black Caribs' part of the island. Bompar prudently advised Rouillé to tell his secretary to give up his claim to the land. The Caribs did not wait for the French response. They burned Perain's house down and destroyed his plantation.[88]

Black Carib complaints of settler encroachment were nothing new to the French. Bompar said he was normally able to placate them by making "spurious promises" or by giving "little presents which flatter their caprice for novelty". But he noted that they had always refused point-blank to countenance ceding any territory in Manacro. Bompar also shed light on his manipulation of Carib politics. "Without the fear that I have taken trouble to inspire in them and with the care I have taken to support the aforementioned Trouya, they would have changed their chief a long time ago."[89] It is surely a sign of Tourouya's close, perhaps too close, relationship with the French that he was granted permission to build houses, and presumably make his home, in the heart of that part of the island settled by Europeans, on the waterfront of what would become the capital of the British colony.

Ill-feeling about French designs on Carib land boiled over in 1755 in the form of what Bompar called an uprising (soulèvement) by the Black Caribs.[90] There are few details—although Bompar also refers to an émeute (riot)—but the governor general was sufficiently concerned to send an official, Monsieur Desligneris, aboard an armed vessel to St. Vincent to restore calm. He imprisoned a few "mutinous and insubordinate" Frenchmen but pacified the Caribs with "persuasion and gentleness" and brought a number of chiefs of their own volition back to Martinique where they asked Bompar's forgiveness. The governor hoped that establishing clear boundaries between the French and the Caribs would diminish tension. But he feared the potential for further trouble if the Black Caribs should incite slaves to run away to their territory.

Red Carib fortunes, meanwhile, continued to dwindle. In March 1749 the Marquis de Caylus received a report which alluded to the "vexations of the Blacks Caribs towards the Reds". The report saw it as an intractable problem: "*il est vray qu'ils les molestent extremement; mais c'est un mal contre lequel l'on connois aucun remede*" ("It is true that they trouble them extremely; but it is an evil to which no remedy is known").[91] Although Caylus issued a proclamation in May promising protection to both the Black and Red Caribs from white settlers, the problems between the two groups did not go away. In 1750 a number of Yellow Caribs were reported to have emigrated to Trinidad. Two years later a French official reported that the Red (Yellow) Caribs were "continually exposed to violence and mistreatment" from the Black Caribs. Many were determined to leave the island altogether and join those who had moved to Trinidad or the mainland. In 1792 Sir William Young, on a visit to one of his estates in Tobago, came across a Carib called Louis. He said he was five years old when, fifty years previously, he had arrived on the island fleeing "the persecutions of the Africans or black Charaibes of St. Vincent's".[92] Estimates about this time put Yellow Carib numbers on St. Vincent at around a hundred people. For the rest of the century the protagonists of the Carib struggle to defend Youroumaÿn would be black.

3. Quel Roi?

"We were greatly surprised to find them in a fixed resolution not to consent to our settling any part of the country claimed by them..."
Report of the Commissioners for the Sale of Lands in the Ceded Islands to the Lords of the Treasury, 16 October 1771

ON 10 FEBRUARY 1763 Paris was witness to a display of diplomatic pomp and circumstance as the representatives of the crowns of France, Great Britain and Spain assembled to put a formal end to seven years of warfare. The negotiations had taken months. John Russell, the fourth Duke of Bedford, had been dispatched to the French capital the previous September and had spent an uncomfortable time troubled by gout and chafing at the restrictions imposed by his masters in London. Representing Spain (and Portugal) was Pablo Jerónimo Grimaldi y Pallavicini, the Italian-born Marquis and Duke of Grimaldi, minister plenipotentiary and ambassador to France. The third participant was César Gabriel de Choiseul, the recently created Duke of Praslin-Chévigny, and secretary of state for foreign affairs. The treaty they signed was breathtaking in the way it redrew the map of the world, with territories changing hands in Europe, Africa and Asia as well as the Americas. The French surrendered Canada to the British and the boundary of British territory in North America was extended westward to the Mississippi river and shifted southward with the acquisition of Florida from Spain. The French handed Sumatra to Britain, which also regained Menorca, and numerous forts changed ownership. Cuba, briefly British, would be Spanish again, as would Manila. France took back the West African slave station of Gorée and, in the Caribbean, regained Guadeloupe, Martinique, St. Lucia and Marie-Galante. And down in Article IX, along with the islands of Grenada, Dominica and Tobago, we find St. Vincent, one of the smaller spoils of a worldwide war, declared to be, "in full right", a possession of Great Britain. A later historian wrote, with particular reference to the provisions for North America, that "half a continent... changed hands at the scratch of a pen." For the Black Caribs, it was their whole world.

51

St. Vincent had not been a battlefield in the war and had been occupied—the French-controlled leeward side at least—without a fight by a British force under General Robert Monckton and Admiral George Rodney in February 1762. The British were in no doubt about the significance of the transfer of sovereignty, which definitively ended, to British and French satisfaction, the "neutral" status of the island. The Caribs were not consulted about nor even mentioned in the treaty. It was never explained how by some diplomatic sleight of hand France could cede an island to Britain which since 1660 both countries had recognized as belonging to the Caribs (a status that had been ratified as recently as 1748). While the French had occupied only the leeward coast, the British had no intention of confining themselves to just a part of the island and quickly set about the business of turning St. Vincent into a profitable colony.

Having seen how the haphazard agricultural development on other British islands had led to soil exhaustion and what today might be called environmental degradation, the Privy Council gave detailed consideration to the best way of exploiting the lands in the four "ceded" islands: St. Vincent, Dominica, Grenada and Tobago. It was decided to limit the size of individual lots to 500 acres to prevent estates becoming too large and conditions were stipulated to encourage white immigration.[1]

A Commission for the Sale of Lands in the Ceded Islands was appointed in 1764 to survey and sell off the newly acquired agricultural land and its members departed for the West Indies by the end of the year. The commissioners were led by Sir William Young, a baronet and leading sugar planter in Antigua and himself the son of a sugar planter of Scottish origin. His son, also called Sir William Young, would go on to write one of the most important histories of the period based largely on his father's papers. He and his three fellow commissioners set about their business energetically—Young said he made some 110 sea voyages over the nine years of the commission's work.

In a prospectus for planters, Young contrasted the bounty of St. Vincent ("remarkably fertile", "plentifully watered") with Britain's more established West Indian colonies: "in our old islands the lands are exhausted and impoverished, the trees all cut down, and their estates become so dry and unseasonable, as constantly to disappoint [the planters] of the crops they expect, and their pains and industry deserve."[2]

In the manner of an estate agent, Young, who had yet to encounter the conditions on the ground, played down the difficulties for potential buyers. The natives, he suggested, were by no means restless and even their longstanding attachment to the French—later one of the principal charges against them—was presented as a positive. The Black Caribs would be no obstacle to profit. "They have been usually represented as turbulent and dangerous, but experience now convinces us, that they are a quiet and well disposed people, speaking French, and instructed by Roman Catholic missionaries, in the principles of their religion. By the last account received from thence, many of them seemed disposed to quit their little cottages, and spots of provision ground, and to remove to St Lucia, or Martinique. But probably, when they are duly apprized of the humanity and generosity of our gracious Sovereign, and assured of the enjoyment of their lands, freedom, favor and protection, they may be gained over to our cause, and even rendered useful."[3]

A byproduct of the land commissioners' work was the beautiful map made by John Byres detailing landholdings on the island, at that stage nearly all in French hands, but also delineating the territory still possessed by the Caribs. This territory, as the British sources unfailingly remark, contained the most fertile land and the most suitable for growing sugar, for which European demand was growing and almost insatiable. Britain consumed five times as much sugar in 1770 as it had in 1710, much of it to sweeten tea, and by 1750 sugar had become the most valuable commodity in European trade.[4] "The eastern, or windward part of the island, through which the Charibbs are at present irregularly scattered," wrote Sir William Young Sr. in 1767, "remains almost intirely unoccupied and in wood, but it is by far, more extensive, more level, and a finer country than the part already disposed of; and as the soil is perhaps the best in the world, and it is admirably supplied with rivers, it would probably soon become a more valuable sugar colony than any possessed by the crown, unless Jamaica, which must be excepted only on account of its very superior extent."[5]

The French settlers on the leeward side had been allowed to repurchase their lands on a forty-year leasehold. In 1763 they numbered some 1,300 with 3,400 slaves and largely grew coffee, tobacco and cacao, along with food provisions and other products such as wood and indigo. This was not purely out of choice. The well-armed and much more numerous Black Caribs had forbidden them to build sugar mills, evidently mindful of the association between plantation agriculture and the appetite for land and the importation of slaves. It was sugar, though, and the prospect of the vast profits that had been generated in earlier sugar booms on islands such as Barbados, that fuelled the British drive to dispossess the Caribs.

Initially, however, the land commissioners' instructions issued on 4 December 1764 were that "no survey should be made of lands occupied or claimed by the Charaibs" until further instructions were sent out.[6] The British had no intention of allowing the Caribs to remain in possession of such potentially productive lands indefinitely but were also aware of the need to proceed with caution, mindful of the Caribs' reputation as formidable warriors, the possibility of intervention by the French and the poverty of intelligence about the true strength and disposition of Carib forces. It may be too that some humanitarian consideration was involved, in Whitehall at least: Lord Hillsborough, the president of the Board of Trade, would later advocate humane treatment of Indians on the North American mainland and in 1763 acknowledged that the Black Caribs "consider themselves to be, and really are, an independent people."[7] The local planters were consistently more aggressive in their views about the Black Caribs than the metropolitan authorities.

The Caribs certainly understood that their independence faced a new threat. Alarmed at the arrival of a detachment of British troops on the island, Tourouya and Bigot ("*qui sont la tête des Caraïbes de St Vincent*") sailed to Martinique to demand of the governor, the Marquis of Fénélon, the protection of the French king and arms to defend themselves against the British colonial government.[8]

On 2 February 1762, a year before the formal transfer of sovereignty to Britain but with the tide of war running to the advantage of the British, a number of Carib chiefs had approached a French cleric, Abbé Dominique Valladares, to advise them and represent their interests to the new British authorities. On their arrival in the island in 1764 the land commissioners assiduously sought him out, hoping through his intercession to persuade the Caribs to acknowledge the sovereignty of the King of Great Britain, and then to agree to sell their lands on the windward side and allow roads to be built on their territory. With the *abbé's* help, they managed to hold conversations with several Carib heads of families and took great pains to explain their proposals. The chiefs listened "with deep attention". A few seemed receptive, others prevaricated but most made little secret of their hostility. Even those few whose attitude had appeared promising to the commissioners were quickly disavowed by their people. In short, the British were left in no doubt that any attempt to acquire Carib lands would be strongly resisted.

Sales of land in St. Vincent began on 28 May 1764 but the windward territories inhabited by the Black Caribs remained for the time being effectively out of bounds. The commissioners were also responsible for disposing of land in the other three "ceded islands"—Tobago, Grenada and Dominica—and the work of surveying and granting land in those territories proceeded in an orderly fashion. By 1767 the commissioners had disposed of 12,507 acres in St. Vincent but all of this land was on the leeward side, inhabited by French settlers, many of whom remained on new leases granted by the crown, and the few Yellow Caribs. As the commissioners noted with some chagrin, though, the Black Caribs, on the windward side, were sitting on "the most fertile part of the island" and, unlike much of the leeward coast, eminently suitable for sugar production. It was flatter, with good soil "consisting chiefly of a fine mould, composed of sand and clay, well adapted for sugar," and well watered by numerous streams which could provide power via water-mills.

It was hoped that persuasion might sway the Black Caribs. The commissioners, led by Young, who was also appointed lieutenant gov-ernor of Dominica in 1768, made great play of their generosity in ad-judicating some minor land disputes in favour of individual Caribs ("The lands of Madame la Croix are declared of right to belong to the Charaib Thuriau [Tourouya?]; the lands possessed by M. Pradiér are adjudged to the Charaib Joannae..." etc),[9] decisions no doubt made easier by the fact that those thus dispossessed were French. Whether this was meant to impress the Caribs into changing their attitude or was directed more at opinion in London is debatable. Leading Caribs were wined and dined as part of the diplomatic offensive. Sir William Young later claimed that during his time as a land commissioner he had spent £1,500 of his own money on presents and entertainment for the Caribs of St. Vincent.[10] (The Caribs themselves later recalled that Young "had never been able to gather more than 20 or 25 Caribs despite giving us all sorts of presents on behalf of his sovereign.")[11] When the governor of the ceded islands, General Robert Melvill, visited in April 1765 he made sure that he "was waited upon by a great number of the French inhabitants of the Island, & the Kings or Chiefs of the Charibbs".[12]

What is clear is that if the commissioners had ever entertained any illusions about the prospect of completing their work with Carib cooperation they were soon disabused and their position quickly hardened against the natives. In a letter to the Lords Commissioners of the Treasury, dated 10 August 1765, they did not mince their words. "[The] Charaibs," they wrote, "are altogether uncivilized, and the *Blacks* particularly of an idle untractable disposition." They went on:

> They live in huts scattered in an irregular manner, at a great distance from each other, without any established subordination, claiming large tracts of wood land intervening, of which they make no use; and are besides possessed of other lands in the cleared parts of the country, which interfere much with the laying out of plantations for sale. They had hitherto occasioned no disturbance, but still we are in doubt if they ever can be made useful; or whether in many instances they may not prove dangerous. The measure that appears to us, from these considerations, to be the safest and most for advantage of the colony, would be as soon as possible to remove as many of them as can *be prevailed upon* to quit, on terms consistent with the humanity and honour of his Majesty's government: and what seems the most probable for accomplishing that end, would be to buy the cleared land, and cottages, of those *who are disposed to sell,* satisfying them with money, or whatever else may be acceptable, and offering at the same time other lands in Bequia, where they cannot be hurtful, in lieu of those they quit; but not permitting them to take up any land again in any other part of St. Vincent's, except in such places, and on such terms, as may confine them to proper boundaries, and subject them to some regulations.[13]

As an insight into the colonists' views this is worth looking at a little more closely. First, their evident distaste at this "uncivilized" people shines through. Also striking is their frustration at their "irregular" living conditions and their lack of any "established subordination", a form of social organization that seemed natural to British subjects but was alien to the independently minded Caribs. Time and again colonial authorities sought to do deals with individual Carib chiefs expecting them, ingenuously or not, to be able to speak for the entire population; the search for a "Carib king" who could deliver a general surrender always proved elusive. Whether the Caribs themselves had any interest in being "made useful" is not considered but the fear that they might prove dangerous was well placed. Despite all the talk of a voluntary process, the commissioners insist that the Caribs must be removed from the island, save for those who might be confined to some sort of reservation; striking because that is exactly what, in time, happened. The idea of the island of Bequia as a potential destination did not last long. It found no support in London, where it was pointed out that the island lacked rivers which were deemed essential to the Carib way of life. Expulsion, though, remained the colonists' preferred solution to the "Carib problem".[14]

The British sought to delegitimize the Black Caribs' inconvenient presence. They were merely runaway slaves, it was said, who had usurped the land from its original owners, the Yellow Caribs, by force, and therefore had no prior claim.[15] But an argument deployed with greater force by the commissioners to their masters in London was that the Caribs claimed much more land than they actually used and that this wastefulness offended "the common law of nations".[16]

It is an argument that, though self-serving, in fact has some pedigree. Sir Thomas More, writing in 1516 at the dawn of England's imperial ambitions in America, depicted the inhabitants of Utopia (an island in the Atlantic) as enthusiastic and enlightened colonists. In founding their colonies, they would join with the natives "if they are willing to dwell with them" but should they refuse they make war on them. "They consider it a most just cause for war when a people which does not use its soil but keeps it idle and waste nevertheless forbids the use and possession of it by others who by the rule of nature ought to be maintained by it."[17]

Applied to St. Vincent this view, deliberately or otherwise, misunderstood the Caribs' use of the land. Fishing was an important source of food but the woods, which to the British appeared as unproductive wasteland, were hunting grounds where the Carib men stalked birds and mammals and lizards with bows and arrows and, by this stage, guns acquired from the French. Furthermore, the women tended gardens where they grew a range of provisions. These gardens were also often hidden some distance away from their *carbets* among the woods, an arrangement that among other things offered some protection for their food supply in case of attack. These plots were also periodically moved as land became exhausted. The houses themselves might from time to time also be abandoned and rebuilt elsewhere, often after a death or some other unfortunate event. The Carib way of life offended the profit-hungry sensibilities of the British but did in at least one important respect have a gentler ecological impact. The forests that the British wanted to clear for sugar cultivation helped maintain rainfall and replenish the soil, precisely where older sugar colonies such as Barbados had run into problems following the felling of their own trees. And the exhaustion of these older sugar colonies was one of the motors behind the search for new lands on St. Vincent.

In 1767 Sir William Young, the first land commissioner, wrote that his original instructions had been issued when the "numbers, dispositions and settlements" of the Caribs were insufficiently known.[18] The commissioners had since discovered that the Caribs' territory on the windward side was "by much the most extensive and finest part" of the island. Young himself had by this time acquired some of the best available land in St. Vincent. The pick of his possessions were the Pembroke Estate on the leeward coast near Buccament and an estate near Calliaqua which took its name, Villa, from Young's opulent residence ("ten large bedchambers")[19] there. His son later felt obliged to defend his father in print from claims that self-interest motivated his work with the land commission.

To acquire the Caribs' lands, though, would require more than just kind words, as the commissioners soon concluded. Back in London Young drew up a plan whose object was explained in the first article: "That the commissioners shall survey and dispose of all the cultivated lands from Ribichi to Grand Sable, and round to Chatteau-bellair (the

Charaib country)."[20] The Caribs were to receive four Johannes or £8 per acre of cleared land (the land was to be sold on for not less than £10 an acre) and be offered other lands elsewhere on the island. They would be granted a grace period of five years in which to build houses and plant crops on their new plots before being required to leave their ancestral land. The Caribs were also to swear an oath of fidelity to the king. Although great care was to be taken to explain the plan to the Caribs and the whole business was "to be carried into effect with the gentlest hand, the mildest manner", there was no escaping the central fact: the Caribs had to go.

The commissioners' plan was submitted to London for approval and on 25 May 1768 was proclaimed in French and English throughout St. Vincent. Two weeks later Abbé Valladares was sent by the British to tour the Carib country, explain the proclamation and advise acceptance of its terms. The cleric reported back to the commissioners that he had drawn some encouragement from his initial contacts which were not openly hostile "but when he arrived at Grand Sable, the richest and principal settlement of the Charaibs, he found the chief Chatoyér at the head of the mass of their people, who sternly asked them—'Quel roi?—what king was this, of Great Britain?—They would listen to the governor of Martinique and no other."[21] A friendly Carib then stepped forward to advise Abbé Valladares' party to retreat while their safety could still be guaranteed.

It is a scene reminiscent of Captain Braithwaite's encounter some 46 years earlier not only in the Caribs' outright rejection of subjugation to the British crown but also in their recourse to help from the French—the balancing third party in the relationship. It also marks the first appearance in the record of Chatoyer,[22] who would be a key figure in the Carib resistance until his death a generation later. It has been estimated that at the time of this conference he was perhaps 28-30 years old,[23] although his date of birth and details of his early life are unknown. An official British document of 1769 describes him as the "Son of Legottes".[24] Nothing more is known of his father, but the fact that Chatoyer is described as his father's son does suggest that he was a relatively young man at the time. From what we know of Carib politics Chatoyer must have already distinguished himself as a leader in some way, possibly warfare, to have achieved his position of authority. His rise coincides with the end of Tourouya's leadership, who appears to have died during the 1760s.[25]

An engraving of Agostino Brunias's painting of Chatoyer and his five wives.

We know what Chatoyer looked like because his portrait was painted a few years later, thanks in part to Sir William Young. Among Young's entourage when he sailed to the Caribbean colonies in 1764 was an Italian artist, Agostino Brunias, who painted scenes of West Indian life in St. Vincent, Dominica and other islands and his work is among the most important visual records of that period. The engraving from his painting *Chatoyer the Chief of the Black Charaibes in St. Vincent with his five Wives* shows the Black Carib chief as a well-built man naked except for a loincloth. He cuts a distinguished figure, straight-backed and smoking a clay pipe. He is barefoot and appears to be wearing an earring in his left ear. A dagger is tucked into his waistband and he is leaning on a sword while on his head is a scarf or turban (as well as arms and ammunition, the Caribs were said to purchase from the French "baubles, shirts and handkerchiefs to hoist around their heads").[26] The five wives in the picture wear short skirts and two of them wear the typical tight bands just below the knees designed to accentuate the curve of the calf. Four of them have racks (*sunana*) for carrying goods which are suspended from a headstrap. The fifth carries a baby in a sling ("They carry their Children in a kind of Basket, which is hung very low; sometimes on the Back and sometimes on either Side. Often also in a Bag so contrived that the legs of the Child spread round the Mother's Body.").[27] At least one wears a necklace and earrings but there is no sign of the "common pins stuck thro' the lower Lip with the Heads inwards, and often thro the Gristle of the nose"[28] that were apparently common at the time. The whole scene is set against a background of lush vegetation and a rocky precipice, an appropriate reflection of the wild ruggedness of the Black Caribs' territory (although the portrait was probably made in the British-controlled part of the island). The fact that Chatoyer is the only named Black Carib in Brunias' paintings is significant in underlining that for the British at least he was their adversaries' most important leader. Brunias also painted a scene of Yellow Caribs who are dressed very similarly to the Black Caribs in this picture: the women's skirts are more like breechcloths and the Yellow Caribs' decorative ornaments appear more elaborate but otherwise their appearance is identical but for details of skin shade and hair.

There is some confusion about where Chatoyer's home was. In the treaty signed between the Caribs and the British in 1773, he is listed among those signatories from Grand Sable, the largest Carib settlement, although unlike the other four from the area he is not described as a chief.[29] However, later British documents state that his lands lay at the northern end of the island where the Caribs' territory curved around to the leeward coast, specifically in the Grand Baleine area.[30] It may simply be that he moved his base at some point or acquired land away from his home district. Yet the fact that he was not considered a chief of Grand Sable may indicate that his chieftaincy was elsewhere and that his association with the most important population centre reflects his leadership in the war. It may be that the Caribs' political structures were evolving in the face of the clear and present danger to their liberty posed by relentless European encroachment. A war leader—*ouboutou*—had traditionally been recognized only for the duration of the conflict,[31] which had more often than not comprised a single raid. But from at least 1763 the evident designs of the British upon their lands must have placed the Caribs on a near permanent war footing. Also it may be significant that the early descriptions of Carib political structures reflect a loose-knit culture spread over many islands; the Black Caribs were now defending a restricted territory on part of a single island. Over the years Chatoyer's age became a factor in his pre-eminence but even at the height of his powers his authority in peacetime was always attenuated.

Despite their flat rejection of the commissioners' terms to Abbé Valladares, the Caribs met again in what was described as a "grand council"[32] to coordinate their response. The result was what would become a familiar strategy of piecemeal formal acceptance, delaying tactics, backed up by attempts to engage French support, and, ultimately, the resort of violent resistance to the handover of any of their territory. So when, on 14 June 1768, the board of commissioners met in Kingstown, forty Caribs from Grand Sable, with Chatoyer and "his prime minister",[33] Jean-Baptiste, appeared and asked that their names be noted "to distinguish them… from the ill-disposed Charaibs, who presumed to resist the King's authority." Of course, it was Chatoyer himself who just a week before had asked "*Quel roi?*" On 17 September Abbé Valladares brought in another 23 names of leading Caribs from the Rabacca area who said they wished to signify their obedience to the proclamation.

This apparent acquiescence lulled the commissioners and other leading men of the colony into believing that the prize of the Carib lands was almost within their grasp. The submission of Chatoyer and the other chiefs would surely induce others to follow their example so that the project could be completed without the use of force. Hastily pressing ahead with the surveying, division and sale of Carib lands at this point could jeopardize that goal so the commissioners decided instead to lay the groundwork by constructing a road into Carib territory, even though their own instructions made no mention of road-building on

Carib land. A road would clearly facilitate the work of the commissioners in the future but the Caribs knew as well as anyone that it could also
serve a military function, allowing troops and artillery to be brought
into their otherwise inaccessible territory. The French governor of Martinique was under no illusions about the reason for the highway: "The
English have begun a road to cross the part of St. Vincent which belongs to the Caribs," Count d'Ennery wrote, "with the aim of making
themselves masters of it and of then hunting the Caribs…"[34]

Construction of the road, which is now part of the Windward
Highway, began in late 1768 and extended northeastward from Kingstown. However, word was soon received from Abbé Valladares that the
Caribs had resolved to oppose it at the point where it met the old
"Barre de l'Isle" boundary established as the limit of their territory by
the French governor of Martinique. The resisters were the Caribs of
Grand Sable led by Chatoyer himself. Robert Wynne, the only land
commissioner then on the island, wrote to Sir William Young at his
governor's residence in Dominica on 28 November, informing him of
this development. Soon afterwards the Caribs stopped the surveyors
and their pioneers at the River Yambou (Jambou). Wynne wrote again
that military assistance would be needed to continue the project but,
with the other commissioners busy on the other ceded islands, work
was brought to a halt.

After a five-month hiatus the commissioners decided it was time to
restart work on the road. This time the surveyors and their slaves were
given a military escort comprising forty men of the 32nd regiment. On
29 April the party arrived at a house on the banks of the River Massarica which they intended to commandeer as a base for their work.
Almost immediately some two hundred armed Black Caribs appeared
on the hillside above, apparently determined to stop them. The troops'
commander, Captain Patrick Wilkie, tried to negotiate and after he
promised that no further work would be done on the road until he
had chance to consult with the authorities in Kingstown the Caribs
allowed the party to cross the river and repair and occupy the building.

If Captain Wilkie thought he had won a tactical victory he was
swiftly disabused. More Carib forces arrived to completely surround
the troops' new hilltop base, cutting them off not only from any assistance from the capital but also from the river below which might have

provided them with fresh water. The military spearhead in an instant had become a party of hostages. Wilkie negotiated an eight days' truce but wrote to the president of St. Vincent's council that "the Charibbs are numerous, well armed, deny any Subjection to the Crown of Great Britain and are resolved to keep their freedom."[35] The surveyor, John Byres, who had had to hide his box of plans in the bushes, was more succinct: "For God's sake endeavour to get the Regiment up here as soon as possible".[36]

The panicked authorities in Kingstown mustered the entire remaining fighting force of the island, one hundred regular troops plus all the civilians capable of bearing arms they could gather, including a number of the "trustiest slaves". The Caribs greeted this new force with a simple and uncompromising message. The stranded detachment would be released only if the commissioners gave up all attempts to interfere in their country, including any ideas of building roads. Assenting to the Caribs' terms, the commissioners belatedly remembered that their terms of reference precluded the use of force. Faced with this determined resistance the armed might of the colony decided that discretion was the better part of valour, turned tail and marched back to Kingstown. The surveyors left "their baggage and every thing behind them". The Caribs then pulled down the surveyors' huts (having failed to burn them, "the Thatch being green")[37] and ripped up those sections of road already built. Subsequently they felled trees to block the routes towards their lands and the jumpy British colonists began to believe that the Caribs were poised to sweep down upon their settlements.

It was a clear victory for the Caribs and one that was achieved without a shot being fired. The status of Chatoyer, who had been central to coordinating the strategy, would undoubtedly have been enhanced. The planters suspected that the Caribs, whose pirogues plied the seas from Trinidad to the Bahamas, had a sophisticated grasp of the strategic situation. The conflict over the road occurred at a time when four companies of the 32nd regiment had been transferred from St. Vincent to Dominica and when a dispute over the Falkland Islands threatened to embroil Britain in a war with Spain and France. In the immediate aftermath the Caribs turned their attention to the man they had looked to for advice but who had become tainted by his apparent advocacy of the British proposals. On the morning of 29 May some 150 Caribs, believed to be from the Rabacca area, attacked the home of Abbé Valladares, injuring his nephew and burning the house to the ground.[38] Their intended target had left early that morning for Chateaubelair and so escaped a bloody fate but he can have been left in no doubt of the consequences of crossing the Caribs. Valladares had in fact been a double agent, employed by the land commissioners to work on the Caribs, and "had by his Influence for a considerable time prevented their Opposition to a Road being made into their Country". For services rendered to the colony he was rewarded with a grant of 36 acres of land in the northwestern parish of St. David after the First Carib War.[39]

The chastened commissioners were not about to accept the status quo. Land sales in St. Vincent had netted £162,854 for the British Treasury and the best, in terms of land, was yet to come, they felt. Sugar production on the land already sold off would rise from a mere 35 tons in 1764 to 1,930 tons in 1770. The commissioners ventured to the end of the unfinished road to seek a meeting with the recalcitrant Caribs but were rebuffed. Retreating to Coubamarou they did manage to get a number of Caribs, including Chatoyer, to put their names to a document in which they gave "the strongest assurance of their pacific disposition and acquiescence"[40] but evidently the commissioners were not convinced that peaceful persuasion would be effective. On 17 July 1769 they wrote to the government in London insisting that there could be no progress on the land issue without the dispatch of a military force "sufficient to restrain and awe [the Black Caribs] into obedience".

The Caribs too knew conflict was inevitable. They sent a "*grande ambassade*" to Martinique to ask the governor, Count d'Ennery, for his support in the form of arms, ammunition and advice. They received a dusty response. Having concluded a peace treaty with the British only five years earlier the French had no intention of becoming embroiled in a war on the Caribs' behalf (although they were more than happy to enlist the Black Caribs as allies in their own struggles when it suited them). The British likewise sent an officer to lobby d'Ennery, seeking a promise that he would prevent French individuals from selling arms and ammunition to the Caribs. D'Ennery replied that that was beyond his powers but that he would not help Caribs directly or indirectly while peace existed between the two nations, even though he was aware of how seriously the Caribs viewed the situation. "The Caribs have even assured me," d'Ennery wrote, "that their intention was, when they felt themselves pushed to a certain point, to cut the throats of their wives and their children and to then perish desperately with arms in hand, because they are persuaded that independently of whether [the British] take their lands, they still want to reduce them to slavery."[41]

Amid a growing sense of alarm, Lieutenant Governor Ulysses Fitzmaurice visited St. Vincent from Grenada (to which the island's government was attached) in June 1769 and reported to the Earl of Hillsborough in London. He noted that those Caribs living on the borders of their territory in close proximity to whites seemed to acquiesce to the government's intentions. But those living farther afield remained deeply suspicious of white settlers "whose gradual and successful intrusions upon their Charibb neighbours they are sagacious enough to have remarked". He also reported that French inhabitants of the islands had worked to heighten Carib suspicions of the British, particularly by spreading the story that the heir of the owner of the original slave ship on which the ancestors of the Black Caribs were believed to have arrived, had applied for them to be sold as his property. Fitzmaurice also noted that: "They have a lively remembrance still of the attempt which was made many years ago by the French to make them slaves; the ill success of the French on that occasion, gives them confidence that future attacks upon them will be attended with a similar event."[42]

Fitzmaurice ventured into Carib country to try to calm the situation, issuing a proclamation in French and English, and was met by a group of about two hundred armed with fuzees, cutlasses and bows and arrows. The Caribs denied the authority of the Treaty of Paris to transfer them and their territory to British sovereignty, declaring "that they owed no Sovereignty to any Prince, that not Being subject to the King of France he could not cede them to the King of Great Britain, that the whole of the Island of St. Vincent had formerly Belong'd to them, that they had gradually given away half or the Leeward part to French Settlers who had come thither from time to time which half might be ceded to the British crown, But that they were Determin'd to Preserve the Remaining half or windward Part to themselves in Perfect Independency[43]." The governor was relieved that the Caribs did not appear to have designs on the British settlements to leeward, but he took immediate action to defend the fledgling colony. He ordered four companies of the 32nd regiment back to the island from Dominica, adding to the five already there, signed an act to raise a local militia and sent artillery from Grenada to defend Berkshire Hill[44] which was to serve as a refuge for women and children and to store valuable records if the situation worsened. A subsequent report put the cost of bringing the island's defences up to scratch at £25,000. As to the Carib forces, Fitzmaurice wrote: "they cannot exceed a thousand fighting men, headed by several intelligent as well as very resolute Chiefs." Faced with the Caribs' effective resistance the council and assembly told the commissioners not to pursue any further steps towards the survey and sale of Carib lands until further notice from the government "for the safety of the colony".[45]

It was with a view to the colony's safety that the local government hired a sloop, the *Ranger*, to patrol the channel between St. Vincent and St. Lucia. The commander was under orders to interdict any traffic in arms or slaves and to intervene whenever he sighted more than two Carib canoes together. In August 1769 the sloop's commander, John Quinland, reported that he had come across four canoes in the St. Lucia channel each carrying at least nineteen Caribs. He claimed he fired on them so they could be stopped and searched and that in response they had pulled down their sails and paddled furiously towards his own vessel. He continued firing, sinking two of the canoes but, undeterred, several Caribs swam towards him with cutlasses in their mouths. The other canoes came alongside and attempted to board the sloop but were repulsed. Quinland said he killed "most of them" and suffered two dead and one wounded aboard the *Ranger*. Such a clash could easily have tipped the island over into open warfare and Lieutenant Governor Fitzmaurice seized upon it to lobby London for action against the Caribs.

It is remarkable, though, that no retaliation was reported for the deaths of up to eighty Caribs in one engagement. Perhaps the story of the dramatic battle on the high seas was too good to be true. The following year a delegation of fifty Black Caribs visited Governor Melvill in Grenada. They told him, among other things, "that the story of the skirmish between the canoes and the English sloop, was an absolute falsehood", with the governor commenting: "as it really appears to have been".[46] Amid a generally pacific message, the Caribs added that their contact with the French was restricted to a small-scale trade in tobacco and that the firearms they received were purely for hunting game in the woods. Unlike the colonists they were not spoiling for a fight.

As the official process of land acquisition showed little sign of progress, other, more enterprising minds took matters into their own hands. Planters or land speculators—some French and from nearby islands—approached leading Black Caribs to make individual deals for tracts of land. The crown had authorized the land commissioners to dispose of all land in St. Vincent so from the British point of view the Caribs did not have the right to sell the land, and it is at least questionable whether they did from the perspective of the Caribs, who had traditionally treated land as a communal resource. The Caribs' motives are murky. Possibly they were duped in some way, but equally they may have been happy to take payment up front knowing that effective possession of the land was another matter entirely. Those adventurers buying the land evidently hoped that by acquiring even a dubious title to the land they could then lobby officials to give it the official seal of approval.

Specifically, a French planter from Grenada, Jean Baptiste Pichery, was accused of having agreed to buy a large tract of fertile land from the principal Caribs of the Morne Garou area. Another Grenada-based Frenchman, named Augier, was said to have agreed the purchase from the family of Touria (Tourouya) of a considerable tract of cleared land in the part of the country settled by the English—perhaps the land at Ouasigany/Kingstown where he had asked the French for permission to build his home. One English gentleman reported seeing Pichery emerge from a meeting with Carib chiefs ("he acted among the Charibbees as a Priest," it was claimed) at the estate of a Mr. Kain with "Joy in his Countenance" and inform him that the Caribs had, remarkably, insisted on making a present of the land he had already agreed to purchase. Pichery defended himself to the British authorities, saying he had bought only a small piece of land and that he had refused the Caribs' offer to buy more, upon which they sold it to others "*qui n'ont pas eu la même délicatesse que moy.*"[47] He claimed that he had warned the Caribs that the sales would not be valid until approved by the king and that he had done the colony a service by advising the Caribs to return runaway slaves. Four Carib chiefs, including Chatoyer, had met Pichery to seek his advice about British intentions. They were concerned that Young's commissioners had already surveyed some of their gardens and feared that the British intended like the French in 1719 to make them slaves. They protested that they could not move to the Grenadines because those islets lacked water and said that while the British could take land in the southeastern districts of Raouacou (Rawacca) and Yambou, the Yambou river should form the boundary. Pichery had given them little cause for solace in his replies and the chiefs left "extremely worried". The authorities in London did nothing while they awaited a report into the illicit sales by its land commissioners. In the meantime, increasingly crazy speculation took place in St. Vincent land. Young claimed that three times the island's total land area had been unscrupulously bought and that one purchaser had done a deal for a staggering 69,000 acres.

Faced with this increasingly chaotic situation the government in London finally issued instructions in December 1770 ruling the Carib land sales invalid. Hopeful that the illicit sales indicated a readiness on the part of the Caribs to give ground, in June 1771 the land commissioners attended a meeting on the borders of the Carib territory at Morne Garou with some forty chiefs "under the conduct of one named Chatoyé, a person esteemed to have the most influence amongst them, and they of Grand Sable the most considerable district".[48] The commissioners had felt encouraged enough by Chatoyer to believe that they had a chance of winning the Caribs over. Young explained the royal annulment of the contested land sales, news which was well received. He then went on to propose that they give up some 4,000 acres "in that part of the island called Morni Garou, extending as far as Point Espagnol, at the north end of the island" in which the commissioners claimed unconvincingly that only two or three "free Negroes" and no Caribs were settled. The Black Caribs would be guaranteed to retain for ever their settlements at "Morni, Espagnol, Rabaca and Grand Sable" and the whole deal would be sweetened with a payment of "one thousand Johannes, or thirty six shilling pieces, to be divided amongst them".

The answer was a firm and repeated no. "We were greatly surprised," wrote the commissioners, "to find them in a fixed resolution not to consent to our settling any part of the country claimed by them, which they steadily adhered to, notwithstanding our endeavours, by many arguments, to prevail on them to alter their sentiments." Jean Baptiste, "a Charaib of high consideration with his people", declared that the governor of Martinique had urged them not to countenance any change in the boundary between their territory and that of the white inhabitants. Furthermore, he said in the name of all the Caribs present "that they were independent of the kings of either of France or England, and would continue so, though indeed attached to the French".[49] The commissioners suggested that Jean Baptiste was biased because he had only recently returned to St. Vincent having lived in Martinique since his infancy and that he had worked as a servant to French officers. However, all the Caribs at the meeting maintained a united front and Jean Baptiste's words closely echoed those heard by Captain Braithwaite in 1723.

For the commissioners this was the last straw. "We are now convinced... that all treaty and negociation... will be fruitless," they wrote on 16 October 1771. "We conceive it to be impossible that so small an island can long continue divided between a civilized people and savages, who are bound by no ties of law or religion; and who, from their situation among woods, are even exempted from fear of punishment."[50] Added to all their previous arguments they now added another in their dispatch to the king's ministers in London: "the honour of the Crown" was now at stake. The Caribs' attachment to the French made it a question of imperial security and pride.

The council and assembly of the island, along with a group of St. Vincent planters in London, joined the chorus demanding action against the Caribs, stressing in petitions to the British government that the Black Caribs were "dangerous and insolent rebels" and effectively agents of a foreign power. Governor William Leyborne of Grenada urged the use of force "since the gentle methods that were practiced by Sir William Young had not the desired effect". The London-based planters suggested the Black Caribs could be dumped on "any unoccupied tract of 10,000 acres of wood land, upon any part of the coast of Africa, having one or more rivers running through it" or alternatively on the island of St. Matthew. (Of all the potential deportation sites for the Black Caribs, St. Matthew is the most bizarre in that although it had featured on charts of the Atlantic since its purported discovery by the Portuguese navigator Garcia Jofre de Loyosa in 1525, it was in fact entirely imaginary.)

Considerations of the Caribs' final fate aside, the metropolitan government had decided that the time for action had come. On 18 April 1772 the Earl of Hillsborough, the secretary of state responsible for Britain's West Indian colonies, communicated the government's view on what to do about the Caribs. "The King," he wrote, had resolved "to take effectual measures for the reduction of them, as the only means of giving security to the settlements of his Majesty's subjects in that Island."[51] The object was to make the Caribs "useful subjects instead of dangerous Enemies". Two days before, the wheels of war had already been set in motion, with Lord Hillsborough writing to the Admiralty asking for the navy to sever communications between St. Vincent and St. Lucia and separately asking the War Office to supply troops for the enterprise, including two regiments drawn from North America with perhaps another from the Leeward Islands. The official view was that once the Caribs had been cowed into submission by force or the threat of it, it was desirable that they should remain on the island albeit on "an allotment of such a portion of the Island as shall be judged necessary".[52] A copy of the treaty signed with the Maroons of Jamaica in 1738 was sent as guidance for the ultimate settlement of the conflict. However, it was left open to the governor of Grenada to determine whether it should be "necessary to remove the Charibbs from St Vincents".[53] The Yellow Caribs were to be exempted from any punitive measures since they had "upon all occasions, behaved themselves submissively to Government[54]."

A Scottish career soldier, William Dalrymple, was appointed as commander of the expedition and promoted to major-general. Dalrymple had studied law at Edinburgh and Leipzig and was sympathetic to American independence. Sir William Young, the lead commissioner and now lieutenant governor of Dominica, was co-opted on to the council directing the whole operation (his son reports that Young was its president but Lord Hillsborough clearly states that direction of the war was to be led by Governor Leyborne;[55] in practice once General Dalrymple arrived it was the military man who assumed full command). Young arrived in St. Vincent on 11 June 1772 along with elements of the 32nd regiment and a detachment of Royal Artillery but delays in assembling the military force meant action was postponed. A hurricane which struck Antigua on 31 August disrupted preparations.

The ships transporting two battalions of the 14th and 31st regiments from New York suffered a number of mishaps, not least of which was the storm that struck the *Elizabeth* on 17 September forcing it to limp to the safety of Bermuda. The *Elizabeth* did not reach St. Vincent until 1 October.

The Black Caribs, rarely caught out in matters of intelligence, were also making preparations for war. Governor Leyborne reported that: "The Charibbs have lately made more frequent excursions to St Lucie and Martinico than is usual, & in greater numbers; they return with arms and ammunition."[56] He added that they appeared determined not to submit to the British king. "The language they hold," he warned, "is very imperious." To counter the perennial preoccupation of Carib communications with the French-held islands, Admiral Robert Man put two frigates and a sloop to work in the waters around St. Vincent but with only limited success. The Caribs "slipped in and out in the night, or watched their Opportunity when there was little or no wind, and with their paddles escaped all the endeavours of the ships to take them".[57]

A tinderbox atmosphere was evident in early July when a planter, William Fitzhugh, ventured by night into Black Carib territory with some armed slaves believing the Caribs were plotting to burn his plantation. A violent clash left several people wounded. But while British troops continued to arrive on the island, putting strain on the local population, Governor Leyborne held back from engaging the Caribs. The St. Vincent government sloop was sent with the chief engineer, Harry Gordon, and the chief surveyor to the windward coast, to map out the lie of the land for the expected arrival of the troops. But when Gordon brought the vessel close to the shore at Rawacca he was met with a volley of shots from the Black Caribs. As the British party was driven off, the Caribs raised the French flag and gave three cheers.[58] However, like his predecessor, the new French governor of Martinique, the Count de Nozières, assured the British that he had advised the Caribs to submit to British authority. Sir William Young visited Nozières on his way from Dominica to St. Vincent and received his personal assurances that he would provide no aid or succour to the Caribs—although the count "observed that it was impossible for him to prevent private Traders in the French Islands from selling arms and ammunition to any person who would bring Money to pay for 'em".[59] The British ambassador in Paris later reported that he had been as good as his word and "done every thing in his Power, to quiet them, and discourage them from undertaking violent Measures".

The colonial authorities were confident that a show of force would be enough to secure submission and felt that the Caribs' words of defiance were mere bravado. Governor Leyborne was impatient that the fine weather was going to waste as he awaited the arrival of the troops. In response to a proclamation issued by Leyborne in early September inviting them to submit, the Caribs held several consultations but their response was that while they would agree to behave themselves no part of their land should be relinquished. Sir William Young, who knew as much about the Caribs as any on the British side, noted presciently that "their best defence will be in delay, and the shelter of their woods & mountains".[60]

Finally, on 28 September Leyborne ordered British troops on to the offensive. But immediately they met with the "determined and spirited opposition" of the Caribs, who seemed to have the better of the initial exchanges. As a squad of the 32nd regiment marched towards the Yambou river, Black Caribs ambushed them from the cover of roadside undergrowth, cutting down a corporal, four privates and a black auxiliary. The Caribs of Mariaqua, "altho' associated with English inhabitants", were among the first to take up arms against them.[61] Also on the 28th a party of thirty attacked Andrew Bruce's plantation in the Washilabo valley on the leeward coast, destroying some buildings and killing livestock. The southern militia arrived in time to save the sugar mill and dwelling house but what was especially alarming about the incident was that the attackers included Yellow Caribs who had been presumed to be pacific. Three days later the Caribs struck in the Warriwarou valley just north of Kingstown where they attacked the property of Jean La Croix, a prominent French planter.

La Croix was perhaps deliberately targeted because he had been appointed commander of a special hundred-man volunteer militia which included French smallholders along with fifty armed slaves who were intended to pursue the Caribs through bush-fighting tactics to which British troops were unaccustomed. As an idea it was far-sighted but in practice the unit was a disappointment. It was disbanded within months after some members refused to fight in the woods, the very job for which they had been formed.

Familiarization with the situation on the ground may have prompted a more sober assessment of the task facing the expeditionary force. On 3 October, shortly after his arrival, Dalrymple was reporting that "a vigorous opposition may be expected, the fatality attending the climate at this season particularly joined with the numbers of the savages, present difficulties only to be overcome by our utmost diligence and perseverance."

Ten days later, the new secretary of state for the American colonies, Lord Dartmouth, placed an order for two hundred complete sets of bedding for a military hospital in St. Vincent, while Governor Leyborne felt that a rum ration for the troops was "absolutely necessary in this unhealthy Climate".[62]

It was not until 18 October that Dalrymple led the British advance north across the Yambou river. At first he found nothing but burned and empty Carib huts and abandoned trenches. Two miles north of the Yambou he came across the intact dwelling of a Carib chief called Louan[63] where he made his headquarters. But after this modest progress the advance ground to a halt amid increased Carib harassment. Caribs shot a sentry cooling himself at the Yambou, which he may have believed was safely behind British lines, and also killed a sergeant who wandered away from his camp. A Carib force also ambushed a group of eighteen sick troops; eight died and three were wounded.

The army quickly found itself bogged down trying to subdue an elusive enemy. Within days of the start of operations, Governor Leyborne, so bullish beforehand, was reporting: "I must confess the conduct of the Charibbs is more serious and formidable, and I see greater difficultys in the execution of His Majesty's Commands than I expected. I very much fear their reduction will be a work of time, for they possess a country very inaccessible, and seem to have a knowledge how to avail themselves of this advantage."[64] For the British, on the other hand, the interior of St. Vincent filled them with dread. "The internal parts are the most wild, broken and inaccessible of any of the [Caribbean] islands, some parts of Dominica excepted, consisting of an aggregate of deep ravines or chasms, perpendicular precipices and conical topped mountains jumbled together in all the forms and appearances that man can conceive from the wildest sportings of nature."[65]

To seize the initiative, Dalrymple decided on a risky amphibious assault on Grand Sable, the largest of the Caribs' communities. The general planned to land the whole of the 31st regiment—about four hundred men—but Governor Leyborne refused to release some troops. The shortfall was made up by marines. On 13 November a flotilla of five vessels—the *Crescent*, the *Favourite*, the *Kennington* and two transports—set sail from Kingstown. Rather than sail directly up the windward coast the flotilla took the long route to leeward via Chateaubelair and Point Espagnol, arriving at Grand Sable on the 18th. The operation almost came to grief immediately as the *Crescent*'s stern ran aground just off the beach. Some brave Caribs ran out from their trenches to fire on the ship but were outgunned. The soldiers' rifles could reach the first line of trenches, a hundred yards from the shore, while the *Crescent*'s guns could bombard the second line, a further hundred yards behind.

In the night the *Crescent* managed to refloat itself and the following day at noon the men of the 31st disembarked amid some confusion. Five longboats were destroyed in the surf, two men were killed by Carib gunfire and two sailors drowned. The major calamity happened a little further down the coast where a boatload of rangers—a unit drawn from regular regiments to replace the bush-fighting militia corps—were shot at from the shore. Some rangers stood up to fire back, overturning the boat. A lieutenant and eighteen men drowned in the "amazing surf"[66] and as the survivors struggled to shore, their arms and ammunition sodden, two more died and nine were wounded as the Caribs rushed from their trenches. Despite this setback the overall operation was a success and the Caribs were driven from Grand Sable, where the British set about establishing a military strongpoint. The British were also encouraged by the Caribs' use of bows and arrows at Grand Sable; they inferred that their adversaries were running short of ammunition for their firearms.

It is unclear exactly how the Caribs' military leadership functioned. It is likely that each chief, or head of family, commanded his own followers, but that there was also an overall commander. Sir William Young (son of the land commissioner) clearly believed Chatoyer was the Black Caribs' general, with Jean Baptiste his closest lieutenant, a view widely shared on the British side. But a later governor of the island, Valentine Morris, felt it was Jean Baptiste who had been the key figure: "although no chief, or if he is, [he] is only a very inferior one among the Caribs, [he] is a person of strong parts, and has infinitely the most weight amongst them of any, or perhaps all of the chiefs, and was the most dangerous enemy the English had among them, long prevented their submission, or even treating, and occasioned most of the trouble, expense and danger which has been incurred."[67] His was the first name to sign the treaty on the part of the Caribs.

It was the first European shooting war on the Caribs' territory since 1719, 53 years earlier. In a curious echo of that campaign an officer of the 32nd regiment reported that the Black Caribs were killing their wives and children in preparation for the fray (as they had intimated to Count d'Ennery).[68] As before, they eschewed meeting regular troops in pitched battle, preferring to use the advantages of the countryside they knew so well to fight a defensive, guerrilla war. By delaying a decisive confrontation they probably hoped to exhaust the British forces, unused as they were to the terrain and the climate. Resupply of troops in the field was a problem for the British despite the use of a hundred mules and six to seven hundred slaves. The soldiers were frustrated that the Caribs would not stand and fight, instead slipping into the woods and adopting hit-and-run tactics. One serving officer, in a letter dated 14 November which was read out in parliament, stated that: "They [the Caribs] act with great caution, and the woods are so thick, that they knock our men down, with the greatest security to themselves, as it is impossible we can see them. We have only been able to penetrate four miles into the country."[69] The St. Vincent rainy season was also dampening the troops' spirits and was felt to be responsible for the high rate of disease: the majority of British casualties in the campaign were the result of illness. Parliament heard that in November of 1,100 soldiers in St. Vincent, two hundred were in hospital and more fell ill every day. Medical attention may not have been of the highest standard either. A major in the 50th regiment later wrote: "I know men have absolutely perished here by the neglect of a villainous set of surgeons."[70]

In stretching out the conflict the Caribs sought to involve the French as allies. Years of gifts and protestations of friendship might have led them to suppose that the French would come to their aid. But the Count de Nozières assured the British colonial authorities that he had not only refused the Caribs any assistance but claimed he had tried to "discourage them from undertaking violent Measures".[71] The British were concerned about the slow pace of the campaign for another reason. A special ten-man council held on 18 December resolved that "a vigorous prosecution of the war" was "particularly urgent from the ill effects a delay may have on the minds of the slaves of all the islands, in one of which they have already shewn a disposition, and even formed a design to make themselves independent, inspired by the idea of the impracticabillity of reducing the Charibbs".[72] Dalrymple told them that "he found the reduction of the Charibbs much more difficult than was either conceived or expected".

The slow progress of the Vincentian campaign did not escape the attention of the British parliament. There the Black Caribs found a surprising degree of support, although much of this will undoubtedly have been opportunistic, coming from opposition figures eager to have a stick with which to beat Lord North's administration. In a debate on 9 December Alderman Barlow Trecothick made a speech in support of the Caribs, calling them "a defenceless, innocent and inoffensive people". The colonists, he claimed, were emulating "the barbarities of the Spaniards against the Mexicans".[73] Colonel Isaac Barré, a former soldier who had lost an eye at the Battle of Quebec, said they were "fighting for liberty, and every English heart must applaud them".[74] Richard Whitworth argued that Britain had no right to the windward part of St. Vincent since France had transferred sovereignty of only that part of the island it had occupied prior to 1763—a point the Caribs themselves had made. The government conceded an inquiry into the Carib expedition but it did not take place until two months later. The delay in communications between London and the Caribbean—the sea voyage could take months—meant that political and military developments got out of step with each other. Mindful of the embarrassment the campaign was causing the government, Dartmouth wrote to Dalrymple urging a rapid end to the war even if that meant making concessions to the Caribs. At the same time Governor Leyborne was removed from his role in running the war and sent back, a disgruntled figure, to Grenada.

Dalrymple ended the year camped at Massarica, the very point where the Caribs had stopped the road surveyors three years earlier. In his report of 26 December he complained of the many "difficulties arising from the obstinate, and well regulated conduct of the Savages" along with the almost impenetrable terrain and the constant rain.[75]

Finally, though, with the worst of the rains over, Dalrymple ordered an advance of his main force on 9 January. He hoped to encircle the Carib entrenchments facing Massarica but typically the Caribs slipped away in the night and took up new positions at the Colonarie river, the island's longest. The following day Dalrymple dislodged them and continued his march northward, joining up with the troops at Grand Sable on 11 January with only modest casualties. One of the prime objectives was to cut the Caribs off from the sea, a source both of food and, potentially, of military supplies from the French islands. Slaves were put to work building forts and the roads needed to keep them supplied.

Back in London the parliamentary inquiry into the Carib campaign began on 10 February. It was hampered by a lack of up-to-date information from the government but heard further criticism of the war. Lord Folkestone condemned "wanton and premeditated acts of cruelty upon a defenceless people". Thomas Townshend pointed out that the Caribs had been perfectly peaceable until provoked by the surveyors' attempts to drive a road through their territory. Lord George Germain, who would go on to become secretary of state for the American department, showed rare understanding of the Carib way of life when he chided another speaker for calling on the Caribs to give up uncleared land. "Is he ignorant that these poor people live chiefly by fowling and fishing?" he asked. "If they are removed from the vicinity of the sea, and into the open country, they must be almost as miserable as if they were actually sent to where he and the rest of his worthy colleagues would willingly dispose of them." Henry Sharp, speaker of the assembly of St. Vincent, spoke up for the planters, calling the Caribs "a faithless people... abandoned to every species of vice". Asked to specify which vices, he replied: "They love a plurality of women, and take pleasure in nothing so much as making themselves beasts by drinking." Colonel Barré shot back that "if they love women and wine, liberty and property, where is the difference, except in colour, between them and Englishmen?"[76] Two motions were put to the vote. The first, that the expedition against the Black Caribs was undertaken without sufficient provocation at the instigation of persons interested in the total extirpation the Caribs, was defeated by 206 to 88.[77] The second, that the expedition was undertaken without direct orders from the government and was so mismanaged as to invite disaster as well as to incur dishonour, was also defeated, by 199 to 78.

By this time, though, the MPs' deliberations were essentially irrelevant. As word of the politicians' speeches and the government's concern at the slow progress of the campaign[78] reached St. Vincent the war was already over. Although even at the beginning of February the Caribs could still mount effective raids, such as that on the coffee plantation of James Blair, surgeon to the 32nd regiment, in which they destroyed all his buildings and killed many of his stock, they had by this time been "pushed to Extremities".[79] The British had failed to engage the Caribs in a decisive battle but the chain of coastal forts and the naval blockade had proved more effective. Ousted from their homes in Grand Sable and other communities, the Caribs were forced to take what shelter they could find in the forest. Some of their provision grounds would have been overrun by the British troops and it would have been all but impossible to fish in the coastal waters. Lack of arms and ammunition was crippling their war effort. Either the Royal Navy succeeded in blocking military supplies from the French islands or the Count de Nozière was true to his word in not arming the Caribs. The time had come to seek a deal.

In the first week of February two Carib chiefs had come into Lieutenant Colonel George Etherington's camp at Chateaubelair to sound him out about a ceasefire. Encouraged, the key leaders of the British war effort, General Dalrymple, Admiral Parry and Sir William Young, travelled up to Chateaubelair on 12 February and held talks with the two Carib headmen along with seven others.

Five days later 26 leading Caribs[80] gathered at General Dalrymple's base at Massarica to sign a treaty ending the war. A painting by Agostino Brunias captures the scene at Dalrymple's camp.[81] The eight Black Caribs in the picture wear loincloths, headscarfs or turbans and earrings. Each has a knife at his waist and carries a gourd or flask. In accordance with article II of the peace treaty they have laid down their arms: rifles, cutlasses and bows and arrows. Their surrender is received by a British officer, almost certainly General Dalrymple, although it could represent Sir William Young, who was the painter's patron. Another officer holds what appears to be a map of St. Vincent, indicating the territorial concessions in the treaty.

The terms of the agreement were in line with the instructions Lord Dartmouth had sent to Dalrymple on 9 December, the day after the

An engraving of Brunias' depiction of the 1773 peace treaty between the Black Caribs and the British.

Carib war had taken centre stage in parliament. Political expediency undoubtedly played a part. The government instructions had alluded to the "welfare and happiness" of the Caribs and also a "desire to end the bloodshed on both sides". They had also expressed some doubts about the prospects of the military campaign, noting that "the King's troops were preparing to enter upon a service hazardous in the execution and uncertain in the event".[82]

For the Caribs, the key provision of the treaty was territorial. The official border of Carib country was moved northwards to the River Byera, transferring some 4,000 acres to the British crown. The Caribs were to remain in possession of all of the rest of their lands, although a coastal fringe of three chains was to be reserved for the crown. The Caribs were to swear allegiance to the king and submit to the authority of his representative, the governor, in all dealings with the white inhabitants. They were to allow the construction of roads, ports, batteries and communications in their territory. No "undue intercourse with the French islands" was to be allowed and any plots or conspiracies were to be promptly reported to the authorities. Runaway slaves were to be returned and the Caribs were to allow slave hunters into their territory. Each chief was to compile a census of the inhabitants of their district. No "strangers or white persons" were to settle among the Caribs without the written permission of the governor. Collaborators, and other Caribs who merely did not fight, were allowed 1,210 acres in the valleys of the Warriwarou, Ribishi, and Coubamarou rivers in the southern part of St. Vincent.[83]

Neither the Black Caribs nor the planters seem to have been entirely happy with the treaty. Governor Leyborne reported that: "the Inferior Charibbs seem very much incensed at the Chiefs for making Peace declaring that they have been sold."[84] But although the Black Caribs formally ceded part of their territory, in key respects it was a better deal than the one they had been offered by Young and the land commissioners which would have forced them to move or live in much-reduced parcels of land. Furthermore, ceding land in principle did not necessarily mean alienating it in practice. Three months after the treaty Governor Leyborne reported: "I found the Charibbs of Ouarrouarrow, Cubaimarou, Jambou, Massaraca & Colonarie returned to their old Quarters, building new houses, falling of wood and cultivating their lands again, without any apparent intention of retiring to that part of the Island allotted them by General Dalrymple."[85] Many "seem'd determined to remain in their Grounds, with a firmness that surprised me".[86] For the British, one of the most important elements was the oath of allegiance, but the Caribs had sworn allegiance to a variety of European monarchs before to little practical effect. Their promises to return runaways and to conduct a census will have carried similar weight. The Caribs also clearly had no intention of severing communications with their allies and trading partners in the French islands. For all the difficulties of the colonial war effort, the fighting had demonstrated that the concerted deployment of British military power could push them to the limit. In these circumstances it would have been little surprise if they had concluded that in future their best chance of being rid of the British was to join forces with the French.

The Caribs themselves later said that they had fought "with a fearlessness and a courage which made the English despair".[87] With only "a few hunting guns and a little powder" they had battled to a standstill, they claimed, 5,000 good regular troops, 1,500 volunteers, plus the militia and black slaves pressed into service (according to British records, the number of soldiers used was 2,275). It was only a lack of arms and ammunition that had forced them to accept the surrender terms offered them or face "extremities". In this letter, written some years later and sent to the French governor of Martinique, 33 Black Carib chiefs led by Chatoyer summed up the campaign of 1772-73. "We were," they wrote: "victims of our enthusiasm and the ambition to become French before the time was right".[88]

The British government insisted to the colonial authorities that the treaty "comes up fully to our wishes and expectation"[89] but for the planters of St. Vincent the terms were deeply unsatisfactory. They called it: "A Treaty vague and uncertain in its Terms, ineffectual in its operation, and inadequate to the expence bestowed on it by Your Majesty."[90] Ten years on from the transfer of sovereignty, and after all the expense in money and lives (British casualties were recorded as 72 killed in action, 80 wounded, 110 dead from disease, 428 sick and four deserted),[91] the Black Caribs were still firmly ensconced on the windward coast—"that fine cream part of this island", as one leading colonial official put it.[92] The war, in the planters' eyes, was meant to have ended in the physical removal of the Caribs from the island. Instead, having given notice of their destructive power during the war when they burned a number of plantations, the Caribs remained as a permanent threat to life and property in the eyes of the planters. Governor Leyborne complained that the Caribs had had their weapons returned to them by Dalrymple and only a small group of Caribs had taken the oath of allegiance demanded by the treaty. (Leyborne also vigorously contested Dalrymple's orders to demolish the military post the British had built at Grand Sable—a position no doubt unconnected to the fact that it had been named Fort Leyborne.) Demand for land on the island was severely dampened by the advertisement of the Caribs' warlike potential. General Monckton, who had received a large grant of land on the southern border of Carib country in the aftermath of the war, put his land up for sale for £35,000. He refused an initial offer of £30,000, and by the time he changed his mind the buyers had changed theirs. He eventually settled for £28,000. All in all, as the island's assembly wrote in a memorial to the British government, the war had been a "fruitless expense".

In the aftermath of the peace treaty, General Dalrymple detected "a very dangerous disposition in the planters towards the Caribs... Such folly and wickedness must produce the worst effects, and I doubt not something very cruel and improper will be done by the people of St. Vincent."[93]

4. Allies of the French

"The Charibs certainly will attempt to rise should any foreign attack be made."
Governor Valentine Morris, 25 August 1778

ST. VINCENT'S planters stewed in resentment at the Black Caribs' continued occupation of the island's prime sugar country but they had another pressing concern. The slaves upon whose work the colonial economy depended were not content to stay on the plantation. Too many were simply taking the chance to run away to freedom.

A country-born male slave cost £75-£80 in St. Vincent compared with £45-50 for a man imported direct from Africa,[1] so the loss of each slave had a significant impact both in terms of the cost of replacement and the labour lost. The government believed that most plantations in St. Vincent were "underhanded" and the phenomenon of runaways, or *marronage*, only exacerbated the problem.

An official survey of slavery in St. Vincent in the late eighteenth century painted a generally rosy picture of conditions for African slaves. However, it acknowledged that whipping or confinement were legal as punishments and "necessary for the preserving of due authority over them". It also recognized that some masters exceeded accepted limits, "either from an avaricious or cruel Disposition". For criminal offences slaves could be tried by justices of the peace (inevitably planters themselves) and sentenced to death for theft of articles worth more than £6. It was conceded that this form of trial was "certainly too summary" but that not more than one or two slaves a year were executed.

The work of a plantation slave was hard, particularly during the period between January and June when activity on the sugar estates was at its most intense. The working day lasted from sunrise to sunset with a break between noon and 2pm at the hottest part of the day. During harvest time the day could be extended even further. Sundays were a rest day and slaves were given three days' holiday a year at Christmastime. Slaves also had an afternoon off a week to grow their own provisions in the steep or broken land on the margins of the plantations on which they worked. Planters might also supplement this with allowances of herring, salt fish or salt beef.

One leading British inhabitant of the time claimed that slaves in St. Vincent were happier and better fed than those in most other West Indian islands because of the abundance of ground provisions, particularly plantains—the views of the slaves themselves are not recorded.[2] One testimony by a former slave did, though, describe the life of a field slave on St. Vincent a generation later. "They were obliged to be in the field before five o'clock in the morning; and, as the slave houses were the distance of from three to four miles from the cane pieces, they were generally obliged to rise as early as four o'clock, to be at their work on time... Before five o'clock the overseer calls over the roll, and if any of the slaves are so unfortunate as to be late, even by a few minutes, which owing to the distance is often the case, the driver flogs them as they come in, with the cart-whip, or with a scourge of tamarind rods. When flogged with the whip, they are stripped and held down upon the ground, and exposed in the most shameful manner." He added: "The work is so hard that any slave, newly put to it, in the course of a month becomes so weak that often he is totally unfit for labour. If he falls behind the rest, the driver keeps forcing him up with the whip."[3] Even during the two-hour midday break slaves were required to collect grass for the plantation's cattle. During crop-time (usually January-June) they might be required to work long into the night. "The work is very severe, and great numbers of slaves, during this period, sink under it and become ill."[4]

Slaves generally lived in huts of roughly twenty by twelve feet thatched with dried cane-tops, housing three or four people. By law slave owners were bound to supply each male slave with "a pair of drawers and shirt or close bodied frock annually and to each female slave a shift and petticoat". Despite this largesse there was no getting away from the fact that among slaves imported directly from Africa a "much greater proportion" would die before the age of fifty than reach it. "Free Negroes" tended to live longer because, as the official response ingenuously noted, they "live more at their ease and enjoy more of the Comforts of Life". Yaws and dropsy were particular problems but less so for free Negroes "perhaps owing to their being better fed and cloathed".

Similarly, slave children were more prone to illnesses such as worms because of their poorer diet.

The official view on the reason why black slaves in the West Indies did not live as long as Europeans in Europe was that "Warm Climates in General are not so conducive to long Life as the colder Climates"— a startling statement when compared to missionaries' awe-struck accounts of the salubriousness of the Caribbean climate and the longevity of the natives. Nevertheless it was felt that there was no alternative to African slavery. "It would be impossible to cultivate the West India Islands by the Labour of Europeans who would be absolutely unable to bear that intense degree of Heat to which they must be exposed: And as to the Labour of Free Negroes, very little Dependence is to be placed upon that in a Country where the necessaries of Life are so few and so easily acquired." In short, no one in their right mind would voluntarily do the work expected of a slave.

For those brave enough or desperate enough to run away, the Black Caribs offered a potential haven. Although colonial authorities occasionally alleged that Caribs sold on runaway slaves in the French islands, an agent for the planters voiced the general complaint that the Black Caribs "entice the slaves of our own plantations, in the island, offering protection and liberty to all who will join them".[5] For the Caribs, too, the threat of enslavement was a constant concern. In 1774 a rumour ran through Carib territory that the English were planning to make them slaves and it was only with great difficulty that Chatoyer and other chiefs were persuaded to come to Kingstown to be reassured by Governor Leyborne. After three or four days of discussions and gifts of rum and clothes, the Caribs left, apparently placated.

The island's new governor, Valentine Morris[6] (St. Vincent's increasing importance had been recognized on 19 March 1776 when the island was constituted as a separate government, having previously been attached to Grenada)[7] identified runaways as one of the biggest problems he faced. He claimed that runaways had been at the forefront of the Carib resistance in the recent war. Morris said the runaways "were the great strength and almost sole reliance of the Charibs then, who ever headed the daring attempts of those & I may say were the chief if not the sole cause of that resistance".[8] His predecessor reported a body of three hundred armed runaways during the war in the heights above Point Espagnol[9]—the territory of the Carib chief Bigot.

Any disunity between the Black Caribs and the slaves was clearly in the interests of the colony's white planters. It was a question of numbers. St. Vincent's 10,391 African slaves were by far the largest component of the colony's population and far outnumbered the island's 1,217 white men, women and children.[10] In addition, Governor Morris estimated that 1,200 runaways were at large on the island, alongside some 5,500 Caribs. (Morris had visited Carib country and been impressed by the large numbers of "Charib youth from ten years old to 16 or 17 [who] swarm & appeared through all the seemingly pathless woods, almost like rabbits in a Warren.")[11]

The question of Caribs harbouring runaways had exercised Morris even before he was appointed to the governorship (he was previously lieutenant governor). He felt that incentives were the way forward and after the Carib war he devised an amazingly elaborate system of rewards for Caribs who might bring in runaways, with four grades for those bringing in 5-10, up to 15, up to 20, or more than 20 escaped slaves. Believing that the Caribs were impressed by finery, he advocated giving each deserving chief a distinctive sort of headgear "something betwixt a grenadiers cap & helmet, with a frontispiece of black tin or white metal, or thin brassplate, on which His Majestys arms to be embossed; with a tuft of feathers in each of one or the other of the following colours, Green, blue, yellow, red, something like the helmets used on the stage". Because of the climate and the Caribs' "aquatic lifestyle" the helmets were to be made of woollen cloth lined with coarse linen. In addition, the state should provide "a silver headed strong ferrelled cane with a string to it, of the same colour as the feather in the cap, to be added to the gift of each helmet or cap". The length of the cane and of the silver head was to increase with each of the four grades.[12] Morris, though, did warn that the Caribs should not be treated in "too high a stile" like North American chiefs or African princes in case they were made "too conceited of their own importance".

Morris, who was to prove one of the most energetic but also most controversial of St. Vincent's governors, saw a challenge in the existence of "the large bodies of dangerous and well armed runaway Negroes, encouraged and protected by the Charibs, and harboured in the mountains in this country, and too successfully calling on other Negroes to quit their masters, and join them, and the Charibs, in a general rebellion[13]." Bands of forty or fifty men, armed with fuzees, pistols and cutlasses, were reported to be terrorizing estates and attempting to carry off slaves, particularly women. The runaways, Morris wrote in 1777, were becoming more and more audacious and were gathered in eight strongholds "that I positively know of". They were being "encouraged, harboured and armed" by the Caribs and the governor, who took to sometimes visiting Carib country in disguise, feared that if the two groups united "they might, nay they must totally destroy the Colony".[14]

The governor did his best to sow distrust between the two groups. He tried to plant the idea that the new runaways would take away the Caribs' lands and attempted to exacerbate feuds between them by insinuating messages to first one side then the other. Some younger Caribs came down to British military posts to offer intelligence on the runaways and, on the governor's orders, were always praised and rewarded, in particular with gifts of beef, pork and rum. Morris hoped that by inviting half a dozen Carib chiefs to dinner he might persuade them to help him track the runaways but admitted that some of those very chiefs' people would probably tip off his quarry. He did manage to persuade some chiefs to help the search for the runaways but was disappointed with the results. The Caribs would head off into the woods, refusing to allow any white people to accompany them, until they had consumed all the provisions they had been issued from the royal stores, at which point they would return professing that they had been unable to find anyone, although the governor assumed they had passed intelligence about troop movements to the runaways. Morris complained that six times he had been fooled into handing out ammunition to Caribs who failed to bring in any fugitive slaves.[15]

Governor Morris looked forward to victory in the American war which had begun in 1775 so that troops could be diverted to tackle what he saw as the enemy within. Certainly, he felt, the situation required a stronger military response. The government in London, though, expressed surprise at what they took to be Morris' alarmist tone, noting that "the Caribs are not only no longer to be considered as internal Enemies, but are actually lending you their assistance",[16] evidently putting the most positive possible gloss on his fruitless dealings with the chiefs. Calls for greater military assistance were brushed off.

In March 1777 the governor announced his intention to personally lead an expedition to capture a group of runaways. Already that year, he claimed, 140 slaves from one quarter alone had headed for the hills "nor is any Estate scarce free from the apprehension of the greatest part of their Slaves doing the same[17]." At first Morris' efforts were frustrated. Even though troops set out in the middle of the night they soon heard conch shells being blown to alert the runaways' settlement of their impending arrival. Consequently all they found were some deserted huts, the women and children having been spirited away further into the interior and the men sniping with muskets from the dense undergrowth.

Morris tracked down one group of runaways and surrounded their remote and inaccessible stronghold in the windward country which had been fortified with help from the Caribs. Seeing that the runaways' force was three times the size of his own and "very well armed", Morris decided to negotiate. In talks with "Chief Peter" he agreed that the runaways would be granted their lives, would not be forced to return to their old masters and that Peter, his wife, and another person named Pierre would be granted their freedom. Later Morris decided to also manumit a certain Dublin for service rendered and resolved to sell the rest of the group off the island. The whole party surrendered and in the subsequent few days another twenty to thirty turned themselves in. In all the three-week expedition returned a total of 120 prisoners to Kingstown. Among the captives were "great numbers of the old determined long runaway ones; many of them out even long before our possession of this island".[18] The British were shocked at the "amazing quantity of provisions in the grounds to the extent of some miles" which were set up and maintained with the help of the Caribs. (This cornucopia was grown on the land that the British maintained had been left criminally underused by the Caribs.)

However, two other significant bands remained at large and were being actively sheltered by Bigot. Governor Morris wrote that this chief was "so uncommonly sensible as by the other Charibs to be called 2 men, implying having double the understanding of one man; very plausible, but whom we have reason to suspect to be inimical". He was one of the signatories of the 1773 treaty and was almost certainly the same chief who challenged the authority of Tourouya in the 1750s. He was not the sort of man to be impressed by a feathery hat. Not only did Bigot give sanctuary to the runaways but he had encouraged them to flee to his lands. Morris described Bigot as "a very capital Chief, &

who by his extream cunning & the strict Order he keeps his people in under him, & from his situation, is certainly the most powerfull, altho' not the nominal first in the Island."[19] Bigot evidently saw the value in swelling the Black Caribs' ranks for what both sides seem to have seen as the inevitable future conflict.

This was not Morris' only dealing with Bigot. In February 1777 he had proposed buying for a "trifle" roughly a thousand acres from the family of a man he described as the chief of the Yellow Caribs because they "dare not reside on it, as they would be in the midst of their inveterate enemies, the present black Caribbs, and very near one of their most daring treacherous Chiefs", none other than Bigot. Morris thought acquiring the land would serve to restrain the daring Bigot.[20] Incidentally, the governor believed that the put-upon chief's family numbered about five and that in all barely forty Yellow Caribs remained on the island.

Bigot eventually agreed to a face-to-face meeting with Morris and consented to give up a couple of dozen of the most recent runaways, including two he had taken as wives. But he still maintained two large bands of escaped slaves on his lands and showed no inclination to knuckle under to the governor's authority. In May the governor accused him of actively dissuading runaways from turning themselves in and of spreading misinformation about the fate of those who had already surrendered. Morris, in the meantime, tried to sow dissension between Bigot and other Carib chiefs.

However, a more direct solution to the problem of Bigot soon presented itself. In circumstances which are unclear Bigot fell into British hands and, in a phrase that is its own condemnation, was shot dead while trying to escape. News of the death of such a powerful and belligerent chief could not fail to spread alarm among the Caribs. In the immediate aftermath "great numbers" of them headed to Martinique and St. Lucia to stock up on weapons. By night the Caribs managed to land "five or six hundred stand of arms" using 22 large pirogues.[21] The secretary of state, George Germain, did not hide his concern when he wrote to Governor Morris on 9 August, tellingly using the phrase "put to death" in connection with Bigot's demise. "I must therefore suppose," he wrote, "that you had such Proofs of his Disaffection and mischievous Conduct that rendered the Step you took unavoidable—I shall wait with much Impatience and anxiety to hear from you what has been the consequence of the Charibbs' application to the Governors of Martinique and St Lucia and the effects of your Endeavours to quiet their Alarms and restore their Confidence."[22]

Despite the rising tension, Morris remained proud of his runaway-hunting activities and asked London to send him six pairs of bloodhounds of both sexes "so great is the terror of both Charribs and Negroes" of dogs.[23] In October he congratulated himself on the "surrender of thirty more Negroes of late Bigoe's desperate gang together with that dangerous & hitherto successful Chief Caesar & I believe I may do the same for a still additional number under their equally audacious Chief Francois".[24] Caesar was based at Point Espagnol and François at Wyarie. The runaway-hunting operations meanwhile became another source of conflict in the already strained relationship between the settlers and the governor when the assembly balked over the question of who would pay for the manumission of Peter and his party. Morris eventually took three of the group in at his own estate but a fourth had already been sold to another planter.

The controversy did not end there. Another recalcitrant Carib chief, Simon, who was also alleged to have harboured runaways, was kept in shackles for months in the barracks (there being no gaol) for allegedly firing at some soldiers and killing two horses. Morris boasted that "I believe not a Carib but is sensible of the lenity of his treatment"[25] but he was released on bail after the intercession of Morris' opponents on the council and assembly. Morris claimed that he had evidence that Simon, a signer of the 1773 treaty, had been involved in the death of a Lieutenant Renton and two other soldiers who had been killed in Simon's territory of Rabacca in early 1775 while trying to advance the much-delayed survey of the island.[26] Renton had been shot in the eye in the act of adjusting his theodolite.

Land had been the most pressing concern for Morris from the first day of his governorship. He enthusiastically set about selling off the territory ceded by the Caribs in the 1773 treaty. Morris proposed setting up two new parishes (three already existed on the island), to be called Chepstow and Monmouth in honour of his Welsh family seat, in the newly acquired land. He also wondered whether "the tracts of land belonging to the Charibbs ought not to be also distinguished into Parishes" since settlers might buy land from them and should be under

British government, so that they could pay taxes. This would also have the effect of expanding the assembly and the council and thus possibly outflanking his opponents. In February 1778 the Lords of Trade and Plantations authorized the expansion of the council from thirteen to seventeen members, including one for Calliaqua, which was growing fast and threatened to rival Kingstown as the colony's principal settlement.

Morris' land grants soon led to conflict with the colonial legislature which accused him of making irregular transactions, many of them to the benefit of himself or his family. In particular, the assembly accused the governor of granting away the large tracts ceded to the crown by the Caribs in the treaty. The governor was also accused of depriving friendly Caribs of land they had been granted by General Dalrymple as a reward for their good services. Among the grants officially recorded are sixteen of Carib lands totalling over 2,000 acres. For example, on 11 April 1777 Dr. Robert Glasgow was awarded in trust for Governor Morris five hundred acres of "Charaib land bounded by Mornagarou & Walliabou Rivers".[27] Another transaction involved land which Morris granted to his sister, Caroline. This was property which the chief surveyor, Levi Porter, claimed to have bought from "one Ramiton a friendly Charaibb" and had then sought to have the transaction legalized under the great seal. Morris claimed his critics were motivated by self-interest and disappointment and that the list of land deals was a forgery. As part of a long charge sheet against the governor the assembly alleged: "That he treats the Black Charaibs in the most arbitrary and oppressive manner and has confined some of the Chiefs upon the slightest surmises and suspicions." They referred in particular to the imprisonment of Simon and the suspicious death of Bigot.

The disarray in the government of St. Vincent extended to the military sphere. Governor Morris was concerned about the need for a new act authorizing the militia, the previous one having lapsed. Of more concern was that Morris quickly found himself at odds with Colonel Etherington, the colony's military commander, despite initially heaping praise upon him. Turf wars between the civil and military authorities were hardly unknown in Britain's colonies but this one was to have serious consequences.

An additional concern which came to have a significance few would have predicted was the private land dealings of Colonel Etherington.

Born in Delaware, Etherington enlisted as a drummer in the British army, rising through the ranks, before his wife purchased a commission for him in the 60th or Royal American Regiment. Following the First Carib War, he acquired a large tract of land in the region above Chateaubelair from none other than Chatoyer in circumstances which were hotly disputed. In Morris' temporary absence, the deal was approved by the president of the council, Mr. Sharpe, who spoke no French, the language in which the Caribs were accustomed to do business (needless to say, he spoke no Carib either), and the only interpreter was Etherington himself. Chatoyer later claimed that he and his brothers had been deceived and that they had never meant to lease more than a few acres. However, the sale of the lands was confirmed by the secretary of state following a visit to London by Etherington himself. The American officer evidently made a favourable impression since Lord George Germain described him as "Superintendent of the Charibbs in St. Vincent, over whom I understand he had considerable Influence, having gained their Confidence, by a humane Attention to their Complaints and a strict Regard to Justice & good faith, in all Transactions with them".[28]

Given his troubles with the British planters, it is perhaps understandable that Morris found his French inhabitants more to his liking. He contrasted the attitude of his fellow countrymen with that of the French who remained on the island. For the embattled governor, the "small and middling white settlers (among which the proportion of those formerly French ones are considerable) may be called the Yeomanry of the West Indies and are by far the most useful and giving the greatest strength to infant Colonies". These smaller landholders stayed on their lands, cleared new land and acted as a buffer on the Carib frontier. "On the contrary the English only think of making a rapid fortune to enable them to return to Europe to spend it there, leaving only servants on their Estates."[29] Absentee planters displayed little commitment to the colony and seemed motivated primarily by the prospect of making a quick profit. Some were selling up to acquire cheaper lands in St. Lucia and Trinidad. Morris also thought the old French settlers were "as usefull a part of his Majesty's subjects if not the most so of any here, as being best acquainted with, & managing the disposition of the Charibs among whom before our possession of the Island they contrived to live in perfect harmony".[30] Morris floated the idea of soldiers demobilized after the eventual end of the war in North America being used to settle lands bordering Carib territory in plots of fifteen acres for common soldiers and fifty for officers. He hoped the veterans would form a more resolute class of settler who might help keep the Caribs quiescent and stop groups of runaways forming. Estates of cocoa, coffee, indigo, ginger and cotton were preferable for Morris because they required only half or a third as much land as sugar and generally employed more white people and fewer slaves.

France entered the American War of Independence on the side of the North American colonists in early 1778. As tensions rose between the two imperial powers, France issued orders in August to the governor of Martinique to seize British possessions in the Caribbean, including St. Vincent. On 6 September the island of Dominica fell to the French without a shot being fired. The authorities in Kingstown were under no illusion but that the Caribs would actively support any French invasion. Carib chiefs later wrote that they had been "impatiently awaiting a revolution" that would put them under the protection of the French king ever since St. Vincent had passed into British hands.[31] On 22 August a meeting was held at Chatoyer's house to concert actions between the Caribs and the French. In early September Morris toured military posts in Carib country on the windward coast and met a number of Caribs bearing French muskets with bayonets fixed. The French had supplied eight hundred guns along with ammunition, and these were not the "fowling fuzils" the Caribs customarily used but the same muskets as used by the regular French troops. The governor picked up further alarming news of preparations for war. The French intended to land a small force, primarily of "*gens de couleurs*" who would join with the Caribs to attack the military posts in Carib country which the French navy would also bombard from the sea. In St. Lucia a former resident of St. Vincent called Frejean Jacques was reported to be raising a force to attack the island and between five and six hundred well-armed Caribs had sailed in their pirogues, wearing French colours, to pledge their support.[32]

Interrupting Carib communication with the French islands was a pressing concern for the British. Two methods were considered: smash their ocean-going pirogues on land in a concerted attack as they were laid up under cover of trees or try to intercept them on the high seas. But, reflecting the paralysis at the heart of the colonial government, in the event neither was put into practice.

To the settlers, the Black Caribs displayed "a menacing and hostile conduct"[33] and Chatoyer was at the centre of their war preparations. In October the assembly heard that the Caribs were by now holding meetings every other day at Chatoyer's *carbet* and kept guard constantly. At Grand Sable another band of warriors was also meeting regularly, particularly on Sundays. In the last days of 1778 Chatoyer entertained the French agent Percin de la Roque and other officials from Martinique to coordinate their plans against the British. Percin, like Coullet before him, earned the respect and friendship of the Caribs and became their advocate and defender. Aware of the potential importance of runaways, Percin asked the Caribs to bring to him "every English Negroe that can be met with within their country".[34] Carib canoes plied the seas between St. Vincent and Martinique bringing in arms and ammunition.

News of Percin's presence reached Kingstown. A British officer was dispatched to arrest the French agents but, approaching at midnight, was surprised by a party of 150 well-armed Caribs. His group was escorted to Chatoyer's house where Percin and another Frenchman told him that the French would very soon be masters of the island. Chatoyer upbraided the British officer, Ensign Hubert Van Hamel, for his temerity in trying to seize these allies of the Caribs and warned that were they to try it again not a British soldier would live to tell the tale. He added that whenever the French descended upon the island the Caribs stood ready to join them. The British party's retreat was cut off by "a very large body of the Charibs" but Chatoyer sent word to let them pass and "had them escorted close to the [British military] post by a body of his own people, who as well as the others were nearly as well armed as the King's Troops".[35] Percin was subsequently arrested by the British when he ventured beyond the borders of Carib country while on a spying mission and put in chains. But he soon managed to escape, perhaps indicating the presence of sympathizers within the British camp.[36] Undeterred, Chatoyer, Jean Baptiste, Salignon and other Carib chiefs kept "a constant intercourse" with the French[37] and the governor reported that Chatoyer's "clan, and some others, that he influences are in arms here".[38]

Invasion fever was only calmed in December with the defeat of a French fleet under Count d'Estaing off St. Lucia by the Royal Navy. Chatoyer had actually given orders for the Caribs to assemble and attack British settlements in support of a French invasion[39] and it was believed they would have done so had news of the naval defeat arrived 12-24 hours later. By January the Caribs were described as "perfectly quiet".[40]

The crisis focused attention on the state of the island's defences. The governor had regularly complained about the poor state of military preparedness he had inherited. The colony was so short of ammunition that he had to abandon all salutes, including, embarrassingly, when before the outbreak of hostilities a French ship had arrived in Kingstown to announce the appointment of a new governor in Martinique. The British plan to defend the island relied on a chain of twenty military posts, including a few such as Owia, Rabacca and Colonarie in Carib country. The chief engineer, in a survey the previous August, had found that none of the island's batteries had their full complement of ordnance. According to the governor, the military posts in Carib country were undermanned and inadequately supplied. Some of the troops were close to mutiny "to prevent which, their killing the stock belonging to the officers and others, and even some plunder of the Charibs, among whom they live, has been forced to be winked at".[41] The Caribs' own feelings about such depredations can well be imagined. American privateers cruised the coasts with impunity, even putting ashore in Carib country. Local requests for a garrison of two regiments and a government sloop were ignored. Just as damaging, the governor and council remained at loggerheads, particularly about who had the right to call out the island's militia.

Despite these difficulties Governor Morris, by his own account, came close to achieving a remarkable logistical success. The difficulty of the terrain meant that communication between the windward and leeward posts involved a detour by road around two thirds of the island. For the British military it involved "a most laborious journey of three days"[42] but even with the twists and turns necessary to scale the considerable gradients Morris calculated that a new road would cut the distance from sixty miles to just fifteen, a half day's march. The case for a route was even more pressing because the only road passed through high ground commanded by Caribs and runaway slaves, who could easily block it by felling trees or tumbling rocks down from the heights above. Anyone trying to clear such obstructions would be vulnerable to ambush. If the winds were unfavourable the sea journey could take a fortnight which meant that sometimes the windward posts went extended periods without resupply. The metropolitan authorities in London had declined to stump up the £50 a mile it was estimated such a road would cost when first mooted, which meant that the Caribs themselves were employed in landing provisions for the troops stationed in their territory. (The government paid out £23 10s 6d to various Caribs for landing supplies at Grand Sable over two months in 1774.)[43] Morris calculated that a single blockhouse would be sufficient to defend his proposed intercoastal road and felt solving the problem would have dramatically improved the reach of the government's forces.

So it was with some pride that in March 1779 Governor Morris reported that "two gentlemen", "a small party of soldiers" and "three faithful yellow Charibs" had succeeded in tracing a path across the middle of the island from the most windward military post to the most leeward. The obvious route would have been along the valleys of the Wallibou and the Rabacca rivers. The Black Caribs jealously guarded the secrets of movement in the mountainous back country and when a group of them came across the trailblazing party they directed their anger at the Yellow Caribs and threatened revenge.[44] It is surely no coincidence that it was in this tract of land that the chief surveyor, Lieutenant Renton, had been killed. To this day, though, no road crosses the island from east to west because within weeks the road project was overtaken by events.

French designs to seize St. Vincent with the help of their Carib allies had been delayed, not defeated. The French drew up elaborate plans to take the island and the Caribs were at the centre of them. A 36-point plan of action[45] stipulated that the Caribs, referred to as "the original and natural owners of the land", were to be treated "more like allies as opposed to subjects" and "all the lands that the British have usurped from them" were to be returned or compensation paid.

Percin de la Roque, who had established such a good rapport with the Caribs through his visits to their territory on spying missions to St. Vincent, was to be entrusted with command of the island. ("I have no doubt that he is the most capable person to make the Caribs happy," wrote Count d'Estaing.) The Caribs would "enjoy the same freedoms that they previously had under French rule. They will even be granted more freedoms in order for them to become even more loyal to the King in order to instil in them the sentiment that they are a part of the same nation as ours."

As Percin had indicated in 1778, the French sought to exploit the colony's runaway problem to their own advantage. "The number of runaway slaves which is significant must be considered an asset that we must use to our benefit." They were to be given land and treated like free blacks in other islands. Slaves deserting British settlers would not be returned, indeed it was proposed to "facilitate their escape tacitly". The French recognized, though, that in the longer term *marronage* was bad for business, noting that "when the number of Free Negroes would have become equal to the number of Caribs, we will apply all our attention to stopping the runaway phenomenon".

The plan provided for prominent British settlers to be held as hostages but warned that the Caribs, who harboured such deep-seated enmity for them, were not to be left in sole charge of them for fear that they might take matters into their own hands. "The word of the Caribs shall not be taken and it is ordered in no uncertain terms and in the most positive way to pay extreme care to the protection of these hostages, whose fate shall be softened as much as it is legally possible without compromising the interests of the Indians." The Caribs were to be given military training and their skills of seamanship were recognized by the provision that Carib canoes were to be used to carry official letters to Martinique. In the event of failure, the joint French/Carib force was to retire inland. It was reasoned that together they must be able to hold out longer than the six months the Caribs had on their own in the war of 1772-3.

With all the pieces in place, a French flotilla, including three captured British vessels which had sailed from Martinique, dropped Percin near Grand Sable during the night of 15 June. The ships continued south around the point of Ribishi until they dropped anchor at ten o'clock the following morning in the bay of Young's Island, between Calliaqua and Kingstown. The British were caught completely off guard. The first the government of the colony knew of the attack was the appearance of three vessels off Calliaqua. The planters mistook them for merchant ships arriving to pick up sugar exports and prevented the Hyde's Point battery from firing on them. The French began disembarking and the post at Calliaqua, defended by six soldiers with two cannons, quickly surrendered.

Because of the political stand-off between the governor and the planters there was no legally constituted militia. Colonel Etherington was later accused of having neglected the windward posts and, more damagingly, of employing a large number of the soldiers under his command to work on his estate on the Wallibou river, more than a day's march from Kingstown.[46] Morris claimed only 43 or 44 soldiers were on hand to defend the capital but said he had it on good authority that a further seventy were working on Etherington's land. Thanks to the spying efforts of Percin and his Carib allies, the French were well aware of these shortcomings in the island's defences, even including the fact that the key to the magazine at Wilkie's battery near Calliaqua was missing.

Percin did not arrive in Kingstown until the night of 17/18 June. Heavy seas had prevented him from landing at Grand Sable itself but despite being chased by British ships he managed to make the shore further along the coast (probably at Byera) where he was saved from drowning by his friends the Caribs. He was accompanied by 46 white Frenchmen and about 25 mulattoes and free blacks, and some six hundred Caribs rallied to his standard. Gathering his forces, he seized the British post at Colonarie after a brief fight. Morris' plan for the defence of the island had called for the posts on the windward coast to respond to a Carib mobilization by attacking the women and children left behind in Carib settlements in the rear so that the warriors would be obliged to return to defend "what they hold most dear". The undermanned military post at Colonarie was overwhelmed before any such plan could be put into action. Pressing on to Carriacoua (Calliaqua), just as the French plans had foreseen, Percin felt it necessary to rein in the Caribs who were "committing disorders" before heading for Kingstown the same night. A history sympathetic to the planters accused the Caribs of "the most flagrant acts of insolence and cruelty" in their initial advance, including "plunder, violence and murder".[47]

The main French force had landed at Calliaqua, two and a half miles east of Kingstown, on the 16th and marched towards the capital. They met an ensign[48] sent by the British governor demanding to know what they were doing there. The French took him prisoner and as they continued towards the capital a force of five hundred Caribs appeared on the heights above them, the air resounding to their war cries. They were led by Chatoyer and other Carib chiefs. According to one planter who was present, the arrival of the Caribs was enough to convince some of his fellow-landowners that the game was up: "At this time a considerable Number of the Charibs appear'd upon the top of Hartley's [Sion] Hill, which alarmed those Inhabitants who had Estates thereabouts, some of whom were at that time in the Fort and they wished for a Capitulation saying, the Charibs would burn and destroy every thing."[49] For the planters the Caribs' "horrid manner of making war, carried such terror... as make them more dreaded than better men".[50] In all some 1,100 Caribs took part in the seizure of the island—by far the largest component of the invasion force.

. With the enemy almost literally at the gates, the British defenders were in disarray. At one point Governor Morris ordered a cannon to be fired at the enemy from the battery on Dorsetshire Hill but Colonel Etherington overruled him, arguing that Ensign Van Hamel was still with the French under a flag of truce. The small British garrison was scattered all over the island and the response to the invasion was marked by confusion, delay and mutual recrimination among the leaders of the colony. Five months earlier Morris had promised to defend his last redoubt above Kingstown "inch by inch to the utmost extremity".[51] The reality was rather less glorious.[52]

Negotiations for the capitulation began between Governor Morris and the French commander Monsieur Canonge at Government House on the afternoon of 16 June, hours after the first appearance of French and Caribs. When Chevalier Durumain, the expedition's commander-in-chief, later disembarked from a frigate in Kingstown bay he demanded changes to the terms already agreed. Principally, he wanted a review of the 1773 treaty to determine what compensation should be given to the Caribs for the transgressions of which they accused the British. Playing for time in the hope of reinforcements, Morris refused and the meeting broke up when Durumain threatened to tear up the capitulation.

When the two sides reconvened the following morning a surprise was in store for the British. Joining the French negotiators were "Chatoyer, and one or two of his brothers, and I think one more Charib Chief", along with their friend and adviser Percin de la Roque.[53] Durumain invited Chatoyer to set forth his complaints against the British for breaches of the treaty. A map was laid on the table and Chatoyer "gave a long history of the Charib war, and the different propositions they made for their boundary which he pointed out very exactly... as he shewed on the map every place". He was particularly concerned about the land that Colonel Etherington claimed to have purchased from them. "Chatoier, the Charib, alledged, that he, and those others who had signed the instrument, never meant more than to *lease a few acres*, not to sell."[54] Morris claimed that the Carib chiefs, in front of witnesses, "told the French Commander that but for their resentment against Col. Etherington for their alledged accusation about the Land, they never would have called them in". This was probably an overstatement but it does reflect the Caribs' extreme sensitivity about their land. Finally it was agreed that the Etherington land dispute was a matter that should be settled outside of the capitulation negotiations and Morris signed over the island into French hands and himself into captivity (British troops were shipped to Antigua but Morris had to wait eight months on St. Vincent before being allowed to join them).

Flushed with victory, the Caribs were alleged to have done "considerable violence to some estates and individuals" on their return home.[55] Over the next couple of days the British troops surrendered their posts and Durumain was obliged to control his Carib allies who were pillaging the British settlements. Slaves on British estates also suffered the Caribs' wrath in these attacks, actions which left a legacy of antipathy. But nothing could dampen the spirits of the Black Caribs. They burnt down all the military posts on the windward coast[56] (with the exception of Byabou in the south) and their *carbets* will surely have resounded to the exuberance of their celebrations.

With the threat to their lands removed, the British and their land commissioners gone and their friend and ally Percin de la Roque a leading figure in the island's new government, the victory of 1779 represented all that the Caribs had fought for. The articles of capitulation stipulated that no Caribs should form part of any military garrisons or be stationed at forts or in towns but should return home. This would have suited them fine: they just wanted to run their own affairs in their own territory. As usual, the Caribs were required to give up any runaway slaves. The terms of the surrender also stated that the Caribs would be disarmed but France's secret plans for the invasion stated quite the opposite and the French had no interest in enforcing this provision. In fact, it was the white inhabitants of the island who were ordered to bring their weapons in to the king's stores on 21 June.

The new French governor of the island, Monsieur Dumontet, reported that the Black Caribs had continued to attack British properties after the seizure of the island, making off with livestock and anything else that took their fancy. He had dispatched troops to block the pathways that led from Carib country to the settled areas but admitted that he had been unable to apprehend the perpetrators. The English inhabitants, he said, "greatly feared them, and with reason, for they haughtily declare that if the island is attacked they will bring blood and fire down upon them; I'll prevent their ferocity as much as I can but I'm not bothered that they fear them..."[57] The British planters would later complain that during the French occupation the Caribs had "pillaged and murdered several of the Inhabitants, destroyed their buildings by Fire and usurped their possessions".[58]

The Caribs were left in peaceful possession of their lands but just a year after their victory they faced a different challenge when a severe hurricane—the first in living memory[59]—tore through the island in October 1780. The storm is considered the most devastating Atlantic hurricane in history, killing more than 27,500 people on its sweep through the islands from Barbados all the way up to Hispaniola, more deaths than in any entire decade of hurricanes (Hurricane Mitch, the most deadly of the twentieth century, which struck Central America in 1998, left some 19,000 people dead in its wake). An official French colonial report argued that the scale of devastation was so vast—the storm's diameter was said to be some 25 times bigger than the average—that it could not have been a hurricane, but rather "an extraordinary fermentation of the elements".[60] In St. Vincent hardly any of the six hundred houses in Kingstown were left standing, likewise almost all churches and other buildings. "Every cane was torn up from the ground—every building was laid low—every property was destroyed."[61] But away from the capital it also caused extreme distress and led to famine in the Carib areas. At the same time an outbreak of smallpox gripped the island; the French garrison was reduced to a "miserable situation" and 51 troops died in the space of four and a half months.[62] The Caribs were grateful to the French governor of Martinique, the Marquis de Bouillé, for sending emergency aid through Percin de la Roque and Philibert Blanchelande, later the governor of Tobago.

The bonds between the Caribs and the French were strengthened two months later when the British made an attempt to recapture the island. A letter from numerous Carib chiefs the following year boasted of the "zeal" they had shown in rallying to the French cause alongside Percin. A British fleet under Admiral George Rodney had left St. Lucia on 14 December and after struggling through the currents down St. Vincent's windward coast landed a force of three hundred plus some marines under General Sir John Vaughan at Warriwarou Bay (now known as Greathead Bay) on the afternoon of the 16th. The French, reinforced by Carib warriors, had erected their defences on Sion Hill which separated and overlooked Warriwarou and Kingstown. General Vaughan marched his troops to the foot of the enemy's works but finding that "the whole appeared in perfect repair, with a numerous and strong garrison", he turned around and marched them back again.

Blanchelande, the commander-in-chief of the French forces, paid tribute to the Caribs' contribution to the island's defence. He ordered Percin to rally the southern militia and the Caribs to harass the enemy's rear. The Caribs exceeded their orders in attacking and burning British plantations, slaughtering livestock and killing five or six English inhabitants in their homes, including the foreman of the planter Duncan Campbell, apparently in revenge for his having previously had one of their number whipped (and making good on their threats as reported by Dumontet). The Caribs harassed the British troops throughout the night and Blanchelande confessed that the sound of gunfire from the Carib detachments in his camp "worried me a little".[63]

A hasty conference between General Vaughan and Admiral Rodney concluded that there was no prospect of taking such a well-defended position. The day after landing the British withdrew without a fight. It was a second humiliation for British arms in St. Vincent in little over a year. For the Caribs it must have increased their confidence that the British, with their land commissioners, their sugar plantations and their designs on Carib land, might be removed for good and that an alliance with the French could guarantee their liberty.

Yet disturbing developments soon began to unsettle the Caribs' peace. Percin, the Caribs' friend and protector, was in fact only second-in-command on the island. In 1781 Duplessis replaced Dumontet as governor. While Dumontet had had a negative view of the Black Caribs, seeing them as untrustworthy drunkards, he also felt they could be useful; Duplessis valued them only as potential slaves. For him the Caribs were a nuisance and, like his British predecessors, he thought the colony would be better off without them. Relations deteriorated so badly so quickly that on 20 September 1781 33 Carib chiefs put their names to a letter[64] addressed to Duplessis' superior in Martinique, the Marquis de Bouillé. The first name among the signatories was that of Chatoyer and it is likely that he, along with Percin, was the instigator of the move.

They reiterated their attachment to the French and their dislike of the English "who had usurped what was ours, contrary to the principles of natural law". Duplessis, they complained, wanted to send them to the Spanish island of Trinidad, "depriving us of our wives and children". Furthermore, they claimed that their children, who should be dedicating themselves to growing crops on their land and "serving us in our old age", were being snatched away from home and attached to French officers to act as their servants, "something we never saw in the time when the English were masters of St. Vincent". The Carib chiefs stated that they had "heard M Duplessis at his table expound his intention to make us captives, casting indignant eyes which revealed clearly his thoughts and which did not lie in the disdainful manner in which he has always looked upon us since he has been here".

They went on to mention presents, including guns embellished with silver, shirts and kerchiefs, which the marquis had sent for them but which Duplessis had allegedly withheld. The letter was hand-delivered to Bouillé in Martinique by three Carib chiefs. Percin endorsed their complaints, saying he had been ordered by Duplessis to advise the Caribs to emigrate to Trinidad or to the South American mainland. He said that he had distributed 482 waistcoats, breeches and shirts, as well twenty hats and some kerchiefs but no guns and no sabres. The Caribs were so exercised by the issue that Percin feared some sort of "violent revolution on their part".[65] In an atmosphere of tension, the Black Caribs remained wary, suspecting that the distribution of presents (valued at fifteen shillings a man) was part of a plan to gauge their fighting strength. "Even when they were receiving these Presents from People whom they considered their Friends, their Jealousy was still manifest; and they could not suppress their Apprehension that Measures had been concerted to discover their Strength and Numbers."[66] They were right to be suspicious. In an official French document written in 1785 it was stated that by means of this distribution it had been confirmed "that the number of men capable of bearing arms did not exceed 500, a secret that few people know and which has been carefully hidden from the English"—although in testament to the Caribs' canniness this was in fact an underestimate.[67]

Bouillé's response was not slow in coming. Demonstrating the high value he placed on the alliance with the Caribs, the governor drafted a reply on 25 September in which he reassured them that there was no plan to sell them to the Spanish Main, an idea he said was being propagated by "people of bad faith". He reassured them over "all the fears that may have been given them by French governors and other officers" and assured them of the French king's "special protection" from anyone who would mistreat or molest them in any way. He reiterated that any Carib accused of a crime against a French or British inhabitant should be turned over to Percin or to the Carib chiefs to be judged, cutting Duplessis out of any role in Carib affairs.

Percin underlined in a letter to the metropolitan government that Duplessis' antagonism towards the Caribs was woefully short-sighted as it threatened to deprive the French authorities of "1,000-1,200 soldiers" who "can be regarded as an inexpugnable rampart for St. Vincent" and who had given evidence of their "valour and heroic courage".[68]

Duplessis defended himself, claiming to Bouillé in a series of letters that he had always treated the Caribs with *"douceur and bonté"*, that he had assiduously distributed the king's presents including two silver-embellished rifles to the *"deux premiers Chefs"* (presumably Chatoyer and Du Vallée or possibly Jean Baptiste) and that the Caribs were being manipulated by "one or two mischief-makers behind the curtain" (Percin).[69] His second-in-command, he wrote, was not of sufficient rank to hold the position he did. "He has never served," wrote Duplessis, "he can barely read or write, he lacks education, he lacks knowledge, he doesn't have the slightest idea of the art of war"—an extraordinary claim to make about the man who had coordinated the crucial Carib component in the seizure of the island and its subsequent defence. (Duplessis was even less complimentary about the Black Caribs, characterising them as duplicitous, lazy drunks. He did, though, concede that "they hate the English".)

Addressing himself to Duplessis two months later, Bouillé upbraided the governor of St. Vincent for "the tone, the style and the content" of his correspondence and for the stream of problems his governorship had generated in just a few short months. Noting that he had sent Duplessis a copy of the Carib chiefs' complaint, Bouillé told him that if he wanted a change of job he was more than ready to offer him one. A few months later Duplessis was replaced as governor of the island. This was not the first time Duplessis had attracted negative attention from the French West Indian authorities. In 1755 the governor general, the Marquis de Bompar, had singled him out after the Black Caribs had revolted against the depredations of French settlers. He described Duplessis, who had moved to St. Vincent from Grenada, as "vain, presumptuous and an inveterate liar". However, Duplessis' attacks on Percin did have an effect in Versailles where it was suggested that the second-in-command should be replaced by a higher-ranking officer and that Percin's pay should be halved.[70]

If Duplessis' removal represented a victory for the Caribs, their strategic position was once again to be undermined by events beyond their control. France's seizure of St. Vincent in 1779 had come as part of the wider conflict between the two European empires occasioned by the struggle of Britain's North American colonies for independence. When that conflict was settled, resulting in the independence of the United States of America at the Peace of Paris in September 1783, St. Vincent was again one of the bargaining chips that changed hands.

For four and a half years in the period of 1779-83 the Black Caribs, despite intermittent hostility from the local French authority, had been largely left to run their own affairs. They could roam the woods, tend their plots, sail their pirogues to the neighbouring islands and visit each other in their *carbets*. Not only had they retained possession of their lands but they had regained effective control of territory lost under the 1773 treaty. The bonds between the Caribs and the French had been strengthened. Now, thanks to diplomatic deals struck half a world

away, they would again have to share their island with a British governor and a planter class casting avaricious eyes on their land.

5. A Pity it Belongs to the Caribs

"Chattoway, as having headed them during the Charaib war, and having a powerful Family, has much Influence amongst them..."
Governor James Seton, January 1789

ST. VINCENT formally passed back to British rule on 1 January 1784. The Caribs would now have to deal directly with their sworn enemies. Undefeated but traduced by the French, the Caribs greeted the arrival of the British troops who arrived to take possession of the island with "visible surprize and consternation".[1] Under the terms of the 1773 treaty the Caribs had promised allegiance to King George III. Clearly, siding with the French over the previous five years had put them in breach of that treaty. The British, however, did not take punitive measures against them. The planters would later deplore what they saw as an example of misplaced humanity, much as they had deplored the 1773 treaty for terms which they considered over-generous. The local authorities once more lobbied for the Caribs' removal from the island but the metropolitan government was more circumspect. British restraint was conditioned by the daunting prospect of launching a military campaign to dislodge the Caribs, with Lord Sydney believing such a measure "to be attended with so many difficulties, that there would be little hopes of succeeding were it to be attempted".[2]

The Caribs adopted a conciliatory stance towards their new, unwanted neighbours and, in the sarcastic phrase of Charles Shephard, "professed themselves enraptured admirers of the mild and benevolent Constitution of Great Britain".[3] The new governor, Edmund Lincoln, reported that to the local military commander, Major Chester, "they appeared well disposed, peaceable and tractable—which I can very readily suppose, as it must be so much to their interest to be so".[4] Carib chiefs came in to Kingstown and promised to behave peaceably provided they were left unmolested on their lands. The view of the ejected French was that "the [British colonial] Government's aim is to win the Caribs' affection through good treatment; and in this way to weaken the hatred

109

and aversion of these people". However, they noted that "this hatred is a feeling which the Caribs suck in with their mother's milk and which has become among them a national prejudice".[5]

For the time being, the Caribs were left to their own devices and life returned to a semblance of normality. Carib women, who remained those responsible for growing the crops, particularly cassava, yams and potatoes, would walk into Kingstown to sell their produce in the market. The men fished and hunted wild pigeon, agoutis and opossums. One of the fishing techniques, in use for hundreds of years, was to poison rivers with juice extracted from plants such as the dogwood or erythrina linn and the sigesbeckia, sometimes damming streams to make the process more effective. In late July the mass spawning of river fish would allow the Caribs to scoop up huge quantities of *tritrixes* (as the fry were known in French). At sea fishermen might use harpoons for larger prey and the Caribs also fished from the beach using huge nets pulled in by up to a hundred people.

George Davidson, a Methodist who pioneered a mission to convert the Black Caribs in the 1780s, wrote his own observations of their way of life. What is striking is how similar his picture of Carib culture is to that painted by the French missionaries a century or more earlier when their observations largely concerned what would come to be called Yellow Caribs. Davidson, like most European observers, was struck by what he saw as the subservient position of women, contrasting their labours in the fields and the home with the "indolent" lifestyle of the men. "No slavery can be conceived more wretched than that of the women," he felt. Given that Davidson actually lived in a slave society, this is a remarkable statement, and one wonders how much better the lot of women in Hogarth's London was. A man could take a number of wives (marriage was usually at an early age) and would establish each new one in a different house but could also simply abandon a wife who he wished to divorce. Female adultery, even the mere suspicion of it, was punished with death and women, it was claimed, were often injured in men's drunken rages. "In no part of the world are women more chaste, owing, possibly, to the severity with which incontinence is punished."[6]

Vengeance remained the principal mechanism of justice and death the penalty. The target would usually be killed when his guard was down, often at a *ouïcou/vin*. Davidson gives as example the case of the chief of Rabacca who was wounded by his nephew, "the latter's being put to death the same evening by his cousin".[7] Grudges could be nursed for many years. However, Percin de la Roque, writing in the same year as Davidson, describes a trial for murder of a number of Caribs by a tribunal ordered by the Marquis de Bouillé where "*tous les chefs de leur nation*" were assembled. They were condemned to death and the sentence was carried out "*sans rumeur ni émeute*" ("without murmurings or disorder") in what may be an example of growing European influence on Carib organization.[8]

One change that had occurred over the years lay in the construction of their dwellings. The houses were originally built with boughs bent over in the form of a semicircle and thatched with the leaves of the *roseau*. Latterly, however, the Caribs had taken to building their houses more robustly, fashioning rectangular structures with hardwood posts fixed in the ground and solid rafters, although still thatched with reed, a change which Davidson put down to European influence (although the influence could conceivably have been African). "The whole furniture of the house consists of seats formed out of logs, their hammocks, the calebash formed into cups and spoons, a cassada-grater, a serpentine press, a wooden trough, and a cassada-iron-plate, and sometimes a few articles of earthen-ware."[9] Logs appear to have replaced the woventopped *matoutou* stools of earlier reports—although another writer, the Scottish curator of the island's Botanical Garden, Alexander Anderson, wrote that their woven baskets were "very useful and always in great demand"[10]—but the iron plate is the only item that is obviously the result of trade with Europeans.

Such trade was generally carried on with the French islands, especially Martinique, which they visited regularly in their pirogues. "Their boats (or Pettiaugres as they call them) are very long and narrow, and sharp at both Ends. They are made of a single Tree, hollowed out with their rude Instruments, at the expence of much time & Labour, and are often dragged from the Woods at a considerable distance, to the Sea Beach. In calm Weather they carry a small square Sail upon a pole, & many of them carry upwards of twenty men. They have no Oars but a sort of Paddles, which the Charaibs use with much Art, and with which they make shift to get on at a great Rate."[11] Their belongings would be lashed to the bottom of the vessel to prevent them being lost when overturned. (Excellent swimmers, the Caribs righted their vessels with little fuss.) They also used canoes for fishing and, according to Percin, although the rough seas to the windward of the island prevented them from doing so for more than two or three months of the year, by exploiting the navigable coasts and rivers, "they easily acquire an abundance of fish not only for their subsistence, but also to salt and trade".[12]

Kingstown—"a small and scattered, but very neat and well-built town"[13]—may have been acceptable as a market for vegetables and poultry but the flourishing ports of Martinique were an incomparable draw for the Caribs. "The comparison of the French island with ours, in respect to wealth, population, shipping, grandeur, etc. is by no means in our favour," thought Davidson.[14] Commerce with the French left its mark on the Caribs' language. Among many loan words in modern Garifuna, all the terms for numbers above three are derived from French. Also, Caribs had increasingly been taking French names, probably adopted from their godfathers as a comparison of the names of those signing the 1773 treaty with those who signed a treaty with the English in 1668 indicates.[15] Tobacco was the Caribs' principal export. They produced a variety known as *macouba*, after a type grown in Martinique, which was much-prized by snuff-takers. They also traded silk-grass nets. The articles they sought were weapons in the form of muskets, ammunition, sabres and cutlasses, other metal objects, plus some wine and the low-grade rum known as taffia. European weapons were certainly the most conspicuous fruits of trade and were the Black Caribs' most treasured possessions ("they take much pleasure in keeping them in perfect order").[16] A knife in the waistband appears to have been the least a Carib man would be seen out with. Davidson maintained that "on all occasions the men carry with them a sabre or cutlass, and a loaded musket, which is ever on the cock".[17] Thomas Coke, who was the superintendent of Methodist Societies in America and who visited St. Vincent twice in the 1780s, wrote: "Even in times of peace they exhibit an armed neutrality; and both sexes display a state of preparation, either for offensive or defensive war."[18]

In such a well-armed society and with vengeance for some earlier offence an ever-present danger, Davidson writes that murders were frequent and that Caribs lived in fear of running into someone who bore a grudge. If this is true, the coordination of this essentially acephalous society into a unified fighting force in time of war is all the more remarkable. "Every district of two or three miles in length, has its peculiar chief, who, however, has not the smallest shadow of authority, except in time of war."[19] Percin describes their political organization in similar terms but seems to suggest that Chatoyer enjoyed extra prestige. "They live communally among themselves on good terms under a chief they describe as a general. Independently of this chief, they have a captain in each cove of their districts when they want to deliberate on some subject all these captains assemble at the house of the first chief who nevertheless seems not to have much authority except when it is a question of executing orders of the French government, to which they seem submissive and affectionate."[20] The British view was more succinct: "This people have no Idea of permanent and fixed Government, nor even of Authority, more than the Circumstance of the Moment suggests."[21]

Davidson felt it would take time and work to wean the Black Caribs from their attachment to the French. The French language was "almost generally spoken by them" and he thought it would be necessary to set up public schools to teach their children English. According to the governor, "Very few of them understand the English language and scarce any of them can speak it."[22] In addition to language instruction, the Methodists felt the boys could be taught a trade and girls schooled in sewing and knitting stockings.

Coke travelled to the edge of Carib country in 1788 and was impressed by the "sweet simplicity and cheerfulness" of the natives. "As we passed by their habitations, they stood at their doors in ranks; and while many of them saluted us '*Bou jou, Bou jou,*' (a corruption of *Bon jour*, a good day) some in broken English cried 'How dee, How dee.'" With great difficulty Coke's party traversed the narrow paths over the mountains separating the Carib country from European settlements to the south, which he judged "the worst and most tremendous I ever rode".[23] His Methodist missionary companion, Mr. Baxter, nearly died when his horse tumbled thirty feet down a precipice. "Full of serpentine involutions, their formation is as rude as their situation is tremendous; opposition and defiance seemed to be presented both by rocks and bushes; and a complication of obstacles threatened to prohibit all access. In short, it appeared to be both the residence and empire of Danger," he later recalled.[24] The Caribs helped them cut their way through the dense vegetation until they were greeted with the sight of the broad plain of Grand Sable, where the largest Carib community lay. This was as far as Coke penetrated but beyond Grand Sable, he wrote, was another larger and very populous plain. "[N]o Europeans, I believe, were suffered to enter" there, he noted.[25] Even visits to Grand Sable were generally only possible after gifts of rum to the Caribs and then in the company of an armed Carib escort.[26]

A Frenchman who spent time among the Caribs in the 1790s described the physical appearance of the Black Caribs as unlike that of natives of West Africa, with smooth black hair, straight, slightly upturned noses and slim lips. Their mouths resembled those of Africans only in "the beauty of their teeth".[27] This may tell us more about the prejudices of the writer, who sought to extol the Caribs in terms of the "noble savage" and saw little such nobility in Africans, than it does about the Black Caribs' actual looks, judging by Brunias' painting of Chatoyer and his wives. But one observation does ring true. "They also had," he wrote, "a supremely proud air, which would change at the slightest reverse to a savage physiognomy full of menace, arrogance and ferocity."[28] Coke also found the Black Caribs "a handsomer people than the Negroes" and agreed that they had a warlike appearance. Governor James Seton remarked only that "the blood of the yellow Charaib is visible in many of the black Charaibs."[29] Davidson said the Caribs formed a "motley mixture... in which the negro-colour and features chiefly prevail."[30] Despite his generally hostile view of the Black Caribs, Alexander Anderson, the curator of the Botanical Garden, did concede that they were "far more intelligent than any other race of savages" (he qualified this compliment by saying this was probably due to "their long communication with Europeans").[31] Certainly, Anderson could not fail to have been impressed by the Caribs' extensive knowledge of healing herbs which were unknown to the island's white people and he duly noted down Caribs cures for such complaints as "*mal d'estomac*" and gonorrhea.[32] The practice of head deformation, which helped differentiate Black Caribs from recent black runaways, earned them the nickname "flat heads" from the slave population. According to Anderson, this mockery caused them to discontinue the practice towards the end of the eighteenth century. The threat of enslavement was an ever-present concern for them and when fishing for shellfish in the Grenadines the Black Caribs would ask the British governor for passports because of their dread of being seized by some ship which might take them for runaway slaves.

Their relationship with runaways, whom Carib captains such as Bigot went to great lengths to shelter in the 1770s, may have undergone a change. Percin de la Roque wrote in 1787 that the Caribs "had been in the habit of hunting" runaways and that "they continue to help the English in this regard, having absolutely no link with the runaway negroes".[33] It was a view shared by the British, and represented a change in policy as remarkable as that observed by Labat at the start of the century.[34] "Whatever has been the case formerly," wrote Governor Seton in January 1789, "it is certain that runaway Slaves do not add now to the number of this People. On the contrary, they are constantly brought in by the Charaibs when found straggling in their Country. This good office, they perform not from regard for the Planters, but for the Sake of a Reward which the Legislature, very wisely, grants them on these occasions." Another factor in the apparent change in attitude may have been demographic. Seton, a navy man from an old Scottish family who succeeded Lincoln in 1787, believed that during the occupation of 1779-83 the French had estimated that the Black Caribs had 1,100 men capable of bearing arms but he thought that "they are now considerably more numerous; and that their numbers are encreasing in an astonishing degree". Seton, albeit recognizing the lack of any hard information, estimated the number of Black Carib fighting men at 1,200, an increase of nine per cent in the five years since the handover. This population growth may have increased pressure on natural resources and led the Black Caribs to look warily on the prospect of sharing their territory with yet more newcomers.

Governor Seton asserted that: "The Slaves bear much ill will and dislike to the Charaibs."[35] He put this down to the "savage cruelties" inflicted upon them by the Black Caribs during the warfare of 1779 and 1780 when "many slaves, who fell into their hands, were wantonly butchered". Anderson agreed that "The negroes bore [the Black Caribs] a great antipathy" but put it down to a different reason. "This no doubt originated from jealousy. The poor slaves, knowing them to be of the same extraction with themselves, yet being free and enjoying more liberty than the lower class of white men, going as gentlemen while they were labouring hard with sweat of their bodies. There was something natural to this dislike and was human nature only."[36]

It is striking, though, that in the 1770s, while Bigot was alive, runaway slaves found a ready welcome and practical support in his lands. By contrast, in the subsequent decade and a half the foremost leaders of the Black Caribs were Chatoyer and Du Vallée, both of whom owned slaves who worked on their plantations.

The Methodists had rented 150 acres of land at Byera on the borders of Carib country to build a schoolhouse and a dwelling for two teachers. The authorities, however, despaired of making good Christians of them. "They do not appear to have any more Sense of Religion than the Negroes lately imported from the Coast of Africa," wrote Governor Seton. Of course, it is very likely that West Africans had a well-developed sense of religion, just not the Christian religion, and with the Black Caribs they shared a penchant for charms which they carried with them to ward off harm. It was also noted that: "They make use of several incantations against Evil Spirits, to prevent their malignant influence."[37] Ultimately the Methodists' efforts to bring Christianity to the Caribs were no more successful than those of the Jesuits. "Among the Charaibees… Mr Baxter saw but little fruit of his labor. To the prospects of a hereafter, they felt an unwillingness to expand their minds."[38]

The English missionaries, like their French predecessors, were also pawns in a wider geopolitical game. On their trading visits to Martinique the Caribs were told by the French that the Methodists were spies sent by the King of England to reconnoitre their land in preparation for an invading army. One day the resident missionary at Byera, Mr. Baxter, found the local Caribs strangely sullen and only after three days of the silent treatment did he get the secret out of them. He tried to persuade them that the missionaries had no such intentions but to no avail. At this point, "he thought it high time to hasten with Mrs Baxter out of the country, with all possible celerity".[39] And that was the end of the Methodist mission to the Caribs. By 1790 Mr. Baxter was living in Kingstown and ministering to a more receptive congregation.

It was not, though, the end of British designs on the Black Caribs' land. The end of the war in North America had produced a flood of loyalist refugees to neighbouring British possessions. William Walker, the governor of the Bahamas, wrote to his newly appointed counterpart in St. Vincent on 8 March 1784 that "Great numbers of unfortunate Loyalists are daily crowding to these Islands..." Apparently believing that the Black Caribs had already been dispossessed, he helpfully suggested that the grant of their lands "would be some recompence to many of those Loyal Sufferers".[40] Two years later this still appeared an elegant solution to those far from the scene. The former lieutenant governor of Georgia suggested that loyalists from the back lands of that colony and of Carolina displaced to East Florida could be given Carib land, with the Caribs being removed to Bequia, an idea that had been rejected twenty years earlier. (Bequia, along with the rest of the Grenadines, had been detached from Grenada and made part of the St. Vincent government in June 1784, an idea that had been proposed by the previous governor, Valentine Morris, years earlier.) While the governor of the Bahamas was dreaming of solving his loyalist problem using Carib lands, the governor of St. Vincent was dreaming of sending the Caribs to one of the Bahama islands.[41]

The British were not the only ones contemplating shifting the Caribs. Their old friend and defender Percin de la Roque, by now stationed in Cayenne, concluded that St. Vincent was not big enough for the British and the Black Caribs to share. He suggested moving them to territory in Guiana on the South American mainland where they might be of service to the French colony there as an example of industry and activity to the neighbouring Indians and where, issued with sabres and guns, they might be useful for the defence of the colony. Percin proposed a detailed plan, involving French ships ferrying groups of Caribs to the mainland where *carbets* and provision grounds would be prepared for them. He believed that far from opposing their emigration, the British would watch them leave with pleasure. Versailles cautiously welcomed the idea but no practical steps were taken.[42]

Following the return of British rule, Governor Edmund Lincoln's approach to the Caribs had seemed to centre on making them take an oath of allegiance to the British crown and interrupting their communication with the French islands. The idea, after all the experience to that date, that the Caribs would feel themselves bound by an oath of allegiance might seem naive but Lincoln made clear that it was not "expected that they can ever be made friends longer than fear operates on their minds, and makes them assume that mask".[43] Lincoln's personal preference would have been to "purchase their lands, and send them to some other Country"[44] but he was constrained by his instructions. Early on he admitted that he had yet to see a Black Carib in the flesh but felt that was probably an advantage as he did not want to reveal his true designs to them. What was needed, he believed, was a military force strong enough to intimidate them into submission, and in particular Lincoln sought reinforcements of black troops "of whom I understand they are extremely afraid". In a postscript he asked for any small arms General Matthew might have to spare to arm the militia "if the Charaibs should make that measure necessary".

In June 1784, just after the handover, the colony was alarmed by reports that the Caribs had been importing arms and ammunition from Martinique and were only awaiting the return of some chiefs from that island to begin hostilities. Governor Lincoln asked for and received reinforcements from the commander-in-chief of British forces in the West Indies. However, several Carib chiefs, including Chatoyer himself ("who is called their leader"), came to see the governor to reassure him that they had no hostile intent. He said that the Caribs who lived on the land around Yambou, Massarica and Colonarie, the ownership of which was disputed by British settlers, and all the way up the windward coast to Owia, had long been urging him to make war against the British and, exasperated by his refusal, had threatened to choose another leader. As a result he dared not pass through their country for fear of his life and was obliged to come down to Kingstown by water. He added that the quantity of arms and ammunition imported from Martinique was not so great and that the anti-British plotting was far from universal.[45]

Lincoln told Chatoyer and the others that the Caribs should retreat behind the boundary set by the 1773 treaty and break off their trade with the French islands. Many Caribs had reoccupied land which had been ceded in 1773 and which white planters had been too scared to develop. Those planters who had toughed it out "were surrounded with mortal enemies who viewed their prosperity with chagrin and jealousy... regarding every foot of land the planter cleared as intrusion on their property".[46] Privately Lincoln determined that only the rebuilding of military posts in Carib country could keep the Caribs in check if they were to remain on the island. The British found the defences left by the French in a poor state, perhaps unsurprisingly, although rather more surprisingly they claimed that they themselves had left these defences in excellent condition[47] in 1779. It was calculated that bringing the French buildings on Dorsetshire Hill ("little more than sheds") up to snuff would cost £19,000. New blockhouses were also required to replace the flimsy structures at the military posts at the Vigie and Byabou, which were seen as important defences against any Carib attack.

The governor hoped that, in addition to the military posts, by gradually buying land within the Carib country and settling Britons among them the Caribs might be weaned from their attachment to the French and eventually become good British subjects. One of the problems for the colony was that "no Englishman has yet been hardy enough to venture"[48] beyond the Carib boundary and so they had little intelligence on what the Caribs were planning.

One exception occurred within two months of the handover of St. Vincent in 1784 when the first ascent by a European of the volcano at the island's centre was completed. An account was published by the Royal Society credited to a "James Anderson, surgeon".[49] In fact the pioneering mountaineer was Alexander Anderson, the second curator of the Botanical Garden who was also a surgeon. Anderson described the lush vegetation changing as he ascended, taking in grass, moss, ferns and finally the bare rock of the summit. Although La Soufriere was at the heart of Carib territory Anderson climbed the mountain without encountering the local people, instead making the ascent in company of a couple of black slaves borrowed from a British planter, perhaps illustrating the divide between the British and the Caribs, who had no desire to reveal the secrets of their mountain passes to outsiders. At the end of the century he revisited the summit and compared the state of the crater then and in 1784. This incidentally provides indirect evidence in support of Defoe's account of an eruption in 1718 since only at the end of the century was vegetation starting to recolonize the bottom of the crater.[50] Also, he adds, the mountain "has always been mentioned to have had volcanic eruptions in it. The traditions of the oldest inhabitant in the island, and the ravines at the bottom, seem to me to vindicate the assertion."[51]

Another notable event occurred in November 1786 when the British inhabitants of the island were honoured with a visit from a royal guest, Prince William Henry, the younger brother to King George III and himself the future King William IV, who was at the time serving in the navy. According to Shephard, the prince met Chatoyer and presented him with a silver gorget which was reportedly found on the chief's body when he was killed. Sadly no more detailed account of this meeting between British royalty and the Black Caribs' foremost leader has survived.

The royal visit coincided with upheaval in the government of the colony. Governor Lincoln suffered a wound to his thigh and died from its effects in mid-November. His successor, James Seton, was appointed the following February, although it was many months before he arrived in St. Vincent, and would be called upon to lead the colony through the most turbulent and defining period in its history. His instructions from London counselled him to keep to the 1773 treaty, attempt to encourage "more frequent intercourse" with the Caribs and to show them "marks of kindness" in an attempt to wean them from their partiality to the French.

In this period of detente the families of Chatoyer and Sir William Young remained curiously entwined even as the Black Carib-British conflict headed for its harrowing denouement. Chatoyer had met the first land commissioner in the 1760s as the two had represented the opposing sides in the struggle for the future of St. Vincent. When the conflict broke out into open warfare in 1772 Young had sat on the special council appointed to run the war on the British side, while Chatoyer had been one of the Caribs' top military leaders and a signatory to the peace. But in the interlude of peaceful coexistence in the 1780s and 1790s relations between the two families were positively cordial. Chatoyer was a frequent visitor at the Young family's estates, receiving "the most flattering attentions and hospitality" and staying as a guest "at the house, and on the estate at Calliaqua". A son of Chatoyer's even lived in Young's household.

Sir William Young had amassed a fortune from his plantations in the West Indies before his death in 1788; among planters in Antigua the Young family ranked tenth in terms of acreage and slave ownership, and the family's holdings in St. Vincent included the Villa estate, near Calliaqua, which is now the centre of the island's tourist industry. Although he was the foremost representative of British power in St. Vincent, through his dealings with the Black Caribs he developed a respect for their leaders. "Many of their Chiefs are very Sagacious and Sensible," he believed.[52] There is a legend that Young was driving in his carriage when he came upon Chatoyer. The Carib chief expressed his admiration for the two magnificent white horses pulling the carriage. Young immediately offered to give him the two animals. In response, Chatoyer looked out to sea and pointing at an island offshore he told Young that he was more than welcome to it. The island still bears Young's name.[53] Given that Chatoyer's territory lay many miles to the north, any such offer would have been playful at best.

Sir William's estates in St. Vincent and other West Indian islands passed to his son, the second baronet, also called Sir William Young, in 1788. The younger Sir William was an educated man, an Oxford graduate, a fellow of the Royal Society and an MP for St. Mawes in Cornwall. He would go on to write a history of the First Carib War, drawing on his father's papers, and the book remains a standard work to this day. On arrival in St. Vincent in December 1791 he boasted of the "mild discipline"[54] in force on his own family estate and was disgusted by the way Africans on the decks of slave ships in the harbour were forced to dance by the sailors. (However, in 1797 he warned that William Wilberforce's parliamentary motion against the slave trade would lead to revolution in the West Indies.)

Young was eager to meet Chatoyer but first entertained two other Carib chiefs: Anselm, from the Morne (Mount) Young area and Brunau, a chief from Grand Sable. Young would only accept presents from chiefs because the giver always required double in return and he complained that he could not afford that rate with all Caribs. Young said he had already received La Lime, one of the chiefs who had signed the treaty of 1773, and a dozen others but this was a more formal affair. The chiefs brought gifts of Carib baskets, fowls and pineapples. Young responded by offering them wine and ordering a keg of rum for each chief. Later "about a dozen of their ladies" were introduced and Young offered these wine but they replied that they preferred rum. The women were naked "saving a petticoat sewed at the corners, and hanging one before and one behind" and were painted red with *roucou*, with pins through their pierced lips, bracelets and bands of leather and beads around their ankles.[55]

The following day Anselm and Brunau returned to discuss more serious matters. They politely asked "*quelles nouvelles de la France?*" and then "*quelles nouvelles de l'Angleterre?*" before steering the conversation around to their concerns about British designs on Carib territory. British settlers had been seen around Mount Young looking longingly at the fertile plain of Grand Sable and remarking, "what a pity this country yet belongs to the savage Charaibes!" A rumour had been heard from some French fugitives from Martinique that Young himself was on a mission on behalf of the British government to dispossess them. Young vehemently denied any such plan and reported that the chiefs seemed very pleased with his response and that they parted "the best friends in the world".[56]

Young was clearly recognized by the Caribs as a person of importance since the following month he received another visit, this time from Chatoyer, his brother Du Vallée and six of their sons. Young describes the two chiefs as well dressed, although he does not describe how,[57] and notes that as a sign of respect they had come unarmed. They brought Young "a stoole of Charaibe workmanship" (*matoutou*) and a wild turkey cock and hen. Chatoyer's status is indicated by the fact that his gift was a sword, "a silver mounted hanger", while Du Vallée received a powder horn. It was presumably this sword which Young later said had belonged to his brother Lieutenant Henry Young, who had died fighting the rebellious Americans at Saratoga and which was engraved with the family arms. Chatoyer and his sons dined that night at Young's villa, putting away a bottle of claret each before departing "in high glee with many expressions of friendship".[58]

It is not clear how many sons Chatoyer had but Governor Seton wrote that two of them were living with the family of "a gentleman" who had intended to take them to Europe but, detained on business matters, had been prevented from doing so.[59] The Methodist Thomas Coke reported that a son of Chatoyer had for some time been under the tuition of the missionaries Mr. and Mrs. Baxter where he went by the name of John Dimmey. Coke was impressed by his refined sensibilities and recounted an anecdote illustrating his graciousness. "Teach me your language," said Mr. Baxter to him one day, "and I will give you my watch." "I will teach you my language," replied the young chieftain, "but I will not have your watch."[60] John Dimmey accompanied Coke and Baxter on a trip to Carib country in 1790 where he introduced them to Du Vallée who regaled them with eggs, cassava bread and punch. Coke had hoped to take Dimmey back with him to England but his father, Chatoyer, was absent at the time and so could not give his permission.[61]

Young clearly saw Chatoyer as the Black Caribs' most important chief—as had his father—but others recognized that, while he had been the key figure in time of war, in peacetime his authority was much attenuated. A decade after leading the Carib force that seized the island in league with the French, Chatoyer was still accorded "personal Respect", "But, as at present they see no Reason for acting in Concert, or under the Command of one Leader, the Interference of Chattoway is not much felt."[62] Governor Leyborne, in the 1770s, had believed that "the Chiefs have really no power, but over those of their own particular Familys".[63] In peacetime different Carib communities could be at odds with each other. A delegation led by Chatoyer once explained to Leyborne that those Caribs in the territory ceded by the 1773 treaty could not withdraw behind the new boundary because "there existed no friendship with those to windward". When Leyborne observed that it was strange that they had managed to combine in war against the British just a few months earlier, they replied that it was true "but every thing at that time gave way to the common danger".[64]

Chatoyer possessed a rich tract of nearly one thousand acres at Grand Baleine, in the north of the island, of which about three hundred acres were cleared for agriculture. Du Vallée, with several slaves belonging to him, had cleared 150 acres of fertile land nearby at Petit Baleine.[65] Both men had benefited from loans and sureties from British gentlemen, probably including Young himself, in making their start in European-style tropical agriculture.

Du Vallée visited Young on at least two further occasions in early 1792 and Chatoyer's brother, who was "next to him in authority, particularly on the Grand Sable side of the country",[66] made a deep and favourable impression on him. The pair exchanged gifts of a bow and arrow and a pair of handsome brass-barrelled pistols. He made a similarly good impression on Thomas Coke who visited the Carib chief at his home and was "treated with the utmost politeness which the savage state could have afforded".[67] To Young he appeared "a very polite and sensible man" who spoke good French. Young felt: "He is the most enlightened of the Charaibes, and may be termed the founder of civilization among them."[68] This may be connected to the fact that he owned nine black slaves who worked on his plantation growing cotton. Certainly Young hoped that drawing the Caribs further into the colonial money economy could eventually make them model members of society. "Money civilizes in the first instance," he wrote, "as it corrupts in the last; the savage labouring for himself, soon ceases to be a savage; the slave to money becomes a subject to government, and he becomes a useful subject."[69]

Caribs were joining the colony's money economy in other ways too as contacts with British planters increased. Emboldened by the return to British sovereignty settlers had cleared some three thousand acres of land on the windward coast in the land ceded by the 1773 treaty, displacing Carib families who had re-established themselves south of the boundary—or who had never left—as they did so. Governor Seton estimated that of the 1,200 Carib men capable of bearing arms that he calculated were on the island, 250 lived on the "British" side of the Byera river. (He estimated that there were no more than thirty Yellow Carib men in St. Vincent.)[70] Their presence caused great uneasiness among the British settlers in the area who accused them of various depredations including attacks on slaves on estates in disputed areas, although Seton's predecessor had noted that they behaved peaceably and "I cannot help thinking them of Benefit rather than disservice to the new settlers."[71] Evictions of Caribs by returning settlers left a legacy of resentment—"frequent murmurings"[72]—as they were displaced to nearby woods. For the planters, the difficulty involved in transporting such a heavy and easily damaged crop as sugar over the rugged, mountainous road to the capital had led them to grow cotton instead, but after six dispiriting years they had concluded that the land was not suitable for the crop. So the planters persuaded the island's assembly to petition the king to build piers and wharves on the windward coast at Byabou and at Sans Souci at the southern end of Colonarie Bay so that they could export sugar directly by sea. This proposal bore no immediate fruit but in the meantime some Caribs were offering a solution to those windward growers who persisted with sugar by ferrying their produce out to ships anchored offshore, as they had done with supplies for British military posts in their territory. Perhaps inspired by this example of cooperation on the windward coast the island's chief justice, Drewry Ottley, in 1791 sought to have "a half hour's chat" with Lord Sydney, the president of the commission on trade and plantations, while in London to discuss the Caribs, "who, I think, from their present disposition towards us, might be effectually attached to our Government and render'd servicable to the Colony at large".[73]

The colony, though, was not about to let down its guard. Beefing up the island's defences was a priority. General Matthew visited in March 1789 and approved new fortifications at what would become Fort Charlotte on Berkshire Hill and at Old Woman's Point directly beneath it, on the western side of Kingstown Bay. He also visited the borders of Carib country and expressed concern that the military post at Byabou was of little use now that the Carib boundary had been pushed northward from the Colonarie river to the Byera.[74] Governor Seton was of a similar opinion since, he claimed, there was not a single soldier stationed within ten miles of the Carib boundary. So a new post was planned for the south side of the Byera. For the planters the Caribs remained a threatening presence, depressing enthusiasm for settling new land. In 1787 the white population over fifteen years of age was only 725 and more than three hundred of these were concentrated in the parish of St. George's around the capital.[75]

Wider worries also impinged on the colony. Following William Wilberforce's introduction of his parliamentary bill for the abolition of the slave trade in 1791 and a slave revolt in Dominica at the start of that year, Governor Seton assured the authorities in London that there had been no reaction in St. Vincent and the colony remained tranquil. "Negro slaves," he wrote, "have not… discovered signs of Discontent or Dissatisfaction."[76] A year later following the successful slave revolt in St.-Domingue (Haiti) and the passing of Wilberforce's bill for a gradual end to the slave trade (ultimately a false dawn for the abolition movement) the colony was less sanguine, the council and assembly passing a joint resolution in intemperate language expressing their "astonishment and indignation" at the measure.[77]

As the slave population continued to grow, the question of feeding them assumed greater importance. St. Vincent's Botanical Garden, believed to be the first in the western hemisphere, had been established with a view to helping planters develop new crops not only for export but also for their enslaved workers' subsistence. In 1793 Captain William Bligh, commanding HMS *Providence*, delivered three hundred breadfruit plants from Tahiti to the Botanical Garden, belatedly completing a mission that had been so dramatically interrupted by the mutiny on his previous ship, the *Bounty*, four years earlier. Breadfruit was seen as a potentially cheap and nourishing foodstuff for slaves, and the plants at the Botanical Garden went on to produce a large crop. (Breadfruit has since become a staple.) St. Vincent's planters were so grateful that they voted Captain Bligh a piece of plate worth a hundred guineas along with two fat bullocks for his officers and crew.

But the winds of revolutionary change were blowing in the wider world and the *Bounty* was not the only site of rebellion. France had been convulsed by revolution since 1789 but conflict with other European powers including Britain reached a new pitch following the execution by guillotine of the former king, Louis XVI, in January 1793. News reached St. Vincent in March that the French had declared war on Britain. Conflict between the two imperial powers could not fail to be of acute interest to the Caribs, who saw in this antagonism an opportunity to advance their own interests. In St. Vincent there was alarm at reports that "this Island continues to swarm with Aliens and Foreigners, who hold illegal Meetings, Clubs and Associations, in the different Quarters of the Island; and who hold and carry on illegal and treasonable correspondence with divers Persons in the French Islands." All such foreigners were called upon to swear an oath of allegiance or given six days to leave the island. French agitators were reported to have landed at isolated bays and "a very high reward" was offered for the capture of any unauthorized white person within the Carib boundary.

Faced with the possible reactivation of what had come to be seen as the enemy within, Governor Seton decided the best thing to do was to call in the Carib chiefs and lay down the law to them. John Carty, a tavern keeper, was engaged to provide dinner for the twenty chiefs on 21 and 22 March. The Caribs were summoned to appear before the council where the terms of the 1773 treaty were read and explained to them, no doubt with particular emphasis on the part which pledged their loyalty to the British crown. The Caribs were invited to raise grievances, after which it was agreed that Chatoyer should be compensated to the tune of £40 for some trees which had been cut down without permission on his land. The Caribs promised to remain neutral in any war between Britain and France, which appeared to satisfy the council. However, repeating a pattern set over previous decades, six days later two chiefs and about fifty other Caribs were reported to have sailed to Martinique, "they being now the Carriers on all occasions for the French Democratic Party".[78] The colonial government was evidently furious but felt powerless to take action against the Caribs.

The atmosphere of impending crisis was exacerbated by the appearance in April of yellow fever in Kingstown which quickly spread through the town, initially striking down the "young and florid".[79] Tension simmered throughout 1793 and the Caribs followed each development in the Anglo-French conflict closely. In June the defeat of a British attack on Martinique saw the Caribs' "gloomy and reserved behaviour" changed to "a haughty and impervious mien, indicating an end to their former wavering and uncertain purposes, and the resoluteness of every future design".[80] In August a vessel was dispatched to the windward coast after intelligence was received that a French officer was planning a landing in Carib country. Repairs were ordered to the fortress at Dorsetshire Hill which blocked the route from Carib country to Kingstown. The optimism that "marks of kindness" might change the Black Caribs' attitude towards the British had completely evaporated. In October 1794, in a dispatch to his superiors in Whitehall, Governor Seton voiced his distrust of "our internal enemy the Charaibs who on all occasions have manifested a strong inclination to favor the views of the French, and who I am convinced would immediately join them, were they to make a descent upon this Island." He was not wrong.

Copy of Chatoyer's declaration in French to launch the Second Carib War. It is signed with the *"marc ordinaire"* of the Black Carib leader.

6. The Cry of Liberty

"The time has come when… the ancient friendship of the French and the Caribs should be renewed; they must exterminate the English, their common enemy." [1]
  Victor Hugues, 13 March 1795

VICTOR Hugues had arrived in the Caribbean in 1794 at the age of about 32. His mission was to spread the fire of revolution through the West Indies and seize whatever British islands he could. The Marseille-born Jacobin[2] was armed with the decision of the French National Convention to abolish slavery although he himself had prospered in the slave-based economy of St.-Domingue (Haiti).[3] Within five months he had taken Guadeloupe from a superior British force and exacted bloody revenge on those he deemed traitors to the new French republic by means of the guillotine he had brought with him from France. Marie-Galante, Les Saintes, La Désirade, St. Lucia and St. Martin were reconquered in quick succession. Now he turned his attention to the islands further south, including St. Vincent. Hugues' success had been based on a strategy of rallying marginalized groups, including slaves who were offered the prospect of freedom, but also free blacks and mulattoes. In St. Vincent, the key constituency for his designs was that of the Black Caribs and there was also a sizeable population of French inhabitants who were believed to be ready to turn on the British.

Hugues looked to Chatoyer, as the leader of the Black Caribs, to spearhead the attack on St. Vincent. His message to the war chief mixed an appeal to the long-standing ties between the French and the Caribs with an exhortation to revolutionary unity. Hugues addressed Chatoyer not just as an ally but as a French general and the leader of the insurrection in St. Vincent. To Chatoyer and his brother Du Vallée, Hugues sent a uniform, a sabre and a hat each as a mark of their leadership. He ordered his French infantry commander, Citizen Touraille, to regard Chatoyer "as your leader in everything".[4]

Chatoyer, who had previously sworn his allegiance to the Bourbon king,[5] now embraced the sanguinary rhetoric of the French revolution. In an appeal to the French inhabitants of St. Vincent drafted on "the twelfth of March and the first of our freedom" at Chateaubelair, he issued a proclamation with the revolutionary fury of a Jacobin:

> Who is the Frenchman who will not join his brothers at a moment when the cry of liberty is heard by them? Let us then rally citizens and brothers around the flag which flies in this island and hasten to cooperate in the great work already so gloriously begun. But if any timid men should still exist, should any Frenchman be held back through fear, we declare to them in the name of the law that those who are not mustered with us within the day will be regarded as traitors to the country and treated as enemies. We swear to them that fire and the sword will be used against them, that we will burn their goods and that we will slit the throats of their wives and children to wipe out their race.[6]

Liberty, equality and fraternity—particularly liberty—were concepts that would be sure to appeal to the Black Caribs, who throughout their brief existence as a people had had to fight to be accepted as free agents of their own destiny. But it is unlikely that the new democratic ideology was a key element of their participation in the insurrection. In the triangular balance of forces in St. Vincent the French had long been their natural allies and Hugues was careful to appeal to the "ancient friendship" between the French and the Caribs. For the Caribs the ambition must have been to return the island to the status quo of a dozen years earlier when the French had ruled over the settled areas to leeward but had largely left the Caribs to their own devices. How the French governed themselves would have been a secondary concern.

British forces in the West Indies were ill-prepared to meet the challenge. The army had been diminished by sickness, and defence was over-reliant on the militia. An official assessment concluded that "no Island could resist an attack even from an inconsiderable Body of Men if led with judgement and spirit".[7]

The Caribs welcomed French troops who were infiltrated into the areas of St. Vincent they controlled. Five Frenchmen were reported to have landed in Chatoyer's quarter on 4 March. Hugues sent wine, salt and currency to Chatoyer, apparently to facilitate a "meeting of your compatriots" which was to take place on 6 March[8] at Grand Sable. A *ouïcou* or *vin* was the established Carib method of planning for warfare. Alexandre Moreau de Jonnès, a young French artillery officer sent to support the Carib rising, later wrote that he had witnessed a type of "national council" involving both Yellow and Black Caribs, although it should be said that no other source gives such a prominent role in the war to Yellow Caribs, who were in any case few in number.[9] As their forefathers had done, the leading Caribs would have debated at length, their deliberations lubricated by copious drinking. "When it's a question of war, they remember the motives of vengeance the nation ought to have preserved since such and such a time towards the enemies they are to fight. They persuade themselves through extensive arguments that these enemies will be exterminated; their own courage is vaunted and the enemy's decried."[10] No doubt their appetite for the fight would have been sharpened by recalling the hardships inflicted by the British in 1772-3 but also the Carib victories over the same enemy in 1779 and 1780.

The overall French plan had been to coordinate attacks against the British colonial forces in both Grenada and St. Vincent. The date was set for St Patrick's Day, 17 March. But on 5 March news reached Kingstown that an insurrection had broken out in Grenada where the lieutenant governor had been seized by insurgents. Governor Seton immediately ordered the alarm to be fired and mobilized the militia who paraded with their arms that evening. A prominent planter with land in Mariaqua on the windward coast, William Greig, arrived in Kingstown with his family saying that a local Carib had warned him that the Caribs planned to exterminate everyone. Another report suggested a French sloop from Guadeloupe had landed at Chatoyer's quarter.

Seton sent a message to Chatoyer and Du Vallée, plus Dufond and all the chiefs residing at Grand Sable and Rabacca, calling on them to attend the governor and council in Kingstown the following Tuesday, as they had done on previous occasions. Chatoyer sent back his refusal, saying that it was now too late for such a meeting. "Such a violation of their Treaty," Seton commented, "indicated too plainly their intentions."[11]

Remarkably, though, the following day, a Sunday, a number of British gentlemen enjoyed a "maroon dinner" or picnic with some Carib chiefs. That same day more Caribs than normal came in to the market in Kingstown with no sign of anything untoward. (Two days later, however, the same Caribs "were foremost in attacking, plundering and demolishing the very plantations… where they had resided in ease and affluence for more than ten years", as one history sympathetic to the planters noted bitterly.)[12] Apparently seeking to bypass Chatoyer's refusal, an aide-de-camp of the governor travelled to Massarica asking local Caribs to come in to Kingstown on Tuesday and to pass the message on to the Caribs of Grand Sable. They expressed astonishment that their loyalty should be suspected, although they said they could not speak for those from Grand Sable and Rabacca.

A black slave named Adam reported that he had met a group of three white Frenchmen in company with several named Caribs who offered to make him a chief, promising him epaulettes and his freedom if he could raise forty blacks to the insurrectionary cause.[13] And that evening the estate of Madame La Croix, a Frenchwoman known for her pro-British sympathies, was attacked by a group of Caribs and French (the estate had also been targeted in 1772).

A party was sent out in the night to search for enemy forces in the woods and returned in the morning with several Caribs and French inhabitants as prisoner. The planters of the windward side needed no further confirmation. By Monday the 9th they and their families were abandoning their homes and heading for the capital. Slaves were abandoned on the estates and denied weapons despite "begging for arms for the Defence of themselves & Masters".[14] Twenty horsemen were sent out to join a militia company left on the windward but meeting a large body of Caribs they were driven back to Kingstown suffering ten casualties out of sixty. The captain of the Windward militia sent word of an impending revolt "by the whole body of Caribs".[15]

The following day, 10 March, alarming reports came in from around the island. The Three Rivers estate was in flames, its buildings and cane fields having been torched by the Caribs. Carib forces led by Du Vallée swept down the windward coast burning all signs of the British presence in their path. Militiamen and volunteers marched out to meet the Caribs at the Massarica river. The Caribs waved their hats as if in friendship before opening up on the British with a volley of musket fire from behind a felled silk-cotton tree. The British retreat to the capital became a rout, some on foot, some on horseback, the stragglers taking circuitous routes after hiding in the cane fields. They left behind 31 dead. The wounded received no quarter, Shephard alleging that they had been "murdered with savage barbarity; some had their legs and arms cut off". As the white inhabitants fled back towards Kingstown, from the Carib boundary to the River Yambou all the sugar works—more than thirty[16]—were set on fire and many cattle were killed as the pent-up fury of the Caribs was unleashed. No white planters who were discovered were allowed to live and a number of black slaves shared their fate. The following day the Caribs who had cut a swathe through the windward territory reached Calliaqua, just two and a half miles from Kingstown. On the 12th Du Vallée's forces occupied Dorsetshire Hill, the commanding height above the capital, and raised the French tricolour. Behind them a line of smouldering ruins marked their path.

On the leeward coast Chatoyer's progress was almost as rapid but less destructive. While on the windward Du Vallée was extirpating all trace of the British presence just as Hugues had urged, on the western coast Chatoyer largely left plantations intact. This was no doubt related to the fact that many French inhabitants, their allies, had their estates there. Hugues' letter to Chatoyer had clearly urged him to "Attack, exterminate all the English; but allow the French to support you."[17] But Shephard suggests that Chatoyer was interested in claiming some of the property for himself, in particular alleging that he had chosen the estate of a Mr. Kearton just north of Barrouallie as his share; "consequently no damage was done, either to the works, or even the furniture in the dwelling house, except one cut on a sideboard with a cutlass".[18]

On the first day of his advance Chatoyer took Chateaubelair, the northernmost European settlement on the leeward coast, where the French inhabitants, along with their slaves, rallied to his leadership. (Slaves of the British planters, in general, did not join the largely francophone uprising.)[19] He continued the drive south, meeting up with the forces led by his brother on Dorsetshire Hill on the 12th. The Carib/French force spent the next two days dragging two pieces of ordnance from the Stubbs Bay battery into position on Dorsetshire Hill while maintaining musket fire against a British advance guard which sought to take up position on Sion Hill. On the morning of the 14th Chatoyer called before him three British prisoners—Duncan Cruikshank, Peter

Cruikshank and Alexander Grant—who had been taken at Chateaubelair. Taking the sabre that had been given to him by Sir William Young he personally cut them to pieces, excoriating the English at each blow.[20] From Dorsetshire Hill, with a united army of Caribs and French at his back, Chatoyer could look down on Kingstown and feel that the goal of kicking the British out of the island for good was within his grasp.

Beneath them the imperial British presence in St. Vincent was reduced to a tiny patch around Kingstown. The governor was holed up with a small force of militia and many civilians in Fort Charlotte on top of Berkshire Hill on the other side of the capital from Dorsetshire Hill. Sugar canes in the immediate vicinity of the capital were set ablaze to deny the Caribs cover. French inhabitants had rallied to Chatoyer's side. A leading French property owner, Toussaint Dubois, wrote to Chatoyer offering his services and asking the Carib leader to protect his family.[21] The fact that Dubois' family were residing in Kingstown makes it clear that he believed Chatoyer would soon be master of the island. The main hope of the besieged British was for reinforcements from off the island. On receiving news of the insurrection in Grenada, Seton had appealed for help to the British army commander in Martinique, Sir John Vaughan, who dispatched forty men of the 46th regiment. They arrived on the 11th with a consignment of arms and ammunition. The following day a navy sloop, HMS *Zebra*, docked in Kingstown Bay. The colonists' spirits were further lifted on the 14th when HMS *Roebuck* appeared offshore.

That same day Governor Seton decided that it was imperative to strike before the French and Caribs could bring their guns to bear on the British positions, particularly Sion Hill. Dorsetshire Hill occupied a commanding position above the town and harbour of Kingstown—it had housed the garrison during the French occupation—and its steep slopes made it "a Spot of Ground very difficult of access".[22] In addition to its fortifications it had barracks and numerous other buildings on the summit. Seton was also influenced by the fear that the insurrectionaries' lightning advance and radical message of emancipation was swaying the island's large slave population.[23] So it was decided that Captain Skynner of the *Zebra* would that very night lead an assault on Dorsetshire Hill at the head of whatever fighting men he could muster. His force comprised sixty men drawn from the *Zebra* and the *Roebuck*, along with thirty merchant seamen, twenty men from the 46th regiment and some armed black slaves. Prisoners later said the hill was defended by 250 Caribs and 120 French troops. It was a desperate gamble.

Under the meagre glimmer of a waning moon, a party of militia and slaves made a diversionary attack on the far side of the ridge while the main force attacked the side nearest the town, advancing up the steep slopes amid bushes and broken ground. "The Hill was stormed near the Flag staff by the Main Body at one o'clock in the morning and every person that made resistance was put to the Bayonet."[24] Twenty-one Caribs and a number of Frenchmen lay dead. Among them was Chatoyer.

Chatoyer's death was a devastating blow to the Carib cause. The great chief had been one of their foremost leaders for more than three decades, years in which they had successfully defended most of their territory from foreign encroachment. He had led his troops in battle, conducted negotiations with friend and foe and managed to combine his fiercely independent countrymen into a unified force on numerous occasions. Both the British and the French had recognized him as the top man among the Caribs, whether as enemy or ally. After his death British writers—no Caribs recorded their thoughts—routinely disparaged Chatoyer in insulting terms, although before the climactic war he had been seen as a civilized interlocutor. "He was brave, desperate and accustomed to warfare and bloodshed," wrote one observer. "Being old, he had far more information than any other of his tribe, which gave him great authority over them."[25] The Caribs would fight on for over a year and inflict serious defeats on the British but with Chatoyer's death went the best chance of winning the war and preserving the Caribs' freedom.

According to Shephard, Chatoyer died in single combat with Alexander Leith, a Scottish officer of the militia, leading some to conclude that something approaching a duel took place.[26] That seems an unlikely scenario, especially as the same author says the fate of the fort was decided within fifteen minutes. In an account recorded years later from a purported eyewitness among the storming party an element of personal confrontation between Chatoyer and Leith remains but the killing itself has a less glorious air. "My informant was within two rank & file of the cruel Carib Commander in Chief,—Chatoyer, when he fell. Major Leith of the Militia advanced upon him, crying out "you him Chatoyer?"—"Oui B_____" was the response, accompanied by a thrust of his sword, which was parried; five bayonets being dashed into the sanguinary monster's breast at the same moment."[27]

Another account, supposedly from an eyewitness, makes no mention of a personal confrontation, painting a more brutal and indiscriminate picture of the mayhem in the blackness on top of Dorsetshire Hill. "It was no fight—it was a mere regular slaughter; and in a few moments the fort was cleared of the enemy."[28] The same source suggested that the Caribs were surprised while carousing on captured liquor, and the disproportionate casualty count (only four seamen were killed on the British side) might be thought to lend weight to this contention. Governor Seton, however, makes clear that the defenders fired at the British forces as they made their assault up the hill so they were clearly not all otherwise engaged.

Chatoyer's body, unusually for the Caribs, was left on the field of the chaotic nighttime engagement on Dorsetshire Hill. But even without a proper burial and amid the dislocation of war he would certainly have been mourned by his kinsmen. "The relatives," according to one eighteenth-century account of Carib grieving, "start drinking, dancing, and smoking, on the mat and round about, singing the praises of the dead man: they recount his brave deeds, praise him to the skies, and claim that he is not dead but merely sleeping, that his spirit has gone behind the mountains and across the sea, where he's now drinking, dancing, and disporting himself with women younger and more beautiful than those he's left behind in the carbet, and that he's preparing a sumptuous feast to receive them all when they rejoin him behind the great mountain across the sea."[29]

The war, though, could not wait. Desperate to maintain some momentum, Victor Hugues wrote to Du Vallée offering condolences over the death of his brother but quickly urging him to redouble his efforts against the English: "Great men after having satisfied nature must think of vengeance."[30] He promised to send supplies to be shared between the Caribs and the French ("*mais le commandement t'est reservé*") and expressed the wish that "we will embrace as conquerors and exterminators of the English". In a separate communication Hugues promised Du Vallée a pair of pistols and one for his nephew, Chatoyer's son, indicating that the latter had inherited some of his father's prestige as a war leader.

Citizen Souhallet was ordered by Hugues to go to St. Vincent and assemble the "Chiefs of the Caribs" and assure them of French support, and specifically that the island would be divided between the French and the Caribs after the expulsion of the British. He was cautioned to at all times act in concert with the Caribs and, with an eye no doubt to Carib morale, told that in military action the French under his command should assume the post of danger.[31]

In the wake of the defeat on Dorsetshire Hill the Caribs withdrew towards their own country "Confounded and dismayed",[32] while most of the French headed to leeward towards the town of Layou. A number were captured en route and Monsieur Dumont, an alleged ringleader, was hanged with twenty others. The military reverse evidently threw up divisions in the previously united front of Caribs and Frenchmen. Victor Hugues felt moved to write to the men he now saw as the leaders of the Carib forces, Du Vallée, Dufond, Durant, Samboula and Jean Pierre of Rabacca, conceding that "You believed for an instant that we were abandoning you in the just war that you and we were fighting against the English barbarians."[33] The time had come, he said, to forget any internal quarrels and attack the common enemy to which end he was sending French reinforcements, along with some salt and a pair of pistols and a sabre for each of the chiefs. In a proclamation dated 11 Germinal (31 March), Hugues and his fellow commissioners named "Citizen Duvalay" as an officer of the army of the French republic and joint leader of the military force in St. Vincent along with two French officers.[34]

The British at this time were in no position to capitalize on their victory and any disunity among the enemy. Deciding that he did not have enough men to defend Dorsetshire Hill, Governor Seton ordered his troops to destroy the buildings there and set up new military posts nearer the town, hoping these measures would suffice as long as the enemy did not bring artillery to bear again. He also ordered the execution of a number of named individuals, mainly French inhabitants but also including four "Marriaqua Charaibs", François, Jean Baptiste, Louis

Pascal alias Joe and Louis Bewa, and, interestingly, "A yellow Charaib, Joseph Gerard".

Both sides prepared for a pitiless conflict. Governor Seton issued a proclamation in which he alluded to alleged Carib atrocities and announced: "To such an enemy I cannot apply the Laws of War". To those of the enemy who fell into British hands he promised "the same Treatment which our Countrymen who are Prisoners, receive from them".[35] Insurgent French inhabitants were given five days to turn themselves in if they were to receive mercy. Privately Seton was echoing Hugues' language of annihilation to his superiors, calling for reinforcements that would "enable me not only to repel but totally exterminate this savage & merciless Race of Charaibs, with whom no Treaties are binding, no Favours conciliating, nor any Laws Divine or human restraining".[36] Flushed with the success on Dorsetshire Hill, Seton suggested that the Caribs could be removed from the island within a fortnight if sufficient force were brought to bear, including, significantly, 5,000 "Negroes of the island".[37]

In the short term, though, the colony was in desperate need of military manpower. It decided to arm two hundred black slaves and send them out to hunt down stragglers from the last battle. As Shephard records, their efforts "were marked with cruelty, hurried on with disorder, and inspired by rapacity, and many innocent persons lost their lives".[38] Another historian, Thomas Southey, makes clear that the excesses referred to included the plundering of the houses of French inhabitants of Calliaqua and that "Neither was English property safe from the hands of these destructive assistants."[39] In response the governor and council ruled out any further such operations by armed slaves but it would not be long before this weapon in all its ferocity would be turned against the Caribs.

Within days of the debacle at Dorsetshire Hill the Caribs were showing that they were far from spent as a fighting force. In the Chateaubelair area black insurgents and small groups of French and Caribs were plundering estates and a detachment of militia had to be sent to restore order. Nearby at Wallibo estate the overseer, a Mr. Grant, was reported to have been crushed between the cylinders of the sugar mill, the symbol of British greed for Carib land. Caribs burned cane fields within sight of Dorsetshire Hill and set up three camps around Calliaqua.

On 21 March they burned the most valuable part of that town. In the middle of the day they advanced to the foot of the fort at Sion Hill and burned the Arno's Vale estate to the ground despite coming under fire from the British guns. Sir William Young's Villa estate, where Chatoyer and Du Vallée had once been dinner guests, also went up in flames and the Belmont and Fairhall estates suffered a similar fate. By the end of March British forces were still confined to a small area around the capital, not just in St. Vincent, but also in St. Lucia and Grenada.

British morale improved with the arrival of the fleet in Barbados on 30 March and the colonists' position was materially boosted on 5 April when two transports arrived from Martinique bearing reinforcements from the 46th regiment from Gibraltar. Three days later nine seamen from Liverpool were put ashore at Greathead's Bay to avoid being pressed into service, apparently unaware that a large Carib/French force was in the area. A rescue party was sent out from Kingstown on 10 April towards the camps around Calliaqua but the vigilant Caribs were ready and waiting for the British. Sodden from heavy rainfall at the start of the rainy season, the attackers moved into position at one o'clock in the morning. "A very smart engagement commenced,"[40] the British were quickly forced to retreat and that retreat became a rout. In the confusion troops trampled upon each other and only straggled back to Kingstown the following morning. It took further reinforcements of regular troops for the British to dislodge the Caribs, recover the sailors and restore some level of order to the area around Calliaqua. But the incident had left the British chastened. "The enemy have been found to be much more numerous in the quarter than they were at first supposed to be."[41] Large numbers could be seen on the hills around Kingstown and another force was camped threateningly above Chateaubelair.

Seeking to radically change the balance of forces, the colony took a step that was to have a decisive effect on the outcome of the war. Blacks had already been armed in a piecemeal fashion but now it was decided to arm slaves from every estate and form them into a fighting force to be known as rangers. Five hundred of the most dependable slaves were initially requisitioned and formed into a body under the command of Robert Seton, the son of the governor. Each slave had his value appraised on conscription, this amount to be paid to the owner in the event of his death. It was a move not without risk. The governor had already expressed fears about the slaves' loyalty, runaways had a long history of joining forces with the Caribs and at that very moment in St.-Domingue Toussaint L'Ouverture stood at the head of an army of slaves who had thrown off their chains and deprived France of the richest colony in the Caribbean. St. Vincent's rangers, however, would soon prove their worth.

The new unit saw its first major action within days and it was an operation that struck at the heart of Carib resistance. Its aim was to harass the enemy in the rear and possibly divide his forces. On 25 April the government schooner set sail up the leeward coast for the northern extremity of the island with a force the major component of which was 64 rangers plus their white officers. Picking up further troops at Chateaubelair the force arrived the following morning at the northern bay where Du Vallée had his *carbet*. The Caribs had thrown up breastworks and had four lightweight swivel artillery pieces positioned at different points above the bay. The British force came under fire immediately on landing. Du Vallée's house was on the top of a precipice above the middle of the bay. The only access from the beach was via a narrow footpath which zigzagged uphill with each turn covered by one of the batteries. Near the top a ditch and drawbridge barred the way.

The Caribs rained down grapeshot and small arms fire and even rolled boulders down on to the attackers. But the rangers, under the command of Colonel Seton, who himself was wounded by a tumbling rock, doggedly forced their way up the slope and, after a fierce fight, overran the village. The Caribs made off into the woods taking most of their dead with them. The victors burned Du Vallée's house and upwards of 25 others and captured the four swivels and another artillery piece. Setting a pattern for the rest of the war, the rangers burned sixteen canoes, some capable of carrying thirty men, and destroyed the Caribs' provision grounds, including a great number of plantain trees.

Seeing his home—situated in one of the most inaccessible parts of the island—burned to the ground, the plantain trees that had sustained his family torn down and his people driven into the woods, all this just six weeks after his brother had been killed, must have been a huge blow to Du Vallée and a bitter foretaste of what was to come. From being on the brink of seizing the whole island, the Caribs now found themselves on the defensive and facing a new and formidable enemy in the black ranger corps implementing a tactic of trying to starve them into submission. For the Caribs the very nature of the conflict had changed. Hugues was spreading the message that the British planned to reduce the Caribs to slavery and distribute them around their West Indian colonies. The Black Caribs' survival in their homeland was at stake.

The Jacobin of Guadeloupe was dismayed at a dramatic change in Carib morale. "We're astonished by the conduct of the Caribs," Hugues wrote to his delegate in St. Vincent. "Aren't they as interested as us or more so in chasing away the English?… We are astonished that these men who were once so courageous are today so feeble."[42] On 11 June he wrote in harsh terms to "the commander of the Caribs" (presumably Du Vallée) decrying the Caribs' conduct and "love of money" which he said had put them in danger of "losing your liberty, that of your wives, your children, your lands, your riches and perhaps of becoming the slaves of the English, your cruellest enemies".[43] Promising to *"oublir vos tortes envers les francais"* ("forget your wrongs towards the French"), Hugues said he would send more supplies and even offered that if the English killed a Carib prisoner he would give up an English captive of the Caribs' choice to be put to death.

Hugues' reference to "love of money" displayed a woeful ignorance of what motivated the Caribs to fight.[44] The rhetoric of liberty came easily to Hugues but for him St. Vincent would only ever be one theatre of war. The Caribs had clearly glimpsed the possibility of an eventual French withdrawal and had to ponder how they would deal with that situation, including ultimately reaching an accommodation with the British. The campaign had also cast into relief the differences in tactics between the Caribs and the French.[45] For centuries the Caribs had specialized in making war through ambush and surprise. On their own ground they were experts at guerrilla fighting, using their knowledge of the wooded, mountainous terrain to pick off the enemy and slip away without exposing themselves to a pitched battle. The defeat at Dorsetshire Hill had come when the Caribs found themselves defending a fixed position. The element of surprise, so important in Carib warfare, had by now been lost. They were more at home striking decisively in a short, sharp conflict than with maintaining an army in the field for the long grind of an extended campaign. In mid-April British forces defending Calliaqua had been surprised to see four hundred or more

Caribs in two bodies "marching in good order[46] and headed by half a dozen Frenchmen. But this display of European military discipline was shortlived and the Caribs retreated before they got within musket range. Since then coordination between the allies had clearly become more strained.

Calliaqua remained an important prize and on 7 May at about nine o'clock in the morning a mixed force of some eight hundred descended towards the town. A parley ensued with a French officer but the defenders, about a hundred regulars with as many rangers, refused his offer to let them return to Kingstown if they left behind their arms and ammunition. Again, the British received timely reinforcements in the shape of the frigate HMS *Alarm* which arrived offshore, shelled the enemy and, after landing 130 sailors, forced them to retreat to another natural strongpoint in the hills to the east of the capital known as the Vigie. It was claimed that had the defenders accepted the French terms a force of Caribs had been waiting in Sir William Young's ruined estate to ambush the unarmed British troops on the road to Kingstown, with the French planning to blame the attack on their "savage" allies. British forces reoccupied Dorsetshire Hill but were taken aback by the ferocity of the counterattack by the Caribs whose numbers were swollen by recently arrived French reinforcements as well as by disaffected blacks and mulattoes. The new French troops were probably those led by Citizen Souhallet whom Hugues had dispatched from Guadeloupe in late April. Dorsetshire Hill fell to a force of three hundred French and Caribs but in a day of confused action was retaken by a combination of British regulars, militia and rangers in the early hours of the morning. The British reported that the retreating defenders left behind 44 killed, including nineteen Caribs, and a further fourteen Caribs were found dead in a valley a mile away; other casualties were believed to have been carried from the field in hammocks. In an attempt to consolidate their newly won position the British evacuated the post at Calliaqua.

The French/Carib force responded to the setback by digging in on the Vigie. The hill was about a hundred yards long by twenty wide and surrounded by steep slopes. The five to six hundred defenders surrounded it with a barricade of sugar hogsheads filled with earth as well as a ditch and could count on four cannon and fifteen swivels. Following a visit by General Sir John Vaughan from the British base at

Martinique at the end of May the forces on St. Vincent were reinforced in the second week of June with one hundred black rangers from Martinique and 488 men of the 60th regiment from Barbados. They were immediately put to work against the Vigie. In the early hours of 12 June British troops set out from Sion Hill to capture enemy strongpoints on eminences around the Vigie while others were posted to cut off potential escape routes. Meanwhile artillery fire was directed against the Vigie itself. After intense exchanges of artillery and musketry, the fire from the Vigie was seen to slacken between seven and eight in the morning as ammunition ran low. A French officer emerged to parley but this appeared to be a ruse to buy time to cover a retreat. Shortly afterwards the combined force of British infantry, Martinique rangers and local militia stormed the Vigie, wreaking carnage among the defenders.

"The scene which presented itself on entering the Vigie could not easily be surveyed with a tearless eye, unless the breast of the spectator was wholly inaccessible to sensibility," wrote Thomas Coke of the aftermath of the battle. "Here lay a leg, and there an arm! Now the foot strikes against the shattered fragments of a head! or, with difficulty, disengages itself from adhering entrails! Yonder is discerned a breathless, disfigured form; while the wounded and dying pour, in every direction, their languishing groans upon the listening ear!"[47] According to Governor Seton, the bodies of 220 defenders were found on the hill, of whom 45 were white, with more killed among the surrounding bushes (but Shephard later put the number of dead at a tenth of that). The French commander, Souhallet, was among the prisoners taken, although no Caribs, to whom Seton had promised no quarter, were listed among the captured.

Most of the survivors retreated towards Carib country. In searing heat a force under Captain Leighton marched northwards after them and eight British soldiers dropped dead, apparently of heat exhaustion, en route. On 15 June Leighton succeeded in capturing the post at Mount Young. He then set about implementing what Governor Seton saw as the most effective strategy against an enemy "inured to the Climate, and accustomed from their Infancy to travel over Mountains and through Thickets almost impenetrable to Europeans"[48]: that is, smashing their canoes, destroying their houses and uprooting their provision grounds. Some two hundred canoes were destroyed at Grand Sable and the black rangers proved particularly effective in digging up provisions.[49] The trail of destruction lasted for five miles from Mount Young all the way up to Rabacca. Moreau de Jonnès describes one action by the rangers, whose leaders, he writes, had experience of hunting runaway slaves on other islands. "These negroes crept through passages believed to be inaccessible, and, getting to the rear of military positions, they reached the redoubt which served as a refuge for women and children and a storehouse for munitions and food. They sacked everything, pitilessly killing the harmless occupants, pillaging and burning the provisions which would have sustained them and the Carib warriors. The warriors, hearing of this disaster, lost courage."[50]

Leighton's grand plan was to lay waste the entire Carib country. Any other tactic, Seton believed, would require a much larger military force. British military planners, in any case, had more than St. Vincent to worry about. At the height of the fighting for the Vigie Britain maintained greater forces in Grenada and Martinique, with barely 1,000 active rank and file in St. Vincent.

For the British this conflict would be known as the Second Carib War (conveniently ignoring the prominent Carib role in the military humiliations of 1779 and 1780) or the Brigands' War. The "brigands" referred to were Victor Hugues' revolutionary fighters, viewed as a contemptible rabble by the British. For the metropolitan authorities it was always principally a struggle against the French, albeit in a new, dangerously democratic guise. The West Indian planters, though, knew this represented their best chance to be rid of the Caribs once and for all. With the fate of the island still in the balance the planters were already planning for the post-war period. Safely in London, Sir William Young in May 1795 wrote a "memorial" to the government urging the implementation of the solution that had been frustrated by the 1773 treaty that ended the First Carib War. Nothing short of deportation of the Black Caribs could guarantee the future safety and profitability of the colony.[51] It was in this context that he published his history of the British-Carib conflict.[52]

The Caribs and their French allies no longer posed a direct threat to Kingstown but as long as their lines of communication with the French-controlled islands remained intact they represented a potent menace to the British. So, while the main body of British forces remained at Mount Young, an amphibious force was sent to reoccupy the old post at Owia, the point on the island closest to St. Lucia. Attacking on 25 June they met with fierce resistance from French artillery but bombardment from the sloop *Thorn* dispersed the defenders. Tradition links the nearby place name Bloody Bridge with this battle. The capture of Owia left the British in control of all the established landing places on the Vincentian coast. However, at almost the same time British forces in St. Lucia, which had taken the colony a year earlier, were forced to evacuate the island by French republican troops. The Caribs immediately dispatched a canoe to the island—some three or four hours' overnight sail away—to re-establish contact with the French and seek resupply.[53] In response to the evacuation of St. Lucia in July the Royal Navy strengthened its presence in the seas around St. Vincent. On 23 August Victor Hugues wrote that French ships had been unable to ferry supplies across from St. Lucia because British warships had made the crossing too dangerous. A month later British naval activity was still playing havoc with resupply, although some material had got through.

The Caribs were unable to strike a strategic blow but could still inflict considerable damage. They responded to the setback at Owia by gathering a sizeable force in the hills near Chateaubelair on the leeward coast and repulsed an attack there on 3 July led by Lieutenant Colonel Prevost of the 60th regiment, inflicting "considerable loss" on the British force of thirty white and seventy black troops. The area around Chateaubelair became the focus of the fighting for the following month. The leeward coast, as well as containing ports that would enable easier resupply from the French islands, also offered the chance of replenishing their stocks of food, including provisions and cattle, from the farms left intact in the area. The British decided to deplete the post at Mount Young on the windward coast in an attempt to dislodge the Carib/French position at Morne Ronde to the north of Chateaubelair, a laborious and time-consuming manoeuvre. The Caribs, in conjunction with the French forces' new black commander, Marinier, outwitted the British by slipping across the mountains to reinforce their positions on the leeward coast. Before their invasion in 1780 the French had sent spies to reconnoitre the Caribs' route across the mountains, which followed the Rabacca and Wallibou valleys, but they had all reported that it was impassable to troops. The British too believed the thickly wooded slopes around the Soufriere volcano were completely impenetrable and although they knew the mountains were "here and there crossed by an Indian Path as narrow as a sheepwalk" it was felt that this was "frequently imperceptible to the eye of a White Man".[54] So the arrival of a force of two hundred on the leeward coast came as a shock.

Having gathered together a force of two hundred regulars and one hundred St. Vincent rangers the British attacked Morne Ronde on the morning of 5 August. The main body of some four hundred Caribs and French was formed up at a pass on a narrow forest ridge leading inland towards the Soufriere. According to Shephard, "a very obstinate engagement commenced here, which lasted upwards of an hour very disadvantageously for the English."[55] The resistance was felt to be too great for an assault by the regulars. Instead the rangers cut a path on either side of the ridge around very extensive mountains to approach from the rear. Dismayed by the appearance of the black rangers, the Caribs withdrew into the woods. The ranking French officer, Massoteau, and twenty others were captured, along with guns and ammunition but very little food. The British lost sixty killed and wounded. In the aftermath British troops pressed home their advantage by making their way north to Du Vallée's and Chatoyer's lands where they destroyed everything they could find.

The victory at Morne Ronde and the rangers' vigorous activity offered some respite for the British troops fighting in an unfamiliar tropical climate against a dogged foe. Morale was fragile. "The troops now here are greatly weakened by constant & hard Duty… who suffer greatly from the Inclemency of the Weather in this season of the year."[56] The officers commanding the regulars and the militia were later criticized for their tactics against the Caribs, "marching with their drums beating, and their colours flying, to fight a savage enemy who crouched like foxes, and glided like serpents, from their foes; yet, at unexpected times, darted like rattlesnakes upon their less vigilant, but better disciplined enemy".[57] This menagerie of animal similes indicates the discomfort that regular British troops felt with the tactics of the Caribs. A small party from the 42nd Royal Highland regiment stumbled across a Carib camp while cutting their way through the forest at night. A sentry's musket shot brought large numbers of people surging from the huts. The troops retreated but halfway back to their base they were ambushed on both flanks and in the rear. "The Caribs were expert climbers, every tree appeared to be manned in an instant: the wood was in a blaze but not a man was to be seen, the enemy being concealed by the thick and luxuriant foliage. As the Highlanders retreated, firing from time to time at the spot from whence the enemy's fire preceded, the Caribs followed with as much rapidity as if they sprung from tree to tree like monkeys."[58]

British spirits were briefly lifted when on 17 August a new commander, Brigadier General Sir William Myers, arrived from Martinique. He planned a pincer movement on the windward coast between a force led by himself up from Mount Young and another led by Major Ecuyer from the post at Owia. Ecuyer advanced but failed to locate the general and finding the enemy gathered around him, returned to his base after a few days. Confusion turned to catastrophe on 3 September when a Carib and French force stealthily approached the post at Owia and seized it almost before the defenders had time to react. Major Ecuyer had earlier boasted to Myers that he could not wait for the enemy to attack so he could take them on—but the calamity claimed his life, along with those of four other officers and 31 rank and file. The British reported that "most of our men [were] cut to pieces",[59] the remainder fled in disarray, some managing to escape through the woods, while other survivors were picked up off the rocks by HMS *Experiment*. The Caribs immediately sent a canoe to St. Lucia to seek reinforcements. Within days four French ships had docked at Owia and landed five hundred troops and a quantity of supplies.

The defeat left the British position in a sorry state. General Myers complained that his soldiers were few and poorly equipped. The troops, he wrote, were "nearly naked" and the Martinique rangers had had to abandon everything in the flight from Owia. Furthermore he had little idea of the enemy's plans or dispositions as "any person that has ever been sent out for intelligence have either been murdered or corrupted as they never returned".[60]

Holed up at midnight in Fort Charlotte on top of Berkshire Hill, Myers wrote a desperate letter on 18 September calling for reinforcements. He had decided to pull back all his troops from outlying posts and concentrate his defences on Dorsetshire Hill. The loss of this redoubt, he warned, "will be followed by the Destruction of Kingstown, and what remains will be cooped up on Berkshire Hill very ill provided with matter for defence or to hold out longer". Describing the scene in the cramped fort overlooking Kingstown, he wrote: "A number of Women and Children are here almost horrified out of their senses".[61]

The British still had a foothold at the Vigie but the Caribs and French controlled most of the surrounding area. A force of four hundred regulars and militia were sent to resupply the Vigie but met with greater opposition than expected. Troops sent to dislodge the enemy refused to obey their commander's orders and fell back "in great disorder" on those marching to resupply: "the Confusion became general".[62] With the relief party dispersed with great loss of life, the entire convoy lost and the Vigie post surrounded the captain commanding the defence used the cover of a very rainy night to destroy his remaining ammunition and abandon the fort, escaping to Young's Island where he died of his wounds. "Our situation," the governing committee wrote, "has become rather critical."[63]

British forces in Kingstown, though, received timely reinforcements from the garrison withdrawn from Morne Ronde on the leeward coast and more encouragingly by the arrival of HMS *Scipio* and a number of transports which brought three battalions of the 40th, 54th and 59th regiments under the new regional commander, Major General Irving. These forces now massed for a counterattack on the Vigie. The two sides fought all day at a distance of barely fifty yards until the British were repulsed with the loss of one hundred killed and wounded. But fearful of another attack, and barely a week after taking the strongpoint, the French and Caribs decided to withdraw from the Vigie, slipping away in darkness towards Carib country after a day of violent showers. In the morning a small party of British troops almost stumbled upon the abandoned prize.

Once again a tactical victory was not followed by a strategic triumph as neither side could bring sufficient forces to bear to deliver a knockout blow. The situation in Grenada, which had been running in parallel with the St. Vincent insurrection since March, demanded the transfer of the 54th regiment which had only recently arrived on the island. The St. Vincent planters beseeched General Irving not to embark the troops. The Caribs, they claimed, would be no match for the British troops while "our other Enemy [the French] is not at present numerous".

They feared that going on to the defensive would leave troops cooped up in garrison and vulnerable to disease and prone to the dangers of strong liquor. The fidelity of the black slaves was also a concern if the balance of the conflict appeared to be swinging. And finally the planters wanted their slaves to return to their estates, the major concern apparently being "to prevent an epidemical distemper being introduced into the town, as was the case at the commencement of our disturbances, when twenty, thirty, and sometimes more died daily for a length of time, and until possession was obtained of the Windward Country".[64] Morale among the troops was low. Battalions which had previously fought gallantly now refused to face the enemy.

General Irving turned down their request. The men of the 54th embarked but after several days aboard ship the general changed his mind and they were disembarked again and marched east to take up positions at Stubbs. Still no decisive action could be taken in the war, a situation which caused some dissatisfaction among the planters at the army's relative inactivity. On the other side intermittent resupply was limiting the offensive capacity of the Caribs and their French allies, who numbered perhaps no more than three hundred at this point and had been reduced to eating their mules.[65]

The mood of heroic unity of March had long since dissipated. Cooperation was now piecemeal and contingent. On 7 November Hugues was still hopefully sending presents to the Caribs but increasingly it is clear from his correspondence that he had ceased to count on them as dependable allies.[66] Leadership of the enterprise was no longer entrusted to a Carib general. At the start of March 1796 Hugues urged his delegate in St. Vincent, Citizen Audibert, for the final time to encourage the Caribs to show "a little more zeal and constancy in their attack".[67]

The military stalemate continued until the end of 1795. General Myers wrote in November that: "A degree of apathy and indifference seems to have overtaken not only the troops but all the people of the island. They complain loudly of neglect and even the news of a force coming out from England seems not to cheer them."[68] Disease, including yellow fever, had taken its toll among the troops. "The British regiments employed at St. Vincent during the whole of 1795... the greatest part of them were reduced to skeletons."[69] It was a posting loathed by the troops. Christmas was an uneasy time for the British settlers. A mood of grim apprehension hung over Kingstown. Although the capital had been saved more than once, the Caribs, the most feared enemy, were undefeated and foraged with impunity in the countryside while the French controlled nearby St. Lucia.

But in August events had been set in train which would alter the whole strategic balance in the Caribbean. General Sir Ralph Abercromby had been appointed to lead a new army to recover Britain's West Indian possessions. Abercomby came from a Scottish Presbyterian family and had studied law but gave it up for a career soldiering. He was an MP, a supporter of American independence and an admirer of George Washington. To him fell the task of reversing French gains in the West Indies and with it the job of finally settling the "Carib problem" by military means. Adverse weather and other logistical problems had prevented him leaving England for some months but the force he was assembling was formidable.

Before Abercromby could arrive in the region, however, British forces again found themselves in desperate straits on St. Vincent. The new year began with a Carib/French force taking the principal British post at Mount William near Mount Young on 8 January, capturing all the fourteen pieces of ordnance present which they then turned on the British. As the British retreated in disarray towards Kingstown, Caribs attempted to pick them off by insinuating themselves in their rear and firing on them from amid sugar canes. The British suffered heavy losses—Brigadier General Stewart reported 54 dead and two hundred missing from the engagement—and Brigadier General Strutt was badly wounded, necessitating an amputation above the knee. Guns and stores were abandoned in the headlong rout. Mount William had been the first action of the 2nd West India Regiment, a new unit formed from blacks already mobilized as rangers (General Myers had to promise the planters that their slaves would not be posted off the island).

According to a clergyman who found himself in St. Vincent at the time, "the Brigands... chased our fugitive troops all the way to Dorsetshire Hill".[70] The debacle and the appearance of Carib forces in the Mariaqua valley had struck dread into the inhabitants as represented on the committee who urged the army to concentrate its forces on defending the capital. In response General Hunter was dispatched from Martinique to replace Stewart as commander on the island and he set about consolidating his forces at the military posts at Dorsetshire Hill, Millar's Ridge, Sion Hill, Cane Gardens, Keane's House, Kingstown and Fort Charlotte, while at the same time abandoning the New Vigie and Morne Ronde, in the leeward country. Contingency plans were drawn up to retreat to a last redoubt at Fort Charlotte if necessary.

A party of Caribs took up position at Bow Wood at the head of the Kingstown valley. On the 20th Caribs pursued some straggling soldiers to their camp at Green Hill. British forces marched out to engage them but after several hours of bush fighting the Caribs slipped away, although not before burning down Bow Wood House. A desperate defence of Millar's Ridge, immediately to the north of Dorsetshire Hill, was required to halt the advance. Being shelled by their own captured guns, a number of British troops refused orders to engage the enemy. But in a night of bloody attack and counterattack the British line held. It meant that by March 1796 the opposing forces were in almost the same positions they had been in June of the previous year.

General Abercromby reached Barbados at the start of April. His orders had laid great stress on St.-Domingue, until recently the region's most profitable sugar colony but now in the throes of becoming the independent republic of Haiti. But his first order of business was to dislodge the French from St. Lucia. With 12,000 troops he succeeded in capturing Morne Fortune, the principal French defensive position. Victor Hugues wrote to Marinier in St. Vincent recalling him to St. Lucia to rally the groups of republicans now scattered in St. Lucia's woods. But Marinier, described by Abercromby as "a Black Man of singular Enterprize, and abilities; very much look'd up to by the Negroes in St Lucia and St. Vincent"[71]—would never take up that command as events moved rapidly towards a climax.

After a brief interlude in which he organized an invasion force for Grenada, Abercromby disembarked his troops in St. Vincent on 8 June. He commanded an army of just under four thousand men, the largest aggregation of military force on the island in the entire war (in fact, the biggest force ever seen in St. Vincent). The following day he marched them in six divisions the eight miles east to Stubbs from where they proceeded to take up positions flanking the main French/Carib post at the Vigie. On the morning of 10 June the British artillery opened up. The defenders held out from seven in the morning until the afternoon.

The Caribs were stationed to the right of the defensive line but, in the face of the overwhelming force ranged against them, were forced to retire, making their escape via the woods. The British lost fifty killed and wounded taking the next line of defence but the remaining French troops were pushed back to their last redoubt at the New Vigie. Finally, after British artillery had been drawn up, at five o'clock in the afternoon Marinier, the French commander, sued for peace. Seven hundred surrendered while a further two hundred insurgents fled for the woods. The terms of surrender specified that all the other French military posts would be turned over to the British.

France's war against Britain on the island of St. Vincent was over. The Caribs were on their own.

7. Calvary of the Caribs

"Posterity will hardly believe the number of lives lost in these islands."
  Robert Bisset, British army, 1796

AFTER his decisive victory at the Vigie, Abercromby turned his attention to "the Object which presses most upon my Mind at this Moment"[1]—the question of the Caribs. The general was under orders to remove the Caribs from the island but the detail of the operation was anything but clear. First, the planters had greatly underestimated the number of Caribs. Abercromby suggested, with impressive accuracy for someone who had been in the country a matter of days, that there were in fact some five thousand men, women and children. The second problem was where to send them. After years of discussion and with ultimate victory in sight the British were no closer to a decision. Abercromby's solution was to send them to St.-Domingue. It had the advantages of being to leeward, making any return to St. Vincent against the prevailing winds more difficult; after the slave revolution there it was doubtful "to whom it is to belong"; and its population was big enough for the new arrivals not to affect the strategic balance. The Samaná peninsula on the east end of the island of Hispaniola was touted as a possibility.[2] What was certain was that this time there could be no place for the Black Caribs on St. Vincent. Abercromby was committed to doing his duty as a soldier but as a newcomer to the scene in St. Vincent he was not untroubled by the responsibility of sending an entire people into exile. "However just the Sentence against these People, I feel personally the Load imposed upon me, in being forced to put it in Execution," he wrote.[3]

While the fight against the French "Brigands" had been decided by a pitched battle at the Vigie, the British attempt to force the surrender of the Caribs would follow the pattern established by the attack on Du Vallée's *carbet* the previous year: displacing the Caribs into the mountainous interior and destroying their canoes and provisions with the aim of starving them into submission.

153

The end appeared to be nigh when on 15 June, five days after the French surrender at the Vigie, three Carib chiefs, named as Desfon, Jack Gordon and Baptiste,[4] sent a flag of truce to the military post at Mount Young seeking an accommodation. They were given a military escort to Kingstown where they proposed an end to the conflict along similar lines to the treaty of 1773. The key element was that they should be left in possession of their lands. They admitted having burned the estates and cane fields of British planters but said that the British in turn had destroyed their provisions. There had been casualties on both sides, each had inflicted and received injury; now there was no reason to continue the conflict. They admitted that they had started the war but observed that in any case "everybody was then at war".[5] For the British, though, the time for compromise had long since passed. All they were prepared to concede was that in turn for their surrender the Caribs would be spared their lives.

The Carib chiefs were shocked at the intransigence of the British. They asked for three days to consult with other heads of families. When the three days were up there was no sign of the chiefs and no word from the Caribs.

The British were surprised at the Black Caribs' continued resistance. It was "generally understood" that after the reduction of the French forces on the island the Caribs "would have surrendered themselves without hesitation."[6] The British negotiators had threatened to bring the whole force of the island against the Caribs if they did not come in but they did not immediately resume the war. Weeks passed with no progress towards a surrender. The British, though, were not prepared to wait indefinitely. On 7 July General Hunter asked the colony for five hundred "Negroes with Bills and Cutlasses to destroy the Provisions in the Charaib Country", insisting that it was "absolutely necessary" that this should be done without delay.[7] In mid-July more chiefs came in to sound out the terms for surrender, some of them promising to bring their people in.

The surrender terms demanded by the British were unequivocal: "Your having been guilty of numerous acts of Treachery, Murder and Treason, and having repeatedly violated your most solemn engagements with the British nation; it is determined you are to be sent from this Island." These terms, which promised humane treatment, were read to fourteen chiefs and ten other Caribs by Governor Seton and General Hunter in Kingstown on 14 July. Still, though, the capitulation proved elusive.

Troops were posted at the passes and on 16-17 July a band of around three hundred Caribs, mainly women and children, were intercepted by Colonel Henry Haffey near Mount Young. They were led by Chatoyer's son of the same name, and camped near the British military post. Here was a chance to bring over a prominent leader and a significant band of followers. On the 18th young Chatoyer addressed his people. "It is no disgrace to Caraibs to surrender to a great Nation," he told them. "The subjects of France and all great nations, even of England, are obliged to submit to each other, when there no longer remains the means of resistance. What else is now left for us? Have we power to continue the War? No, we have not the power. Tomorrow morning I will set you the example of submission by bringing my family to Col Haffey that he may lead us immediately to the General. You may do as you please, I can only be accountable for my Family and myself".[8]

The following day the younger Chatoyer did indeed set an example but it was not one of submission. Instead of surrendering he led his people away into the woods that evening. Chatoyer's speech was heard by Colonel Haffey and his officers. The British would not have understood the Carib language so presumably he spoke in French, a language in which most Caribs (or at least most Carib men) were fluent. The possibility does exist that he spoke in English since he had lived in the home of Sir William Young in his youth. If so, it might indicate that the speech was for the benefit of the British more than for his own people. However, his contention that he could speak only for himself and his family was true to Carib custom.

Some on the British side felt that an opportunity had been missed over the previous six weeks by not pursuing an aggressive war against the Caribs. It was believed that the Caribs had taken advantage of the truce to shift their families to strongholds in the mountains where they were believed to have a number of artillery pieces, which is perhaps what young Chatoyer was doing when he was intercepted by Colonel Haffey. Now, with General Abercromby having left the island, General Hunter resumed hostilities on 21 July. A force of three thousand men was employed principally in hemming the Caribs in and denying them access to the sea. Of these, five hundred were black rangers from the island with a further hundred recruited from Martinique. The conflict became again what one British officer described as "a horrid butchering war with the Caribs who neither give nor receive quarter".[9] The same writer described how military tactics, in the face of effective Carib resistance, had changed. "Since the first days operation which was not upon the whole in our favor, the Mode of Carrying on the War has been changed. We now confine our selves to the destruction of their provision grounds being assisted at each Post by the Working Negroes who perform this Service with great pleasure while covered by the Troops in front. By this means it is expected that the Savages will be starved into Compliance." Nevertheless to those on the ground the outcome looked anything but certain. "How all this will terminate God knows. Posterity will hardly believe the number of lives lost in these islands."[10]

Young Chatoyer's actions and those of the other Carib chiefs showed that they were determined to stay at liberty on their lands. They probably hoped that if they could hold out long enough there might be a change in the strategic position, particularly in the balance of forces between Britain and France. But there was to be no respite, no salvation. And this time there were no pious expressions of support in Westminster. The French artillery officer Moreau de Jonnès maintained that at this time some Caribs sailed away surreptitiously to Trinidad. These may have been among the French republicans—for the most part "mulattoes and negroes"—who the Spanish governor of that island reported had fled in pirogues to wild and inaccessible coasts of his territory, eluding British warships.[11]

British troops could not be sure if Caribs they met in the field were ready to give up or were determined to fight on. A detachment was sent to Grand Sable to receive the expected surrender of a large band of Caribs. On arrival at the settlement, however, Lieutenant Laborde found houses deserted and two hundred armed men massed on a small hill declaring their continued defiance. They said "that they never would submit to the English, and they did not revolt so much from the prospect of death, as from the idea of submission".[12] Laborde, like Captain Braithwaite more than seventy years earlier, prudently retreated.

Along the Colonarie river British troops came across a large party of Caribs at a strongly fortified position. The British thought they were

156

prepared to talk but when the soldiers advanced they were met with a volley of gunfire which caused several casualties. More skirmishes ensued and the rangers set about the grim business of systematically dehousing the Caribs and smashing their canoes. Some thousand homes went up in smoke. The British occupied more and more of the Caribs' settlements. After a battle the Black Caribs were forced to abandon their position above Grand Sable and their camp four miles above Rabacca also fell to the British.

The first breakthrough came almost as young Chatoyer was heading for the hills. The British took 280 prisoners, including 102 who were intercepted retreating to Colonarie. These may have included some French "brigands" but on 21 July 276 Carib men, women and children were shipped from Calliaqua to a holding camp on the tiny Grenadine island of Baliceaux. A few prominent Caribs, named as Letrailled, Delaprade and Jean Toulie, turned themselves in. After the first shipment of Caribs to Baliceaux a steady trickle of surrenders and captures added another 177 by the end of August. The authorities decided to allow one man from each family to go back to St. Vincent to persuade their kinfolk that they were being treated well and that they too should surrender. Fighting still continued, for example at Turama a couple of miles north of Rabacca, but at the same time Caribs were coming in on a daily basis.

By mid-September the beleaguered Caribs were described as "Wretches... reduced to the brink of destruction, deprived of every resource, and experiencing the most complicated misery and distress". Their line of communication to the French islands cut off, "they are so continually harassed, that their sufferings must be great both from fatigue and hunger, all their Provisions being nearly destroyed".[13] The British were under no illusion that it was only the very real threat of extinction brought about by their own scorched earth policy that was forcing the Caribs to surrender. "[T]he strongest necessity alone," wrote General Graham, "has influenced their present Conduct, and impelled them to a measure, to which they would never have submitted, had not the preservation of their existence, been so nearly connected with it."[14]

The whole of September was spent attempting to surprise and capture the straggling parties of Caribs, and to destroy their provision grounds, "in which the Rangers distinguished themselves by their unceasing activity and perseverance".[15] When they made contact with the Caribs who tried to harass them in their efforts they offered no quarter. St. Vincent's slave army was what ultimately pushed the Black Caribs to desperation. Reflecting on their effectiveness some years later, Sir William Young observed: "A negro militia of such description, I must pronounce, on experience, to be most valuable."[16] Alexander Anderson was even more forthright: "On negroes depended the preservation of the colony of St Vincent from being separated from Great Britain."[17] The Caribs were compelled to retreat further and further into the mountainous interior of the country, their freedom of movement confined to smaller and smaller areas. Carib morale suffered a serious blow when a party of rangers ascended the Soufriere volcano from the leeward side and crossed to the windward descending down the bed of the Rabacca river. The Caribs had always guarded the secrets of the pathways of their mountain fastnesses. Now it seemed that they had nowhere left to hide.

On 2 October Marin Padre,[18] the brother (or brother-in-law) of the French general Marinier, surrendered near Rabacca. He was allowed to return to persuade a further three or four hundred "Brigands" to surrender, which meant that the last remnants of the Caribs' foreign allies had deserted them. Shortly afterwards the Carib chiefs Thunder, Toussaint and Emanuel came in, followed by perhaps the biggest names, Du Vallée and young Chatoyer. In September more than a thousand Caribs were shipped to Baliceaux, including over six hundred on a single day. The figure for October was 2,664.[19] As the starving, desperate Caribs trudged into captivity, the British were amazed that so many had been concealed in St. Vincent's rugged interior: "their number appears to be much greater than has ever been supposed".[20] On 18 October General Hunter could write to his superiors: "I have now the satisfaction to inform you of the total reduction of the Brigands and the Charibs on this Island."[21]

In November many of the rangers—so crucial to the British victory—were demobilized and others recalled from service by their owners. For them there was little honour and much less reward for their services. Many of the black troops who had played such an important role in forcing the Caribs to surrender called on their former commander "extremely dissatisfied at not receiving some gratuity for their Services".

He reported that: "they say they have not even been offered thanks, and turn'd off like a parcel of useless dogs."[22]

Still there was no decision on where the Caribs would ultimately be sent. In October, with hundreds already in captivity, the secretary of state for war, Henry Dundas wrote to Abercromby reminding him of an earlier plan to send the Caribs to "any part of the Continent of America under the Dominion" of Spain. Any scruple about this course had been removed by Spain's recent alliance with France against Britain. Therefore, the Caribs should be sent "to such part of the Coast of the Bay of Honduras, or elsewhere" as might seem advisable to the military and civil authorities in St. Vincent. Despite the Caribs' "atrocious conduct", Dundas went on, the deportation should be carried out according to the principles of humanity.[23]

Defeated and starving, the Caribs now found themselves captives on a tiny island of barely 320 acres, some five miles south of Bequia. Baliceaux had only been decided upon as the site for the Caribs' holding camp about three weeks before its first inmates arrived. On 30 June a meeting of St. Vincent's principal inhabitants at the house of James Hartley in Kingstown, having been informed that vessels were not yet available to deport the Caribs, resolved to house them on Baliceaux, one of the smaller Grenadines. Still wary of the threat the Caribs posed even in defeat, they called for armed guards to be stationed on Baliceaux; the navy sent the sloop *Beaver* to patrol the nearby waters. Ever mindful of the rights of property they called on the legislature to indemnify the owner of the islet, John Campbell, for any damage incurred by the Caribs' occupancy.[24]

Baliceaux today is a lonely speck whose only permanent inhabitants are a dozen cattle and countless yellow-spotted tortoises. The island is a little over a mile from north to south but the only flat terrain is a low saddle of land at Baliceaux's pinched waist where a grey, stony beach, as in 1796, provides the landing place for visitors, willing or unwilling. Towards each end of the island rise steep slopes largely covered with low, scrubby trees and cactus plants. For anyone arriving by boat Baliceaux first reveals itself as a red-brown cliff rising abruptly from the open sea. There are no streams or springs on the island. To meet the Caribs' needs one Richard Davies was engaged by the colony to supply water at a cost of fourteen shillings a puncheon (seventy gallons)—the gentlemen of

159

the island were soon complaining about the expense. Today Baliceaux is quiet, bar the twittering and bickering of the birds. With its sister island, Battowia, it lies within sight of the millionaires' playground of Mustique with nothing to indicate that somehow, more than two hundred years ago nearly four thousand Caribs were crammed in here. That is close to the current population of nearby Bequia, an island about fifteen times the size of Baliceaux.

Now the only evidence of a human presence is a small farmer's hut but Baliceaux in 1796 had a modest number of buildings: a large, boarded and shingled house with a gallery, a large thatched cotton house and about thirty "negro houses". It was suggested, perhaps optimistically, that the island had sufficient wood and thatch to build huts for all the Caribs. The colony promised to provide huts and the necessaries of life for the Caribs, which was vital as the island produced none of the vegetable provisions on which they depended.[25] The colony's leading figures were later forced to deny claims that they had not provided sufficient food for the captives. Indeed, the authorities said that if anything they were guilty of providing too much for the Caribs to eat.[26] In this context an earlier comment by Governor Seton acquires a bitter irony. Referring to "the Carib," he wrote: "I am told it is incredible how small a portion of food will serve him."[27]

The Carib population of Baliceaux grew from the first arrivals on 21 July until 2 February when two men, a woman and a child were shipped there. The British reported that a total of 4,776 prisoners were taken to Baliceaux over a six-month period.[28] That figure included 1,080 men, 2,003 women and 1,693 children. Of those, 4,633 were classified as Black Caribs (1,047 men, 1,943 women, 1,643 children), 102 as Yellow Caribs (including three born on Baliceaux) and 41 as "Negroes the Property of the Black Caribs". Eighty-three Yellow Caribs were sent back to St. Vincent which may indicate that 22 died on Baliceaux. Although the British took these figures as definitive, in fact their own running tally of prisoners shipped to Baliceaux suggests a lower figure of 4,336 (1,002 men, 1,779 women and 1,555 children), the discrepancy possibly arising from faulty arithmetic or transcription errors (see Appendix 3). Abercromby suggested that the Yellow Caribs, "who are few in number, and innocent of the late War", should be allowed to remain in St. Vincent and be allotted land but should not be "allowed to intermarry with the Blacks upon pain of forfeiture of their lands and being sent away".[29]

At first, when only a few hundred were confined on Baliceaux, no problems were reported. In August, though, as more and more Caribs were crammed into this confined space, people started falling sick and, in short order, dying. According to the account of the British doctor on the island,[30] assistant surgeon N. Dickinson, a dozen Caribs and one British soldier died as a mystery disease took hold on Baliceaux. In September a hundred Caribs died. The following month that figure quadrupled and continued to rise until the end of the year when 950 Caribs died in the month of December alone. Most of those who fell ill died, which must have struck terror into the Caribs, especially as no one knew how the malady was communicated. The physician concluded that the disease was "pestilential" in nature but provided few details on the symptoms or the precise identity of the malaise. He believed that the disease had its origins in the desperate state the Caribs had been reduced to before their captivity. The dying, he maintained, had begun in the interior of St. Vincent before the Caribs' surrender. "When the Soldiers entered the deserted huts of those Charib men—who had left their families and situated into the woods—they in general found the Hammocks occupied by their deceased Wives and Children." Alexander Anderson said those who surrendered presented "a dreadful spectacle of distress and misery. A number of them when they first came in were so weak as not to be able to crawl."[31] Dickinson maintained that the disease had been introduced to Baliceaux by the later arrivals on the island who had been in the worst condition after being hunted through the woods of St. Vincent. The prisoners arrived in an "emaciated state" which left them in a weakened condition exacerbated by "continual fear and apprehension" and the "dread of an indefatigable pursuing enemy". This judgment was broadly echoed by Abercromby: "A considerable mortality which has taken place chiefly among the Women and Children, must be attributed to the Extremities to which they were reduced before they surrendered, and the sudden change of Diet and Situation."[32]

After the death of a British officer who had been sleeping downwind of several Carib women and children who themselves also succumbed to the disease, the authorities took preventive steps—to protect the health of the troops. A new barracks for the guards was built on a high point to windward and a hospital was constructed some distance away. The mortality rate among the troops was a fraction of that among the Caribs. Thirteen soldiers are recorded as dying on Baliceaux, although the death rate off the island appears to have been higher. (General Abercromby wrote in January 1797: "The great Sickness which has prevailed in these Colonies since the Month of August, has reduced our Force beyond any possible Calculation.") Sick Caribs were allowed a ration of wine, rice and sugar but the majority of those who fell ill died within days.

The British said they had done everything possible for the Caribs' welfare. Dickinson insisted he had afforded them "every medical attention within my power". The doctor placed the blame for their predicament firmly on the Caribs themselves for their obstinacy in holding out for so long and he felt that the epidemic's subsequent "dreadful Consequences are in great Measure to be attributed to their own Inhumanity". He accused Carib men of turning out sick women and children and of appropriating the "indulgences" allowed to the sick. Dickinson said the Caribs had to be forced to bury their dead. Since the Caribs were known to make every effort to carry their dead away from the battlefield, perhaps this reflects the horror of living in a confined space with a deadly epidemic disease whose means of communication were unknown.

Periods	No. of sick		No. that died	
	Troops	Caribs	Troops	Caribs
August	12-18	20-35	1	12
September	30-45	40-60	2	100
October	50-70	160-400	5	400
November	75-80	500-800	3	750
December	80-30	800-1200	2	950

Source: N Dickinson, *History of the Causes of a malignant Pestilential Disease, introduced into the Island of Baliseau, by the Black Charaibs from St. Vincent.* WO1/82

At this distance it is impossible to say with certainty what the disease was. Garifuna tradition preserves a story of the British mixing lime with the Caribs' bread, which, although unlikely and unsupported by any other evidence, does perhaps convey the psychological impact of the disaster on an already suffering population. It has been suggested that the epidemic may have been typhus or yellow fever. Although the disease is rare in the tropics, a typhus epidemic had been recorded in Barbados in 1795.[33] Sometimes known as gaol fever because it was common among prisoners huddled in filthy conditions, typhus is communicated by lice and spreads rapidly in crowded, unhygienic conditions. Dickinson noted that: "Baliseau being entirely destitute of water was by no means favorable to the comfort and convenience of its new inhabitants—who regard the luxury of immersion in fresh Water an indispensable necessary of Health." It is also a disease which has accompanied famine elsewhere, such as during the Irish potato famine.

Yellow or Bullam's fever had broken out in St. Vincent in 1793 and was described, like the Baliceaux epidemic, as a "malignant pestilential fever".[34] Some 80,000 cases were recorded in the region over the subsequent three years in what appears to have been a particularly devastating epidemic, making it a prime suspect for the Baliceaux deaths. Moreau de Jonnès, incidentally, believed that it was yellow fever that killed so many Caribs before they reached their place of exile, an infection he blamed on the ships used to transport them.

One other possible cause of the dreadful mortality on Baliceaux should perhaps be noted, "and that," according to Alexander Anderson, "was the agonizing reflection that they were to be forever transported from their native country to another they never saw".[35]

With disease taking its toll, the navy made preparations to carry 3,500 Caribs from the island but only 2,248 were left in March 1797 when they were finally deported.[36] It was nothing short of a cataclysm and its scope was much greater than those figures indicate because they do not reflect the casualties of the armed struggle and the deaths from hunger and disease before the surrender.

Friday 3 March was a day of fresh breezes and rain showers, the weather providing a suitably unsettled backdrop as the surviving Caribs were loaded on to HMS *Experiment* and a flotilla of other vessels at Baliceaux. Relief at leaving the patch of land that had meant only death and misery for them must have mingled with sadness and foreboding at the prospect of abandoning for ever the islands they had called home for generations. The destination had finally been decided upon: the Spanish-ruled island of Roatán in the bay of Honduras, some 1,700 miles[37] to the northwest.

It was four days before the convoy set sail and then it was only as far as Bequia, within sight of St. Vincent. Then on Thursday 9 March the remains of the Black Carib nation caught their last glimpse of Youroumaÿn's green mountains as, unwilling passengers on the ships of their conquerors, they left their homeland behind for good.

8. Aftermath

"Who can avoid melancholy sensations on a whole race of mankind transported forever from their native land inhabited by them for many generations and not conceive there has been something radically wrong in the principles of that government necessitated to that act?"
Alexander Anderson

THE ten-strong convoy of ships[1] headed first for Grenada where they took on water. From there the flotilla, which also carried three hundred British military invalids, sailed to Port Royal in Jamaica where it spent two weeks taking on supplies and troops and conducting repairs. One ship, the *John and Mary*, was so disabled that the Caribs aboard were transferred to other vessels. The voyage was not without incident. Two ships, one Danish and one Spanish, were captured and one of the transport ships, the *Prince William Henry* with some three hundred Caribs aboard, was lost to the Spanish near the island of Guanaja and taken to the nearby port of Trujillo. On Tuesday 11 April the island of Roatán was sighted and the following day, faced with this floating expression of British military might, the commander of the Spanish garrison at Port Royal prudently decided to surrender. At sunset the Black Caribs of St. Vincent were set ashore on Roatán.[2]

The 2,026 Black Caribs who landed at Roatán included 664 men and 1,362 women and children. That number was 222 fewer than the 2,248 who had set out from Baliceaux[3] just over a month earlier. It is likely that disease had continued to take its toll on the voyage (although it may possibly reflect the number of Caribs carried off to Trujillo aboard the *Prince William Henry*). This small band represented virtually all that was left of the Black Carib people, less than half the number who had surrendered in St. Vincent just a few months earlier. The number who had died in the period since war broke out in 1795 is unknown but the doctor treating the survivors on Baliceaux believed their pre-war population was between eight and nine thousand

(Anderson estimated the latter figure).[4] If that were the case, up to 77 per cent of the Black Carib population may have died in the space of two years.

Of the chiefs who had distinguished themselves during the war, Du Vallée, young Chatoyer and Durant made the journey to Roatán.[5] The Sambula listed in Spanish records is apparently the son of the Carib general who was said to have been killed in the war.[6] With them the British landed supplies deemed sufficient to last the Caribs six months. Among the food items were flour, beef, saltfish, biscuits, sugar, oatmeal and rum. Indian corn, guinea corn, "pidgeon pease", sweet potatoes, yams, okra, pepper and cassava were provided for the Caribs to grow in their new lands. Livestock included fifty hogs, thirty goats and a variety of poultry.[7] They also had fishing tackle, griddles, graters and other tools, plus three hundred muskets with ammunition.[8] The British officer in charge of the operation, Colonel John Wilson, considered the provisions "very inadequate".[9]

The British flotilla headed to the mainland port of Trujillo where the captured *Prince William Henry* had been taken. After a confused engagement against the Spanish forces in the fortress there the vessel, with the Caribs, was recovered on 27 April. The British said they received assurances from the Spanish that the Caribs would not be disturbed in their new settlement. En route back towards Roatán Captain John Barrett of the *Experiment* sighted enemy ships and ordered his flotilla to sail at once to Nova Scotia, simply abandoning the *Prince William Henry*, "which I was obliged to leave with the Caribs".[10] The vessel reportedly foundered on reefs at Roatán and oral tradition suggests a number of Caribs died as a result.[11]

The British intended that the Black Caribs should build on Roatán a settlement based on agriculture supplemented by fishing and hunting. The surrounding sea was said to be full of fish and the woods contained a few wild hogs. Only a very small part of the island had been cleared for cultivation but British officers reported that in their first days on Roatán "the Charribs had begun clearing the Woods and appeared extremely active and indefatigable". But Wilson warned that it would be a long time before the Caribs' crops could provide sufficient for their sustenance, and worryingly the cassava, the essential staple of the Carib diet, had been much damaged on the voyage and it was feared it would not germinate. Without relief from the British government, Wilson wrote, they would "be soon in the greatest distress".[12] Wilson's plea was answered: on 23 October he was ordered to take command of the transport *Calypso* loaded with all the supplies he had requested and take them to the Caribs at Roatán, "furnishing them with every requisite for their comfortable subsistence and for their defence".[13] By the time this order was issued, however, the Caribs were already gone.

The surrender terms had promised the Black Caribs would be taken to "a good Country, where there is plenty of Water, and a good Soil".[14] In fact, they had been landed on the relatively arid southern coast of Roatán in the driest season of the year. Water would have been scarce and the sandy soils did not compare to the fertile lands they had left behind in St. Vincent. The British had hoped the Caribs would defend the strategically placed island against the Spanish or at least be a nuisance but with at least some of their number having seen the Spaniards close up in Trujillo, the Caribs saw the possibility of forging a new tactical alliance with another European power.

A Spanish colonial official, José Rossi y Rubí, sailed from Trujillo with a dozen officers to parley with the Black Caribs. They quickly agreed to surrender, doing so formally on 17 May, in return for transportation to the mainland. The fact that black, French-speaking veterans of the revolution in St.-Domingue—who had been at the forefront of the defence of Trujillo against the British in April—accompanied the Spanish delegation may have encouraged the Black Caribs as to the sort of reception they would receive in the Spanish-controlled port. An entry in Rossi y Rubí's diary after the encounter on Roatán records a declaration that could have been made by any Carib captain of the previous two hundred years. "I do not command in the name of anyone," the man said. "I am not English, nor French, nor Spanish, nor do I care to be any of these. I am a Carib, a Carib subordinate to no one. I do not care to be more or to have more than I have."[15]

Within months Black Caribs had moved in large numbers to the mainland port.[16] On 23 September 1797 a census of the Caribs who had been brought to Trujillo recorded 1,465 people, of whom 722 were male (496 labelled "men") and 743 female (547 "women"). By 16 October only 206 Caribs remained on Roatán.[17] From this exodus to the Central American mainland stems the current distribution of the

Garifuna population. Within a few years Blacks Caribs were migrating along the Caribbean coast of Honduras and on to Belize, Guatemala and Nicaragua.

The final paragraph of Defoe's *Robinson Crusoe* hints at a continuation of the tale of the colonists on Crusoe's island in which a force of "Caribbees" fought them and "ruined their plantations, and how they fought with that whole number twice", killing many and, after the destruction of the Caribs' canoes, the planters of Crusoe's fledgling empire "famished or destroyed almost all the rest, and renewed and recovered the possession of their plantation, and still lived upon the island".[18] So in St. Vincent after the ravages of war the colony settled down to enjoying the fruits of victory.

Initially, though, planters were slow to exploit the opportunity of the newly available lands in Carib country. Correspondence between London and Kingstown repeatedly fretted over the danger of the former Carib territory being left vacant and potentially becoming a base for runaway slaves or French agents. Sir William Young signed a letter urging the government to act quickly to prevent subversion from nearby St. Lucia. The colony's leading citizens were also concerned about security and were determined to deport the remaining Yellow Caribs even though the governor believed they were "innocent in the late War".[19] On the contrary, the council and assembly wrote in a petition to Governor Seton that they had evidence from a brigand captured in St. Lucia and a black informant, as well as from certain items of food and ammunition found in Black Carib camps, that the Yellow Caribs had maintained "a regular correspondence" with the insurgents still at large.[20] Seton promised to pass their petition on to the Duke of Portland in London and said that provision was being made to house the Yellow Caribs in huts beneath the walls of Fort Charlotte.[21] The following January the Duke of Portland authorized the governor to deport the Yellow Caribs to Trinidad—which had been captured by the British in 1797—from where it was presumed they might migrate to the mainland.[22]

The Carib lands were officially estimated to include 27,078 acres (excluding 550 acres controversially acquired by Colonel Etherington in 1775), of which 10,000 were suitable for sugar cultivation, and 7,000 would serve for coffee, cocoa and provisions, the remainder being uncultivable.[23] Progress in settling and developing the lands was, however, slow. By the end of 1798 the governor was warning that in the two years since the Caribs' eviction the cleared parts of their territory had become overgrown and were "absolutely impassable".[24]

It soon became clear, though, that not all the Black Caribs had been shipped to Roatán. In April the new governor, William Bentinck, reported the capture of a Carib chief, Augustine, and nine others in the woods. Two Caribs died in the encounter. Augustine's first question was whether the French had yet landed in England, indicating that even now they hoped for a change in the strategic balance. Augustine offered to bring in others who were still living in the mountains. Bentinck, echoing his predecessors, observed that "their numbers are much greater than we thought".[25]

Despite the recent crushing victory, the colony was reported to be in "a continual state of alarm". Jumpy witnesses spotted "Brigands" operating in the area around the governor's country house near Layou and a gentleman named Samuel Clapham, who had planted between sixty and seventy acres of former Carib land at Grand Sable, was apprehended and killed by "savages" near Rabacca while on a fishing trip.[26] The unfortunate Mr. Clapham's "whole Face, Head, Neck, and Body was only one Scene of Gashes, Stabs, and Cuts".[27] Three months later a private of the West India regiment was also allegedly killed by Caribs.

The major planters expressed dissatisfaction that the rangers had failed to root out the last of the Caribs. In early 1799 it was decided to definitively disband the rangers and deploy the regulars of the 4th West India regiment (another black corps) in Carib country, but military measures proved ineffective.

At the start of the year a prominent Carib, Cuffy Wilson, turned himself in, joining "Tuscany... Augustine and the Black Caraib Prisoners and others now in Confinement, who were in Rebellion in this Island".[28] By August 1800 28 Black Caribs—three men, thirteen women and twelve children—"who in part surrendered themselves, and in part were made Prisoners about eighteen months ago, or longer" were still housed in Fort Charlotte and the authorities were deliberating about what to do with them.[29] They were supported at public expense and had relative freedom of movement, only being required to sleep in the fort at night. Their number had been increased by births in captivity. Later that year the metropolitan government authorized the local military commander to dump them on some foreign shore—the usual options of the Spanish Main and Trinidad were canvassed, as was Martinique. At this time it was estimated that fifty Black Caribs were still at large.

In August 1801 three Carib men were sent to Trinidad through the offices of Admiral John Duckworth, having been taken on as fishermen aboard ship. The St. Vincent authorities sent a further 29 women and 30 children after them with a view to them being received by the missions on that island.[30] Four years later they were said to be living in "comfort and security" there.[31]

In November 1804 Bentinck was replaced by Major General George Beckwith for having fought a duel with Henry Sharpe, whom he wounded in the belly, conduct thought unbecoming of His Majesty's representative on the island. One of Bentinck's last acts as governor was to grant Chatoyer's former lands in the northwest of the island to Henry Haffey, the man who as a militia officer had witnessed Chatoyer's son's oration to his people eight years earlier. Du Vallée's lands were assigned to a Mr. Thesiger.[32]

On 28 January 1805 the council heard testimony from a female slave who had been taken blindfolded to a camp composed of a great many houses built of roseau and made up of half runaway black slaves and half Caribs in the heights above Washilabo. The assembly resolved to raise a force of thirty black slaves from the leeward estates to find the camp. Meanwhile the council called on the governor to arm "certain Yellow Charaibs in the neighbourhood of Mr Ross's plantation" to hunt the Black Caribs and runaways.[33]

For eight years Black Caribs who had survived the war had continued to roam the wooded interior of St. Vincent occasionally clashing violently with official forces sent against them.[34] Now Governor Beckwith determined to use negotiation to solve the Carib problem once and for all. Two Carib children had been brought in by one of the parties sent out to scour the back country. The mother in due course came in with a babe in arms and was well treated. She in turn was followed in by her husband. Beckwith sent him back out with some trifling presents and some provisions to try to bring the rest of the family in. A brother and a nephew took the opportunity to come in and over the subsequent days several others overcame their fear. Six men, three women and six children came in, and Beckwith estimated that seven men, six women and ten children were left in the forest. He sought a royal pardon for all of them, calling them "all along the Dupes of French Intrigue".

On 15 May 1805 the local legislature passed an act pardoning those remaining Caribs in St. Vincent who surrendered. And so it was that on 10 June Beckwith reported to London that the Carib war was finally at an end. Forty-five men, women and children, the nucleus of whom were two groups of brothers, had surrendered. The oldest was a fifty-year-old called Joseph, while the youngest was a baby boy aged just five days. The surrender revealed the Caribs' numbers, once again, to be greater than had ever been thought. Beckwith was astonished at how they had managed to remain concealed for so long. "[I]t affords no mean proof of their judgement and enterprise that their last position where they raised their Vegetables of every description, was in the gorge of a Mountain within three miles and a half of a flourishing plantation, from whence they were never discovered."[35] The Black Caribs were to be given land, 270 acres, at Morne Ronde and provided with provisions, including blankets and clothing, and a small canoe for fishing. Even at this late stage the colonial legislature insisted that there was no place on the island for Black Caribs however few in number and petitioned unsuccessfully for them to be deported to Trinidad.

The following year a Yellow Carib called Gabriel petitioned the military commander at Owia for permission to settle 19 men, 28 women and 58 children at Great Sandy Bay. The Privy Council advised against taking "any immediate measures respecting the Yellow Charaibs"[36] but soon Yellow Caribs were allowed to settle there and Sandy Bay remains the largest Carib community in St. Vincent.

A year later Beckwith, acting on direct orders from London, granted six thousand acres of the best land in Carib country to Thomas Browne,[37] a large landowner in the Bahamas and a veteran of the American war. This grant would be argued over for years until in 1809 the land was broken up into eight different estates.[38] Gradually, though, the fertile plains of the windward country were turned over to sugar production. Exporting the stuff was more of a problem. The windward coast had no good, natural harbours and there were no Carib navigators left to ferry the harvest through the crashing surf out to waiting ships. The Windward Highway, the attempted construction of which had led directly to the war of 1772-3, was eventually extended up to the sugar plantations beyond Mount Young. Even then the contorted topography of the island meant that tunnels had to be blasted in order to iron out the most precipitous inclines. New wharves were built and in the plain around Grand Sable, which was once the Caribs' largest community, arose a new urban centre, Georgetown, which briefly threatened to overtake Kingstown as the foremost metropolis on the island.

In 1812 the Soufrière volcano erupted causing widespread damage, particularly in what had been the Caribs' stronghold. The sugar plantation which stood on Du Vallée's former lands was "entirely covered in ashes and sands".[39] Caribs from Morne Ronde fled to Kingstown, "abandoning their Houses, with their live stock and everything they possessed",[40] as a torrent of lava swept down towards them. The colony provided relief supplies for the island's Caribs (whose population the governor calculated as 130 Yellow Caribs and 59 Black Caribs) but most of the Yellow Caribs, led by a Captain Baptiste, asked for help in migrating to Trinidad "where they say they have numerous Relatives".[41] The colony paid more than £300 for about 120 men, women and children to be shipped to the island, leaving St. Vincent behind for good.

At the time of the abolition of slavery in 1833 the Grand Sable estate, once the centre of Black Carib independence, was worked by 693 slaves.[42] The sugar boom, though, did not last. Even before abolition, sugar was in decline. The peak year of production was 1828, after which it fell 32 per cent in five years.[43] Today St. Vincent imports sugar.

After the war of 1795-6 a number of British officers were presented with swords and other honours for their part in defeating the Black Caribs. When St. George's Anglican cathedral was built in Kingstown in 1820 a stone slab was laid commemorating Major Leith, the supposed nemesis of Chatoyer, who outlived the Carib leader by less than three years. In New York in 1823 a play was presented called *The Drama of King Shotaway, founded on Facts taken from the Insurrection of the Caravs on the Island of St Vincent*. It is described as "written from Experience by Mr. Brown", hinting that the author, William Alexander Brown, might have taken part in or witnessed the Second Carib War.[44] However, the fact that a year earlier Brown had premiered the play as

Shotaway; or the Drama of the Caribs of St Domingo suggests that his knowledge of the actual events was sketchy. No text of the play is extant.

A visitor to St. Vincent reported in 1830 that the Caribs in the colony "would hardly amount to one thousand, including men, women, and children" and that their numbers were decreasing. "The Charaibs have still a king in their little village, who passes in Kingstown by the name of Charaib Daniel. He is a very old man, and on account of some service which he did for the government in the late war, he is recompensed with rations from the Commissariat stores." The writer made no distinction between Black and Yellow Caribs and the suggestion that he served the government during the Second Carib War perhaps suggests that Daniel came from the latter community. However, a man named Daniel was among the Black Caribs who surrendered in 1805 and he would have been 59 in 1830. Daniel, like Chatoyer, was said to have five wives and "has still a little authority among his subjects; but their way of living is so peaceable and inoffensive, that there is seldom any occasion for his interference". The Caribs were by now seen as marginal to the life of the colony. "They keep completely to themselves, and it is quite a rarity to see one of them in Kingstown."[45]

The story of how the Black Caribs/Garifuna settled the Caribbean coast of Central America after 1797 could easily fill a book of its own, so what follows is merely a brief sketch.

Following their arrival in Trujillo, the Caribs soon distinguished themselves, one hundred of them defending the town on 14 May 1799 against their old adversaries, the British. But their Spanish hosts seemed unsure whether their presence was a boon or a problem. Black and francophone, their allegiance to the Spanish crown was suspect. In 1804 the governor of Comayagua (roughly modern Honduras), Ramón Anguiano, advised that all black people should be removed immediately from the coast of Honduras, preferably to France or its colonies, before their numbers became too great. The British had a presence in what is now Belize and, through their alliance with the Miskitos, on the Caribbean coast of eastern Honduras and Nicaragua, so the Spanish authorities were concerned that they might extend their influence all along the sparsely settled Honduran and Guatemalan coast in between.

It is likely that as the Caribs spread along the coast they moved in extended family groups each headed by a "captain" as they had on St. Vincent. They soon began to disperse along the shore of the Bay of Honduras, preferring secluded villages to urban life. Village sites tended to be near the beach, facilitating fishing and trade, where they would also have access to fresh water and land for growing provisions, but also, to a much greater extent than on St. Vincent, close enough to potential sources of wage labour, in terms of soldiering, mahogany cutting, agricultural work and trading in markets.

Some headed east. A traveller in 1804 found Black Caribs living in the territory of a prominent Miskito leader between Black River and Caratasca. A British account reported that in 1807 the Caribs living in a suburb of Trujillo ("called the Barrio de Caribes") rebelled and headed east to the territory of the Miskitos but the Spaniards pursued and brought them back along with a number of Miskitos who had joined them.[46] Others headed west. Livingston (Labuga in Garifuna) on the Caribbean coast of Guatemala is believed to have been founded by Caribs led by Marcos Sánchez Díaz in 1802 or 1804. Díaz himself may well have been a black Haitian, possible evidence of the way that members of different black minority groups were incorporated into Garifuna culture in Central America. A French traveller, Alfred Valois, writing in 1861, recalled an encounter in Livingston with an old Carib called "Tata Marco" who spoke good French and claimed to be the founder of the port.[47] Caribs established themselves at Stann Creek (now known by the Garifuna name Dangriga) in British Honduras to such an extent that it was known for a time as Carib Town.

In 1807 Britain abolished the slave trade. Among other things it meant that in Belize (then British Honduras) colonists could no longer import slaves from Africa. The woodcutting business which was the main reason for the British presence in Belize needed a new labour supply. They turned to the Caribs who quickly proved themselves to be excellent woodcutters. With the Second Carib War still fresh in the memory, the authorities were wary of this influx and went so far as to issue an ordinance prohibiting Caribs—or French or Spanish blacks—from entering the territory. But the woodcutters went on hiring Caribs. At their early base of Trujillo Black Caribs continued to play an important military role. In 1820 when the port was attacked by a flotilla from South America under the French corsair Louis-Michel Aury, Caribs were part of the defending force that repulsed the attack. Garifuna troops also manned the fort at San Felipe on the Río Dulce in Guatemala.

It was a time of upheaval in the Spanish empire which would culminate in independence for its Central American colonies. Carib fighters formed an important part of the royalist armies in this period. They were the mainstay of the Battalion of Olancho, led by General Pedro Gutiérrez, who wrote that they struck fear into all, including those on their own side.

In 1822, four months after the break with Spain, the Central American provinces were annexed to Mexico which soon generated a new movement for independence. The result was a federation of Central American states, whose first president was José Manuel Arce. He in turn was overthrown in 1829 by Francisco Morazán, who was subsequently elected president. Morazán was a modernizer and throughout his rule, which lasted until 1840, Arce's followers, who included the elite and the Catholic Church, mounted a series of counterrevolutions. Black Caribs formed an important part of these counterrevolutionary forces, probably less out of political conviction than as a form of paid work.

In addition to woodcutting and soldiering, Carib men also found work as sailors and on fruit and sugar plantations. They fished offshore and some hunted deer to sell their skins. With their disdain for governmental authority and expertise as navigators they took readily to smuggling, exploiting their familiarity with a coastline carved up by first the British and Spanish and latterly (after 1838) by the new Central American republics. As in St. Vincent women cultivated the fields, once cleared by the men, and sold their surplus in the market. They did all the work associated with maintaining the home and family and during the nineteenth century also began to take on some waged work. In the early years, while the men were wearing shirts and trousers, women in 1820 were still dressing much as they had in St. Vincent. By the 1830s they were dressing in calico bodices, patterned skirts and headscarves on their trips to market and in the second half of the century adopted similar attire at all times.[48]

In 1832 three counterrevolutionary armies attacked Morazán's government at Trujillo, the coastal fortress of Omoa and in the interior, and in all three Caribs were prominent. All three were eventually defeated. Fearing reprisals, the Caribs fled the territory of the Central American federation for British Honduras (Belize) where they were welcomed by the woodcutters who had discreetly supported Arce's rebellion. As had happened 35 years earlier the Caribs were uprooted after ending up on the wrong side of a war. It was a time of cholera in the region which may also have played a part in the exodus. A visitor to Livingston in 1834 found "only two or three families because two years earlier all the Caribs emigrated, because of the uprising in Trujillo and Omoa".[49]

This time the exile, at least for some, was not permanent. Seen as good workers, the Caribs were encouraged in 1836 to resettle in a number of places in Guatemala and Honduras. Many Caribs returned to settle in the region of the ports of Puerto Cortés, Tela and La Ceiba.

In the east, in the Mosquitia, other Caribs had migrated from the central Honduran coast. A British traveller wrote in 1842 that the reason for their move had been "the unceasing demands upon their labour" and that they had been welcomed by the local Miskito "king", "who well knew the immense advantage of having a race of brave and industrious men in his territory. From that time they have increased greatly, all seeming perfectly happy; preferring the climate to any other, enjoying health and vigour, and living to a great age."[50] The traveller Thomas Young also reported on the Caribs' diet, noting in particular their liking for pepper-soup, which was placed in large basins for diners to dip their cassava bread into: "This being one of the St Vincent customs, is held in great esteem." Carib feasts still involved heavy drinking although at this time, it was noted, "they seldom quarrel". Like their forebears on St. Vincent, when families met "they greet each other with much warmth and cordiality".[51] Ephraim Squier passed through the same area in 1855, noting that: "The Caribs... now occupy the coast from Trujillo to Carataska Lagoon, whence they have gradually expelled the Sambos or Mosquitos. Their towns are all along the coast near the mouths of various rivers."[52] From this region, sometimes known as Costa Arriba, Juan Sambola (possibly a descendant of the war leader from St. Vincent) travelled to the shores of Pearl Lagoon to found the first Garifuna settlements in Nicaragua.

By this time the Caribs had spread to virtually their entire current Central American range, from Nicaragua to Belize, although some earlier settlements appear to have been subsequently abandoned. A traveller in British Honduras in the 1870s reported that: "The Caribs are timid and shy. Their women principally supply the local markets with yams and starch, the men are good sailors, and contribute in some degree to the labour market. Their ambition is to be left alone, and live as their forefathers have before them, and if disturbed or annoyed, simply move to another place."[53]

In the 1870s Caribs participated in small-scale "*poquitero*" banana production in Honduras. Adept navigators, they would ferry their produce out to waiting ships off the north coast in dories. When, from the 1890s onwards, US fruit companies started buying up coastal lands for banana plantations Caribs formed a significant part of the workforce. In 1913 the United Fruit Company established railways as Honduras was transformed into the original banana republic (the railways crisscrossed the northern fruit-growing regions but never made it to the capital, Tegucigalpa). In 1915 *morenos*—a term commonly applied to Black Caribs in Central America—made up ten per cent of the Standard Fruit Company's employees. In 1929 out of 5,125 employees of the Trujillo Railroad Company, 463 (or nine per cent) were described by the company as Honduran Caribs.[54] This was near the peak of the Honduran banana industry. Its subsequent decline had a major effect on the Black Caribs.

A century after their involvement in political strife led to their exodus, in 1939 local politics could still have a drastic effect on the Black Caribs of Honduras. Soldiers came to the community of San Juan Durugubuti near Tela to inflict collective punishment for their alleged facilitation of an exiled liberal leader's entry into the country. The men were marched to the beach and shot. The survivors, including those men who were at sea fishing at the time, fled to British Honduras where they swelled the community of Hopkins.

The Second World War brought new work opportunities just as they were disappearing locally with the decline of the banana industry. Carib men migrated to the United States to fill jobs, for example in manufacturing, vacated by new soldiers. Caribs also found work as merchant seamen aboard US or other countries' ships. It was the start of the Caribs' most recent displacement, to the major cities of the United States, a process which gained new momentum in the 1960s with the lifting of race-based restrictions on immigration and the growth of the service sector in the US. Carib migrants from Honduras and Guatemala, increasingly identifying themselves by the term Garifuna, tended to congregate in New York while those from Belize headed in greater numbers to Los Angeles. Other cities such as Chicago, Houston and New Orleans also have Garifuna populations. Some Garifunas also found a home in London. From the days of the woodcutting camps, where men might be absent for up to eight months at a time, Garifuna villages had long been the province primarily of women and children for much of the year. Migration to the United States exacerbated the scarcity of men in Garifuna villages but remittances increasingly came to play an important part in the local economy. The Bronx is now said to be home to the world's largest Garifuna community. Of course, not all Garifunas joined this movement and in Belize, for example, Garifunas have developed something of a tradition as schoolteachers and have taken on roles in the civil service.

Efforts to convert Black Caribs to Christianity were more successful in Central America than they had been in St. Vincent. In 1813 the Catholic Church sent missionaries to Trujillo to save their souls and in the second half of the nineteenth century the work of Father Manuel de Jesús Subirana earned him the soubriquet "the Apostle of the Caribs". Most Garifunas today are at least nominally Catholic—although the Church of Rome has to share spiritual space with traditional Garifuna beliefs. In Central America the Black Caribs also acquired the Spanish surnames which most have today. From the 1980s evangelical churches have had some success in making converts among the Garifuna where Protestants of previous centuries largely failed. Although the evangelicals have encouraged literacy in the Garifuna language they have been less tolerant of traditional religious practices, such as the *dügü*, a major ritual held some time, often some years, after a death in the family. The ceremony, which requires the offices of a *buyei*, typically takes places over three days and involves offerings of food, dancing and spirit possession. It also demands the attendance of the whole family, even those now resident abroad.[55] If anything, international migration has increased the frequency and lavishness of *dügü* ceremonies.

Migration may have a less positive effect on the other most striking aspect of Garifuna culture: the language. It remains to be seen if a form of communication which was preserved in relatively isolated villages in Central America will survive through the generations in the cities of the US. In Central America too the language, like many minority languages, is under threat. When the Nicaraguan government conducted a literacy crusade in the native tongues of the Atlantic Coast in the 1980s they found that only a few older people in Garifuna communities retained their native language. The arrival of electricity to many Honduran Garifuna villages in the 1980s brought with it an influx of Spanish-speaking culture and a loss of the mother tongue among some of the younger generation. In Belize Creole English has in some places displaced Garifuna as a first language.

Nevertheless Garifuna is still widely spoken and unites people otherwise divided by national boundaries. The language, which was largely unwritten until the second half of the twentieth century, has been given increasing prominence by Garifuna musicians. In the 1980s punta rock, a souped-up version of a Garifuna ritual dance rhythm, became wildly popular in Belize. Subsequently Andy Palacio, who made his name in punta rock, brought a range of traditional Garifuna styles sung in Garifuna to international attention and acclaim, and after his untimely death Aurelio Martínez from Honduras has picked up his mantle. Garifuna culture, for so long marginal in all the countries where it is present, is increasingly visible, reflected in the fact that the word Garifuna—the people's own name for themselves—has progressively displaced the range of other names (Carib, *moreno*, *negro*, etc) largely applied by others. The colours of yellow, black and white have been adopted as the Garifuna flag. In 2001 Unesco, at the behest of Belize and supported by Honduras and Nicaragua, proclaimed Garifuna language, dance and music a "masterpiece of the oral and intangible heritage of humanity". Garifunas have also distinguished themselves in the sporting field: of the 23-man Honduran football squad at the 2010 World Cup in South Africa eight were Garifuna.

In 1977 Belize established Settlement Day, 19 November, as a national holiday to officially commemorate the arrival of the original Garifuna population and Garifuna communities in Honduras, Guatemala and Nicaragua also have special days on which they celebrate their settlement. Numerous Garifuna community and cultural organizations now function in the various Central American countries and in the North American diaspora. In 1992 the Garifuna were admitted to the World Council of Indigenous Peoples after overcoming resistance in that body to accepting black-skinned people in the Americas as indigenous. The decision marked one point in the shifting definition of Garifuna identity between the poles of indigenous and African. In recent years the tendency among Garifunas to view themselves as essentially African has come increasingly to the fore, affected in part by the exposure of migrants to US culture.

Following independence for St. Vincent and the Grenadines in 1979 Chatoyer was embraced as a symbol by the new nation. He became Right Excellent Joseph Chatoyer, First National Hero of St. Vincent and the Grenadines. His image, taken from the Brunias painting, adorns postage stamps and even phonecards, and a simple obelisk stands as his monument on top of Dorsetshire Hill. Major Leith's memorial in the cathedral is now covered by a carpet.

Several communities which identify themselves as Carib remain on St. Vincent. The largest is at Sandy Bay but others include Petit Bordel, Owia, Rose Bank, Greiggs and Fancy.[56] There is some debate among them about which are descended from Yellow and which from Black Caribs, and whether that distinction is meaningful. The people of Greiggs maintain that their community was founded by holdouts from the Second Carib War who had remained hidden for years in the shadow of the Petit Bonhomme mountain at the head of the Massarica valley. In all these communities there has been considerable mixture with the general population over the course of the past two hundred years and in none of them is the Garifuna language spoken.

The language is, though, spoken and the name of Satuye (Chatoyer) remembered in communities all along the Caribbean coast of Central America and also in certain cities in the United States. There is no reliable tally for the world Garifuna population but a figure in the region of 300,000 has been suggested, along with higher and lower estimates.

In 1997 a Garifuna anthropologist, Joseph Palacio, interviewed a woman in Dangriga, Belize, who told him a story she said she had heard from her grandmother, who in turn had heard it from her grand-mother, who was called Gulisi. According to the informant, Mrs. Felic-ita Francisco, Gulisi had not only been one of the original Black Carib deportees from St. Vincent but was the daughter of Chatoyer himself and had arrived in Roatán at the age of 24. Part of the story, told as if in Gulisi's own words, recalls the uprooting from their original home-land: "Running away from danger would seem to be my destiny in life. It first started in St. Vincent where we had fought back the British who wanted to take away our land. It was especially dangerous for my family because my father Joseph Chatoyer was the leader of our people in war. In the battle he was killed along with my brother and several other rela-tives. It was the British who eventually loaded the survivors into men o' war and set sail this way... The war was devastation to our way of life."

Gulisi's narrative emphasized the importance of telling the story of the life that had been left behind: "Having experienced the massacre of our people in St. Vincent and the miraculous way how we survived the surrender, the diseases, the inhuman conditions, and the long period in the belly of men o' war on the way to Roatan, I wanted the little ones to know the very strong mettle of their forefathers and to be proud of them."[57]

Hundreds of years after the arrival of the Europeans and generations after the extermination of most of the archipelago's indigenous inhab-itants, on St. Vincent in the late eighteenth century the Black Caribs fought the last battle of any people in any of the Caribbean islands to maintain their traditional way of life on their own land. Defeated, decimated, uprooted from their homeland, and dumped on a foreign shore, the Black Caribs might easily have been erased from history. But they survived.

Appendix 1

The Anglo-Carib Peace Treaty of 1773

I All hostile proceedings to cease; a firm and lasting peace and friendship to succeed.

II The Charaibs shall acknowledge his Majesty to be the rightful sovereign of the island and domain of St Vincent's; take an oath of fidelity to him as their King; promise absolute submission to his will, and lay down their arms.

III They shall submit themselves to the laws and obedience of his Majesty's government, with power to the Governor to enact further regulations for the public advantage as shall be convenient. (This article only respects their transactions with his Majesty's subjects, not being Indians, their intercourse and customs with each other, in the quarters allotted them not being affected by it.) And all new regulations to receive his Majesty's Governor's approbation before carried into execution.

IV A portion of lands, hereafter mentioned, to be allotted for the residence of the Charaibs, viz. from the river Byera to Point Espagniol on the one side, and from the river Analibou to Point Espagniol on the other side, according to lines to be drawn by his Majesty's surveyors, from the sources of the rivers to the tops of the mountains; the rest of the lands, formerly inhabited by Charaibs, for the future to belong entirely to his Majesty.

V Those lands not to be alienated, either by sale, lease, or otherwise, but to persons properly authorized by his Majesty to receive them.

VI Roads, ports, batteries, and communications to be made as his Majesty pleases.

VII No undue intercourse with the French islands to be allowed.

VIII Runaway slaves in the possession of the Charaibs are to be delivered up, and endeavours used to discover and apprehend the others; and an engagement, in future, not to encourage, receive, or harbour any slave whatever; and carrying off the island a capital crime.

IX Persons guilty of capital crimes against the English are to be delivered up.

X In time of danger to be aiding and assisting to his Majesty's subjects against their enemies.

XI The three chains to remain to his Majesty.

XII All conspiracies and plots against his Majesty, or his government, to be made known to his Governor, or other civil magistrates.

XIII Leave (if required) to be given to the Charaibs to depart this island, with their families and properties, and assistance in their transportation.

XIV Free access to the quarters allowed to the Charaibs, to be given to persons properly empowered in pursuit of runaway slaves, and safe conduct afforded them.

XV Deserters from his Majesty's service (if any), and runaway slaves from the French, to be delivered up, in order that they may be returned to their masters.

XVI The chiefs of the different quarters are to render an account of the names and number of the inhabitants of their respective districts.

XVII The chiefs, and others Charaibs, inhabitants, to attend the Governor when required for his Majesty's service.

XVIII All possible facility, consistent with the laws of Great Britain, to be afforded to the Charaibs in the sale of the produce, and in their trade to the different British islands.

XIX Entire liberty of fishing, as well on the coast of St Vincent's, as at the neighbouring keys, to be allowed them.

XX In all cases, when the Charaibs conceive themselves injured by his Majesty's other subjects, or other persons, and are desirous of having reference to the laws, or to the civil magistrates, an agent, being one of his Majesty's natural born subjects, may be employed by themselves, or if more agreeable at his Majesty's cost.

XXI No strangers, or white persons, to be permitted to settle among the Charaibs, without permissions obtained in writing from the Governor.

XXII These articles subscribed to and observed, the Charaibs are to be pardoned, secured, and fixed in their property, according to his Majesty's directions given, and all past offences forgot.

XXIII After the signing of this treaty, should any of the Charaibs refuse to observe the condition of it, they are to be considered and treated as enemies by both parties, and the most effectual means used to reduce them.

XXIV The Charaibs shall take the following oath, viz.

We A.B. do swear, in the name of the immortal God, and Christ Jesus, that we will bear true allegiance to his Majesty George the Third, of Great Britain, France, and Ireland, King, defender of the faith; and that we will pay due obedience to the laws of Great Britain, and the Island of St Vincent's; and will truly observe every article of the treaty concluded between his said Majesty and the Charaibs; and we do acknowledge, that his said Majesty is rightful Lord and Sovereign of all the Island of St Vincent's, and that the lands held by us the Charaibs, are granted through his Majesty's clemency.

On the part of his Majesty,
W Dalrymple.

On the part of the Charaibs.

Jean Baptiste	Simon
Dufont Begot	Lalime, Senior
Boyordell	Baüamont
Dirang	Justin Baüamont
Chatoyér	Matthieu
Doucre Baramont	Jean Louis Pacquin
Lalime, Junior	Gadel Goibau
Broca	John Baptiste
Saioe	Lonen
François Laron	Boyüdon
Saint Laron	Du Vallet
Anisette	Boucharie
Clement	Deraba Babilliard
Bigott	Canaia

Signatories by home district

Jean Baptiste*	Grand Sable
Dufont Bigot*	Grand Sable
Boyerdelle* [Boyerdel]	Grand Sable
Matthieu*	Grand Sable
Du Vallette* [Du Vallet]	Grand Sable
Chatoié [Chatoi]	Grand Sable
Dirang*	Massaraca
Simon*	Rabaca
Laline* [Laline Snr]	Coubamarou
Baiamont* [Bauamont]	Baüra [Bauara]
Justin Baiamont*	Baüra
Doucre Barimont*	
[Douare Bauamont]	Baüra [Bauara]
Laline* [Laline Jnr]	Coubamarou
Broca*	Coubamarou
Païoe* [Saico]	Coubamarou
Clement*	Jambou
Francois Loian*	Colonorie
Saint Loian*	Camacarabou
Anisette*	Baüra [Bauara]
Clement*	Massaraca
Louis Pacquin*	Camacarabou
Gadel Goibau	
[Gadel Goiberie]	Baüra [Bauara]
Jean Baptiste*	Oanaarow [Ouarawara]
Louen* [Louan]	Jambou
Boyidon*	Rabaca
Bouchire* [Boucherie]	Massaraca [Macaraca]
Deruba Babilliard*	
[Deraba Babilarde]	Baüra

| Canaia• [Cania] | Colonorie [Colonerie] |
| Bigot | Point Espagnol |

*Marked a chief

Alternative spellings of names and places occur in the different copies of the treaty in the British archives (CO101/17: 68 and CO101/17: 87)

Appendix 2

Return of the Charaibs landed at Baliseau from July 26th 96 to Feb 2nd 1797

DATES	MEN	WOMEN	CHILDREN	TOTAL
July 21st	65	89	122	276
27th	12	-	7	19
Aug 8th	1	6	7	14
15th	22	48	26	96
	15	18	15	48
Sep 6th	1	6	5	12
	6	1	1	8
9th	4	2	4	10
10th	7	19	14	40
15th	5	31	15	51
	80	186	286	552
	5	8	6	19
27th	3	10	11	24
29th	12	26	30	56[a]
30th	46	80	104	230
Oct 7th	61	130	116	307
9th	16	15	15	46
	70	80	52	202
11th	14	16	52	126[b]
12th	57	75	85	217
	40	60	103	203
13th	68	162	90	320
14th	136	253	78	467
15th	33	96	33	162

DATES	MEN	WOMEN	CHILDREN	TOTAL
16th	24	33	21	78
	24	55	45	124
17th	11	30	24	65
19th	16	21	19	56
21st	22	61	38	161[c]
23rd	14	16	21	51
26th	29	26	18	73
Nov 4th	1	4	2	7
	4	8	19	31
12th	10	13	3	26
	42	63	26	131
16th	1	-	3	4
18th	10	2	6	18
19th	3	3	8	14
21st	1	4	3	8
28th	10	15	15	40
1797 Jan 17th	1	7	5	13
25th	-	-	1	1
Feb 2nd	2	1	1	4
Total	1080[d]	2003[e]	1693[f]	4776[g]

a Sum of figures for men, women and children for this date is 68
b Sum of figures for men, women and children for this date is 82
c Sum of figures for men, women and children for this date is 121
d Total for first column (men) is 1004
e Total for second column (women) is 1779
f Total for third column (children) is 1555
g Total for fourth column is 4410. However, total of cumulative totals for men, women and children is 4338

These figures presumably include 102 Yellow Caribs and 41 black slaves noted elsewhere.
Source: WO1/82

Appendix 3

Numbers, Names and Ages of Charibs Surrendered, taken the 28th May, 1805

1 Joyett 36
2 Myeas 23
3 Boison 32   } Brothers
4 Daniel 34
5 Viteau 30
6 Watchman 25

7 Joseph 50
8 Lewis 40   } Ditto
9 Levilliea 30

10 Lorain, son to Joseph 18
11 Francis 36
12 Barbanoe 40
13 John, Nephew to Joyett 16
14 Henry 45
15 Morgan 24
16 Castilliea, Nephew to Morgan 14
17 Marginear, Son of Morgan 7
18 Mary Ann, Wife to Joyett 36
19 Conna, Her Daughter 3
20 Hessea Ditto Son 1
21 Pelestiea, Wife to Morgan 27
22 Aberdeen, Her Son 4
23 Money Chambo, Ditto 1

24 Nanett, Wife of Lorain 27
25 Callisadee, her Daughter 4
26 Cauba, Ditto 1
27 Bassac, Henry Wife 23
28 Sommica, her Daughter 3
29 and an infant male aged 5 days
30 Margreet, Wife to Levillea 20
31 Labeth, her Daughter 5
32 Cannana, Ditto 3
33 and an infant Female aged 3 Months
34 Mary Jean, Francis's wife 26 Years
35 Reuma, her Son 4
36 and an infant Boy I month old
37 Meimo, Wife to Myeas 26 Years
38 Medison, her Son 4
39 Sacamo, Wife to Lewis 22
40 Frances, her Daughter 3
41 Celeist, Ditto 2
42 Mary, Wife to Daniel 27
43 Lamisair, her Son 7
44 Fanny, Daughter 5
45 An infant Female, 4 months old

Source: CO260/19

Appendix 4

The Indigenous Population

Over the course of the seventeenth and eighteenth centuries French and English colonists made various estimates of the indigenous population of St. Vincent. The following is a representative sample:

1667: St. Vincent is "all Indians, and some negroes from the loss of two Spanish ships in 1635" – Under-Secretary Williamson

1672: "the Indians in St. Vincent, Sta Lucia, and Dominica are 1,500 bowmen, whereof 600 are negroes" – Governor Stapleton (Nevis)

1674-5: "St Lucia, St. Vincent, Dominica, Grenada, Bequia, inhabited by 1,500 Indians strong in bowmen; in St. Vincent are 600 escaped negroes" – Calendar of State Papers

1676: "St. Vincent is possessed by the French, where are about 3,000 negro inhabitants, and in no other island, are as many Indians" – Colonel Philip Warner

1719: "Negroes there [St. Vincent], which are in number about 4,000" – J Chetwynd, Charles Cooke, P Dominique, T Pelham, D Pulteney

1719: "the negroes at St. Vincent's are now computed at 4000" – Thomas Weir

1719: "our small number in comparison to our capital enemies the Negros" – Yellow Carib chiefs

1720: St. Vincent "is possessed by red savages, and by blacks who have taken the language and the custom of that nation, the latter outnumber the former" – Inhabitants of Martinique petition

1726: "about 1200 Men, Negroes and Indians, with some French" Uring map

1742: "the *Indians* being computed to be near 8,000, and the *Negroes* 5 or 6,000 when Mr *Egerton* sent out on his Embassy [1722]" John Oldmixon, *The British Empire in America*

1750: St. Vincent's "savage" population estimated at 4-5,000 – De Poincy

1752: 100 Red Caribs and 3-4,000 Black Caribs (some have estimated 7-8,000 but people who know put the figure lower) – Maximin de Bompar

1760: "Over time the Blacks' colony has grown to the point where there are now more than 20,000 of them just on St Vincent (even though there were were no more than 200 of them when they arrived) as opposed to three or four thousand Red savages at the most" – Marquis de Lambertye

1761: 7,000 Black Caribs, of whom 3,000 bear bows or guns; 300 Red Caribs, including women and children – Prevost

1767: "their numbers consist of about 2000, including women and children; some few of them are of a yellow complexion, descended from the original natives, the rest are the descendants of a cargoe of negroes who were brought from Africa, and destined for sale at Barbadoes about a century ago" – Sir William Young Sr.

1769: Black Caribs "cannot exceed a thousand fighting men" – Lieutenant Governor Fitzmaurice

1773: "they are much more numerous than I had any idea of": 1,200 capable of bearing arms – Governor Leyborne

1774: "the truest information I can get, their whole number of all ages (exclusive of runaway negroes)… cannot be less than five thousand five hundred, or even approaching to six thousand" – Governor Valentine Morris

1774: Caribs: 1,500 or 1,600 fighting men exclusive of runaways – Governor Morris

1777: "the original possessors of the Island, or real Charibs… scarce forty of these now remain alive" – Governor Valentine Morris

1781: Caribs: "at least a thousand to twelve hundred soldiers" – Percin de la Roque

1784: "the lowest account I can collect from the best informed Persons here, make them [the Charaibs] seven hundred fighting Men, the highest Twelve hundred, which implys a Population of from three to five thousand. When some presents were made them by the French, upwards of seven hundred men came in at one time to receive them, it is therefore safe to fix upon that, as their least number…" – General Mathew

1785: "the number of men capable of bearing arms did not exceed 500" – French colonial estimate

1787: French colonial estimate of Caribs: 2,000

1787: "few have fixed their numbers below five thousand: I should rather suppose even that calculation to be short" – Davidson

1789: "I must suspect that, taking them all together, the number of Men, throughout the Island, capable of bearing arms, will fully amount to twelve hundred. Of these, I do imagine two hundred and fifty reside on this side of Byera River, and nine hundred and fifty on the other side of it" – Governor Seton

1789: "At present, I do not conceive that the number of Yellow Charaibs exceeds thirty men; and they live in a state of subjection to the black Charaibs" – Governor Seton

1795: Black Carib population: 8-9,000 – N Dickinson

1795: Black Carib population: 9,000 – Alexander Anderson

1795: "The Carib population of St Vincent exceeded, in 1795, 6,000 inhabitants of the indigenous red race, with about 1,500 Black Caribs" – Alexandre Moreau de Jonnès

1790s: Yellow Caribs number "two or three families only" – Alexander Anderson

1796: Caribs sent to Baliceaux: 4,633 (including 102 Yellow Caribs) – General Hunter

Notes

Introduction

1 Governor James Seton letter, January 1789. CO260/9
2 Others say the name derives from a term meaning "cassava eaters".
3 Quoted in Miller (1979), *The European Impact on St. Vincent 1600-1763*, p16
4 Anderson, Alexander (1983), *Alexander Anderson's Geography and History of St. Vincent, West Indies*, p98

1. Youroumaÿn

1 Joseph, EL (1838), *Warner Arundell, the Adventures of a Creole*, pp97-98
2 Le Breton, Adrien (1998), *Historic Account of Saint Vincent, the Indian Youroumaÿn*. Raymond Breton (no relation), another missionary living mainly on Dominica a generation earlier, recorded the name as Iouloumain. Numerous other variants occur; among modern-day Garinagu, Yurumein is probably the most common spelling. Rochefort, Charles de (1666), *The History of the Caribby-Islands*, p8. Little is
3 known of Rochefort; his book is based on his own observations and the writings of previous authors.
Labat, Jean-Baptiste (1931), *The Memoirs of Père Labat 1693-1705*, p137
4 Le Breton (1998), p20
5 Hulme, Peter, and Whitehead, Neil L, eds. (1992), *Wild Majesty, Encounters with*
6 *Caribs from Columbus to the Present Day*, p129; Du Tertre, Jean Baptiste *(1667), Histoire General des Antilles*, Vol 2, p357
Le Breton (1998), p19
7 Hulme & Whitehead (1992), p109
8 Rochefort (1666), p251. Du Tertre found them "of good stature and well-pro-
9 portioned build, stout, powerful, strong, and robust". Hulme & Whitehead (1992), p129; Du Tertre (1667), p357
In modern Garifuna the words for numbers above three are derived from French,
10 no doubt reflecting the extent of trading links in the colonial era.
Breton, Raymond (1978), *Relation de l'Ile de Guadeloupe*, p72
11 Terms applied by Europeans, naturally.
12 Du Tertre (1667), p130
13 ibid. (1667), p373
14 Labat (1931), p77
15 Rochefort (1666), p300
16 Rouse, Irving (1963), "The Carib" in *Bulletin of Bureau of American Ethnology*
17 *Smithsonian Institution*, Vol 143
Labat (1931), p112
18 *Hippomane mancinella.*
19 Le Breton (1998), p18
20

21 Du Tertre called the original inhabitants of the Lesser Antilles Ygneris (otherwise rendered as Igneris or Iñeris). Arawak properly describes a language group and the extent to which widely dispersed speakers of Arawak languages represented a unified culture is hotly disputed.

22 Bullen, Ripley P and Adelaide K. (1972), *Archaeological Investigations on St. Vincent and the Grenadines West Indies*. It should be noted that this interpretation rests on the widely but not universally accepted identification of the "Island Carib" population with the so-called "Suazey" type of pottery. Unfortunately, perhaps the most distinctive elements of Carib material culture, namely their basketware and their boats, have generally not survived. For an alternative if controversial view of Carib origins see Allaire, Louis (1980), "On the Historicity of Carib Migrations in the Lesser Antilles" *American Antiquity* 45:238-45. Rochefort, incidentally, suggested that the Caribs had not migrated to the islands from the south but from Florida, in the north.

23 Rochefort records a different if unlikely tradition, which he says was recounted by Vincentian Caribs. According to this version, the Caribs had been the Arawaks' slaves on the mainland but had rebelled and fled to the islands, which were, it was said, uninhabited, landing first at Tobago. This story curiously parallels another concerning the later separation of the Black and Yellow Caribs, also on St. Vincent.

24 Taylor, Douglas M, and Berend J Hoff (1980), "The Linguistic Repertory of the Island Carib in the Seventeenth Century: The Men's Language–A Carib Pidgin?" *International Journal of American Linguistics* 46(4) 301-12; Pelleprat, Pierre (1655), "Relation des missions des PP. de la Compagnie de Jesus dans les Isles, et dans la terre ferme de l'Amerique Meridionale" in Jesuits, *Voyages et Travaux des Missionnaires de la compagnie de Jésus*, p67; Du Tertre (1667), p361; Rochefort (1666), pp208-9

25 Writing about the modern Garifuna population of British Honduras (Belize), Taylor stated: "the Black Carib speak a language whose morphology and syntax are mainly Arawak, and whose vocabulary is Ignerian Arawak, with Galíbi (Cariban family), Spanish, French and English overlays". Taylor, Douglas (1951), *The Black Carib of British Honduras*, Viking Fund Publications in Anthropology, 17, p138. Taylor found only two words of African origin in the Garifuna language.

26 Seton letter, January 1789. CO260/9

27 Morris letter, 13 November 1777. CO260/2

28 Young, Sir William, *An Account of the Black Charaibs of the Island of St. Vincent's*, 1971, p5

29 Letter from Colonel Philip Warner, *Calendar of State Papers 1675-1676*, p384

30 *Journal of the Council for Trade and Plantations 1718-1722*, pp108-9

31 Lafleur, Gérard (1992), *Les Caraïbes des Petites Antilles*, p161

32 Hulme, Peter (2006), "French Accounts of the Vincentian Caribs" in Palacio, Joseph O, ed., *The Garifuna A Nation Across Borders*, 2nd ed., p33

33 Rober letter, 12 February 1700. CAOM F3/58

34 Young, Sir William (1764), *Considerations which may tend to promote the settlement of our new West-India Colonies By Encouraging Individuals to embark in the*

Undertaking, p9
35 Later Archbishop of Chiapas.
36 Hulme and Whitehead (1992), p40
37 ibid., p43
38 Rochefort (1666), p324
39 Labat visited Barbados at the turn of the eighteenth century and observed: "The English do not look after their slaves well and feed them very badly... The overseers get every ounce of work out of them, beat them without mercy for the least fault, and appear to care far less for the life of a negro than for a horse." Labat (1931), p127
40 Labat (1931), pp83-4
41 Governor Crowe letter, 8 August 1707. *CSP 1706-1708*, p525
42 Coullet letter. CAOM F3/58, 43-47
43 Governor Stapleton to Council for Trade and Plantations, 17 July 1672. CSP, p392
44 Gonzalez, Nancie L (1988), *Sojourners of the Caribbean: Ethnogenesis and Ethnohistory of the Garifuna*, p118
45 Kiple, Kenneth F, and Ornelas, Kriemhild C (1996), After the Encounter: Disease and Demographics in the Lesser Antilles, in Pacquette, Robert L, ed., *The Lesser Antilles in the Age of European Expansion*
46 Fitzmaurice letter, 10 June 1769. CO101/13
47 Crawford, MH (1984), "The Anthropological Genetics of the Black Caribs (Garifuna) of Central America and the Caribbean", in *Yearbook of Physical Anthropology 26*
48 Of course, some of the Amerindian genes may have been acquired in Central America post-1797.
49 Anderson (1983), p43
50 Rochefort (1666), p202
51 Coelho, Ruy Galvão de Andrade (1995), *Los Negros Caribes de Honduras* (2nd ed.), Tegucigalpa, pp217-221. Ancestors also played a part in Island Carib religious beliefs. Taylor (1951), pp141-2
52 "They do not appear to have any more Sense of Religion than the Negroes lately imported from the Coast of Africa. Like these, they have the most absurd notions about the Power of Enchantment, and set a high Value upon many trinkets made by their own cunning Conjurors, and which they carry about them to guard them against harm." Seton letter, January 1789. CO260/9
53 Labat (1931), p104

2. Good Friends, Cruel Enemies

1 Rochefort (1666), pp267-8
2 Montagu (1725), pp104-109
3 ibid., p109
4 ibid., p109

5 Cohen, JM (1969), *Christopher Columbus The Four Voyages,* pp58-9
6 See Arens, W (1979), *The Man-Eating Myth*
7 Crouch, Nathaniel (1685), *The English Empire in America,* p183
8 Scott's "Description of Grenada" (c1688), British Library, Sloane MSS 3662, 49-53, quoted in Williamson, James A (1926), *The Caribbee Islands under the proprietary patents,* 15-18, p107
9 Labat (1931), p103
10 ibid., p102
11 Breton (1978), p48
12 Quoted in Ross, Charlesworth, "Caribs and Arawaks", *Caribbean Quarterly,* Vol 6, No3, p52
13 Warner, Aucher (1933), *Sir Thomas Warner Pioneer of the West Indies A Chronicle of his Family,* p39
14 ibid.
15 Boucher, Philip P (1992), *Cannibal Encounters: Europeans and Island Caribs 1492-1763,* p48
16 Rennard, J (1935), *Baas, Blénac, ou les Antilles Françaises au XVII siecle,* p177
17 Governor Stapleton to the Council for Trade and Plantations, 9 January 1674, *CSP 1669-1674,* p547
18 Du Tertre (1666), pp384-5
19 Breton (1978), p71
20 Philip Boucher estimates the Island Carib population in the early seventeenth century at 7-15,000. Boucher (1992), p35
21 This may or may not be his real name. *Baba* means "father" in the Island Carib language and may simply describe his relationship with one of the abductees. He may also be the "Grand Brabba" referred to in the 1668 treaty with the English.
22 Pelleprat (1655), p71
23 ibid., p76
24 Rochefort (1667), p286
25 CAOM C8A9, 31/3/1699 f20, in Lafleur (1992), p75
26 Pelleprat (1655), p73
27 These were not the only Christian martyrs in St. Vincent. French sources also record the killing in 1679 of a Capuchin, Father Epifanne, by Caribs on St. Vincent. One Jalinanan killed the priest on the orders of a certain Tia, grabbing him from behind and slitting his throat and then drinking the priest's communion wine at his *carbet* at Masirara. M de la Paire to Comte de Blénac, 11 July 1679. CAOM F3/58
28 Labat (1931), p81
29 ibid., p79
30 Adams, Edgar (2007), *Saint Vincent in the History of the Carib Nation 1625-1797,* p19. It also noted that "the Caribs who are now present on the island are not the same ones that lived there previously" which may be a reference to the rise of the Black Caribs.
31 Labat (1931), p140
32 *Boyé* is sometimes recorded as *piayé.* In modern Garifuna the equivalent is *buwiye*

or *buyei.*

33 Crouch (1685), p178

34 Hulme & Whitehead (1992), p134; Du Tertre (1666), pp414-5

35 CO101/17: 7-13

36 Instructions to Willoughby, 4 February 1666/7. CO260/3

37 *CSP 1661-1668,* p587

38 ibid., pp554-5, CO260/3

39 Dutton letter, 3 January 1682. *CSP 1681-1685,* p181

40 *CSP 1675-1676,* p384

41 Adams (2007), p18

42 King to Sir Richard Dutton, November 1683. *CSP 1681-1685,* p556

43 Dutton letter, 3 January 1682. ibid., p181

44 Stapleton letter 15 June 1683. ibid.

45 Lieutenant Governor Stede letter, 18 September 1686. *CSP 1685-1688,* p244

46 ibid., p345

47 Agents of Barbados to Council of Trade and Plantations, 30 December 1699. *CSP 1699,* p584

48 In January 1718, an English sea captain, Christopher Taylor, reported that his ship carrying building materials along with money and silver worth £8,000 was seized by pirates at St. Vincent. CAOM C8A 24, 211 MIOM 32

49 Governor Crowe to the Council of Trade and Plantations, 8 August 1707. *CSP 1706-1708,* p525

50 ibid., p528

51 The agreement was signed on 22 October 1707 "with Totem marks, of Carib Chiefs; Malego Bay, Capt Bugecent, Capt. Sanson; Wilary Bay, Sanson; Valevo Bay, (?) Destee, Capt. Abell; Rebecco Bay, Capt. Nicloa; Marco Bay, Capt. Winiam". ibid., p619

52 Coullet letter, 1707. CAOM F3/58. Each chief received a hat, two axes, two billhooks, ten large grains of crystal, six knives, a pack of fishing hooks of different sizes and two razors, along with eau-de-vie, ribbon, cloth and gunpowder. "They were so happy that nothing could be added to their joy."

53 Bennet to Montagu, *CSP 1728-1729,* p25. Alexander Anderson later offered a similar assessment: "The French, having that insinuating address and ready mode of adopting the habits and customs of savages that they attract their attention and friendship much sooner and more readily than any other nation of Europe, by these means they easily got admittance into St. Vincent." Anderson (1983), p45

54 From Myst's Journal, 5 July, 2 August 1718, in William Lee (1869), *Daniel Defoe, His Life and Newly Discovered Writings,* Vol II, pp48-55

55 Shephard, Charles (1997), *An historical account of the Island of Saint Vincent,* p184

56 Rober letter, 12 February 1700. CAOM F3/53

57 Labat (1931), p138

58 Hulme &Whitehead (1992), p176

59 Labat (1931), p138

60 Letter from Thomas Weir, 20 June 1719. CO260/3

61 *CSP 1719-1720*, p244
62 CAOM F3/23: 056
63 Pichery letter, 16 October 1770. CO101/15: 233-8. The chiefs were Louan, Chatoyer, Canailly and Céladou Yamousa.
64 George Lillington to Council of Trade and Plantations, 31 October 1719. *CSP 1719-1720*, p247
65 Petition of inhabitants of Martinique, 1720. CAOM F3/58
66 *CSP 1722-1723*, p4
67 ibid., p127
68 Montagu (1725), p28
69 ibid., p44
70 *CSP 1722-1723*, p233
71 Laborde, Sieur de (1712), *Voyage dans L'Amerique*, p532
72 *CSP, 1728-1729*, p26
73 ibid., pp561-2
74 Governor Matthew to Mr Popple, 18 June 1735. *Journal of the Commissioners for Trade and Plantations 1734-1735*
75 JCTP to Duke of Newcastle, 4 November 1736. ibid.
76 Oldmixon, John (1742), *The British Empire in America*, p185
77 Caylus letter, 24 August 1748. CAOM F3/23
78 CAOM F3/58: 95-100
79 He may also or alternatively be the Thuriau involved in a case adjuducated by the land commissioners in the 1760s but his name does not appear beneath the 1773 peace treaty so presumably he was dead by then.
80 Hulme (2006), p33
81 Lambertye also says he had in his possession a detailed narrative dictated by the leading Red Carib chief, Vincent Prat, recounting the history of the Caribs' possession of the islands and of their relations with the Black Caribs. This too has not survived.
82 CAOM F3/23
83 In fact Petit Louis outlived Tourouya. The former was still alive in 1769 while a land commission document of that year refers to the land held by the "heirs of Touriau". CO101/1, CO106/11: 33
84 Lambertye names the "sovereign cacique of the Red Caribs" as Vincent Prat. Hulme (2006), pp32-4
85 Maximin de Bompar to Rouillé, 24 July 1752. CAOM F3/58: 117-120
86 Lafleur (1992), p165
87 Young (1971), p15
88 ibid., pp15-16
89 Bompar letter, 14 August 1752. CAOM F3/58:112
90 Bompar letter, 23 August 1755. CAOM F3/58
91 Prevost to Caylus, 1 March 1749. CAOM F3/58
92 Edwards, Bryan (1818-19), *The history, civil and commercial, of the British Colonies in the West Indies*, 3rd ed., p275

3. *Quel Roi?*

1 A minimum of one white man or two white women per hundred acres was stipulated.

2 Young (1764), p32

3 ibid., pp9-11

4 "In Britain sugar consumption had reached a point at which the Jamaican planter Edward Long could claim in 1770 that it was 'so generally in use, and chiefly by the assistance of tea' that even the poor wretches living in almshouses will not be without it." Duffy, Michael (1987), *Soldiers, Sugar, amd Seapower: The British Expeditions to the West Indies and the War against Revolutionary France.* pp7-8

5 Young, William Esq, Memorial to the Lords of the Treasury, 11 April 1767, in *Authentic Papers relative to the Expedition against the Charibbs and the Sale of Lands in the Island of St. Vincent* (1773)

6 Young (1971), p20

7 Fabel, Robin FA (2000), *Colonial Challenges, Britons, Native Americans, and Caribs 1759-1775*, pp150-1

8 Fénélon letter, 31 August 1763. CAOM F3/58: 148

9 Young (1971), p24

10 Sir William Young memorial, 7 January 1774. T1/500.

11 Carib chiefs' letter, 1781. CAOM C10D2

12 23 May 1765

13 Young (1971), pp27-8

14 On 18 December 1765 the commissioners reported: "removing them from St. Vincent... we look upon as a very important Object". CO101/1: 214

15 However, Alexander Anderson, no friend of the Black Caribs, later conceded: "They certainly had a prior right to any European power to the island." Anderson, Alexander (1983), p51

16 Young (1971), pp21-2

17 More, Thomas, Utopia, quoted in Pagden, Anthony (1985), *The Lords of All the World, Ideologies of Empire in Spain, Britain and France c1500-1800*, pp76-7

18 *Authentic Papers* (1971), p5

19 Edwards (1817-18), p248

20 Young (1971), p34

21 ibid., p38

22 Also recorded as Chatoller, Chatawae, Chattoway, Shotaway, and numerous other variants. In Central America the name became Satulle/Satuye.

23 Fraser, Adrian (2002), *Chatoyer (Chatawae), First National Hero of St. Vincent and the Grenadines*

24 CO106/11: 32

25 CO106/11: 33, CO101/16: 221.

26 Morris letter, 13 June 1777. CO260/4

27 Seton letter, January 1789. CO260/9

28 Seton letter, January 1789. CO260/9. See also, Anderson (1983), p64

29 However, Governor Leyborne referred to Chatoyer as "the Chief of Grande "Sable".

Chatoyer's brother Du Vallée is described as a chief of Grand Sable in the 1773 treaty. CO101/17: 149-153

30 CO260/17, Bentinck letter, 29 October 1798, CO260/19. The "Tract of Land contained about Two hundred and Eighty Acres and is situated on the North West Coast of the Island… and is surrounded by an high chain of Mountains except where bounded by the sea at which a landing is impracticable for six Months of the Year". CO260/24: 64.

31 Rochefort, however, suggests that in the mid-seventeenth century: "He is during his life, from his first election to that charge, the General of their armies, and he is always highly respected by them." Rochefort (1667), p314.

32 Young (1971), p39

33 ibid.

34 D'Ennery letter, 29 May 1769. CAOM F3/58:150-151

35 Wilkie to Harry Alexander, 30 April 1769. CO106/11: 8

36 Byres letter, CO106/11: 11

37 Memorial of Richard Maitland, 11 July 1769. CO101/13: 75

38 Young claims that Valladares' black servant was killed.

39 T1/500: 120

40 Land commission minutes, 26 May 1769. CO106/11: 32

41 D'Ennery letter, 23 May 1769. CAOM F3/58: 150-151

42 Fitzmaurice letter, 10 June 1769. CO101/13: 107-116, *Authentic Papers* (1773), p30

43 ibid.

44 Sir William Young (the younger) believed Berkshire Hill to be "scarcely assailable". Its flattened summit accommodated "most commodious barracks for a complete regiment, stores, regiments, etc., all bomb-proof". Edwards (1817-18), p261

45 *Authentic Papers* (1773), p32

46 *Authentic Papers*, Extract of a letter from Gov Melvill to Lord Hillsborough, dated Grenada, 5 July 1770

47 Pichery to Melvill, 15 October 1770. CO101/15: 218-231

48 Report of the Commissioners for the sale of lands in the ceded islands to the Lords of the Treasury, dated Dominica, 16 October 1771, *Authentic Papers* (1773)

49 Young (1971), p77

50 Land commissioners' report, 16 October 1771, *Authentic Papers* (1773)

51 *Authentic Papers*, (1773), p71

52 Lord Hillsborough to Governor Leyborne, 18 April 1772, *Authentic Papers* (1773), p73

53 Letter from Earl of Hillsborough to the Lords of the Admiralty, 16 April 1772, *Authentic Papers* (1773)

54 Earl of Hillsborough to Governor Leyborne, 6 May 1772, *Authentic Papers* (1773). After the war Governor Leyborne sought permission to reward with lands "some Charibbs who continued in the Militia during the War, some few that were very serviceable to us in assisting to land Provisions, & serving as Guides, and others both Black and Yellow, that were neuter". Leyborne to Dartmouth, 20 July 1773, CO101/17: 183

55 *Authentic Papers* (1773), p72

56 Leyborne letter, 17 June 1772, SP78/286

57 Leyborne letter, 30 November 1772. CO101/17: 44-46

58 Governor Leyborne to Earl of Hillsborough, 25 August 1772, *Authentic Papers* (1773)

59 Sir William Young letter, 28 July 1772. CO71/3

60 ibid.

61 Anderson (1983), p54

62 Leyborne letter, 9 October 1772, WO1/57

63 Louan would sign the 1773 peace treaty.

64 CO101/16

65 Anderson (1983), p6

66 Leyborne letter, 30 November 1772. CO101/17: 44-46

67 Fabel (2000), p186. Both the Jean Baptistes who signed the 1773 treaty are recorded as being chiefs.

68 Letter from an officer of 32nd, dated St. Vincent 9 August 1772, published in London Chronicle 6 October 1772. Quoted in Fabel (2000)

69 Cobbett, William (1813), *Parliamentary History of England*, Vol 17 1771-74, pp722-3

70 Major Gordon letter, 27 February 1773. WO1/57

71 James Rochford letter, 11 December 1772, SP78/286

72 CO101/17:37

73 Cobbett (1813), p569

74 ibid.

75 CO101/17: 33

76 Cobbett (1813), p727. "The House laughed out, and the Speaker for a moment lost his presence of mind."

77 Horace Walpole observed: "206 to 88 gave them up to the mercy of their persecutors." Quoted in Thomas, J Paul (1983), "The Caribs of St. Vincent: a Study in Imperial Maladministration 1763-73" in *The Journal of Caribbean History* Vol 18:2, p67

78 Lord Dartmouth wrote to Dalrymple on 3 March 1773: "The little Progress that has been made in bringing the Expedition against the Charibs to a final issue has in some sort disappointed our Expectations." CO101: 35

79 James Blair's claim for compensation, T1/500: 291

80 Their names are Jean Baptiste, Dufont Bigot, Boyerdel, Matthieu, Du Vallet, Chatoi, Dirang*, Simon, Laline Snr, Bauamont, Justin Baiamont, Douare Bauamont, Laline Jnr, Broca, Saico, Clement, Francois Loian, Saint Loian, Anisette, Clement, Louis Pacquin, Gadel Goiberie, Jean Baptiste, Louan, Boyidon, Boucherie, Deraba Babilarde, Cania, Bigot. Two copies of the treaty exist in British archives – CO101/17:68 and CO101/17:87 – with slightly different spellings of these names. This version is taken from the latter. General Dalrymple believed that "almost all their cheifs, are amongst the killed and wounded" but prominent named chiefs such as Chatoyer, Bigot and Louan all clearly survived the war. Dalrymple letter, 22 February 1773, CO101: 66

81 In Bryan Edwards' *History of the West Indies*, however, this image is accompanied by the legend "Pacification with the Maroon Negroes".

82 Dartmouth to Dalrymple, 9 December 1772. CO101/16: 218

83 Fabel (2000), p200

84 Leyborne to Dartmouth, 10 May 1773. CO101/17: 149-153

85 ibid.

86 The following year Colonel Etherington met a number of Carib chiefs at Fort Leyborne and reiterated that all Caribs should withdraw north of the boundary. Chatoyer told him "they would do what they could to bring the other Charibbs to reason, but, that it could not be expected they would assist to destroy their own relations, having many among the Charibbs in question". Etherington to Leyborne, 12 January 1774. CO101/17: 234

87 Alexander Anderson agreed: "They fought with great courage and resolution." Anderson (1983), p53

88 CAOM C10D2: "la victime de notre enthousiasme et de l'ambition de devenir francais avant le tems".

89 Dartmouth to Leyborne, 10 April 1773. CO101/17: 78

90 Memorial of planters, 5 May 1773. CO101/17:172-3

91 CO101/17: 72

92 Harry Alexander letter, 3 May 1769. CO101/13

93 Dalrymple to William Barrington, 21 April 1773, Manuscripts of the Earl of Dartmouth, quoted in Fabel (2000)

4. Allies of the French

1 CO260/8. A female slave would cost £45-£50 if country-born and £35-£40 if imported from Africa. Except where noted, the details in this section are taken from an official question-and-answer survey of the conditions of slavery in St. Vincent.

2 Anderson (1983), p72

3 Warner, Ashton (2009), *Negro Slavery Described by a Negro: Being the Narrative of Ashton Warner, a Native of St. Vincent's*, pp33-4

4 ibid., p38

5 *Authentic Papers*, Memorial of Richard Maitland, esq, of Mark-Lane, London, agent for the Island of St. Vincent to the Right Honourable, the Earl of Hillsborough

6 Morris was born in Antigua but spent most of his early life at his family's Piercefield estate in Monmouthshire.

7 Born in Antigua in 1727, Valentine Morris had acted as lieutenant governor since 1772.

8 Morris letter, 14 May 1777. CO260/4

9 Leyborne to Dartmouth, 10 May 1773 CO101/17:149-153

10 Population estimate, 19 March 1777. CO260/4

11 Morris letter, 11 July 1774. CO101/17: 281-2

12 Morris letter, 12 July 1774. CO101/17: 284-291

13 Morris memorial, 15 February 1783. CO260/3

14 Morris letter, 5 March 1777. CO260/4

15 Morris letter, 6 September, 1777. CO260/4

16 Germain letter, 2 July 1777. CO260/4

17 Morris letter, 9 February 1777. CO260/4
18 Morris letter, 14 May 1777. CO260/4
19 Morris letter, 25 March 1777. CO260/4: 86-87
20 Morris letter, 11 February 1777. CO260/4
21 Morris, Valentine (1787), *A Narrative of the official conduct of V. Morris Esq*, p21
22 Germain letter, 9 August 1777. CO260/4: 132
23 Morris letter 13 June 1777. CO260/4. Moreau de Jonnès claims the Caribs them-selves used large, wolf-like dogs, but no other witness mentions these. Moreau de Jonnès (1858), p267
24 Morris letter, 13 October 1777. CO260/2
25 Morris letter, 7 October 1777. CO260/5
26 At the time, runaway slaves had been blamed and Bigot and Simon had "brought two negroes heads who were of the number of those who killed Mr Renton" to the British military who had them set on sticks outside their fort. Lieutenant Sloper letter, 22 March 1775. CO101/18
27 Morris had proposed to his superiors that one thousand acres should be set aside to provide the governor with an income. His income was in fact to be provided from the four and a half per cent duty on exports, one of the main bones of con-tention between the governor and the leading planters.
28 Germain letter to Morris, 31 October 1777. CO260/4: 167. Governor Morris wrote of Etherington: "he has an Ascendancy over very many of them [the Car-ibs] little inferior to what their Chiefs have, & they chuse him as their Agent to negociate any of their concerns with the Chief or Lieutenant Governor having a well grounded confidence & almost implicit faith in whatever he assures them of." Morris letter, 11 July 1774, CO101/17: 281-2
29 Alexander Anderson agreed that: "The genius of the English and the French dif-fer much in this part of the world. The ambition of an Englishman is to be a great man at once. In aspiring to this he often reduces himself to worse than when he began, but a Frenchman goes on from little to mediocrity, from that to affluence, by slow but sure gradations, and ever keeps himself independent." Anderson (1983), p20
30 Morris letter, 2 July 1776. CO260/4
31 Carib chiefs' letter, 1781. CAOM C10D2
32 Morris letter, 17 September 1778. CO260/5
33 Morris (1787), pp54-5
34 CO260/2
35 T1/552: 65
36 Young (1971), p100
37 Council meeting, 9 January 1779. CO260/6: 138
38 Morris report, 1 January 1779. T1/552
39 T1/552: 65
40 Morris letter, 16 January 1779. CO260/6
41 Morris (1787), p434
42 Morris (1787), p6n
44 T1/510: 114

44 CO260/6

45 Quoted in Adams (2007), pp78-89

46 Captain Kelly, who commanded the troops at the estate, testified that to reach Kingstown: "It would have been a great march to have effected it between Sun rising, and setting, the Roads were so bad." Harburn, Dr Todd E, and Durham, Rodger (2002), *"A Vindication of My Conduct" The General Court-Martial of Lieutenant Colonel George Etherington of the 60th or Royal American Regiment*, p103. Etherington's court martial heard that the troops were on official business, building a military post on his land.

47 Shephard (1997), pp40-41

48 The same Ensign Van Hamel who had been frogmarched out of Carib country by Chatoyer's men the previous year.

49 Dr Robert Glasgow testimony, in Harburn and Durham (2002), p88

50 Morris (1787), p167

51 Morris letter, 1 January 1779. CO260/2

52 Who was to blame for the ignominious loss of St. Vincent was argued over for years. Valentine Morris was exonerated after an inquiry into his conduct. Colonel Etherington, whom an initial court of inquiry found had "lacked zeal" in his defence of the island, faced a court-martial held in St Lucia in 1781. Morris, his main accuser, was unable to attend as he had been imprisoned for debt in Antigua. Etherington was cleared of all charges. Etherington had also been the officer commanding Fort Michilimackinac (in modern Michigan) when it was captured with the loss of half the garrison during Pontiac's rebellion in 1763. Despite this unfortunate record, Etherington continued his military career in the West Indies until his retirement from the army in 1787. He apparently made no attempt to recover his disputed land in St. Vincent. Morris spent years unsuccessfully attempting to recoup expenses he believed he was owed by the government from his time as governor of St. Vincent, including for his Carib intelligence activities and his runaway hunting expeditions. He spent five years in a debtors' prison and after being forced to sell off his Piercefield estate in Wales, his wife having been confined to a madhouse, he died at his sister's house in London in 1789.

53 Morris (1787), p174

54 ibid., pp174-6

55 ibid., p180

56 Chester letter, June 1784. CO260/8

57 Lafleur (1992), p193

58 Memorial of Planters, Merchants and Other Person's concerned in the island of Saint Vincent, June 1783. CO260/3

59 Tableau de l'Isle de St. Vincent, 1 May 1785. CAOM C10D2

60 ibid.

61 Southey, Thomas (1827), *Chronological History of the West Indies*, London, Vol II, p475

62 CAOM C10D2: 20

63 Lafleur (1992), p191

64 CAOM C10D2. The full list of signatories is: Chateauguet [Chatoyer], Pierre

iBabillard, Duvalet, Salliman, Joseph Founouchau, Lalime, Duchatet, Bruno, Palanquet, Duroebet, Marie, Anisette, Baramont, Saglou, Louison, Auearné, St Laurent, Fiolin, Romain, Bayoura, Smit, Honesset, Youbia, Fauchin, Baraota, Salignon, Bellet, Dupont, Sandousse, Clement, Antoine, Basseme and Alpha.

65 Percin letter to Castries, 2 December 1781. CAOM C10D2
66 Seton letter No55, January 1789. CO260/9
67 Tableau de l'Isle de St. Vincent, 1 May 1785. CAOM C10D2
68 Percin letter to Castries, 2 December 1781. CAOM C10D2
69 CAOM C10D2
70 Lafleur (1992), p198

5. A Pity it Belongs to the Caribs

1 Chester letter, June 1784. CO260/8
2 Sydney to Lincoln, 6 August 1784. CO260/7
3 Shephard (1997), p51. Shephard's book is dedicated "To the survivors of the Carib War".
4 Mathew letter, 15 February 1784. CO260/7
5 Tableau de l'Isle de St. Vincent, 1 May 1785. CAOM C10D2
6 Davidson, George (1787), *The Copy of a Letter from a Gentleman in the Island of St. Vincent*, pp10-12
7 ibid., p13
8 Percin letter, 21 November 1787. CAOM F3/58: 188
9 Davidson (1787), p15
10 Anderson (1983), p67
11 Seton letter, January 1789. CO260/9
12 Percin letter, 21 November 1787. CAOM F3/58: 188
13 Sir William Young's "Tour of the Islands", in Edwards (1817-18), p249
14 Davidson (1787), p19
15 The Caribs, at least those of an earlier generation, did not necessarily use these names among themselves. Raymond Breton reported that: "They never call anyone by his name, particularly if he is a relative. If they are forced to name him, they say just half the name." Breton 91978), *Relation*, p49. This reflected a wider delicacy about names. They feared the dead and never mentioned their names. When sailing, Caribs never named or pointed at the land which they were approaching, for fear that they might not be able to get ashore. Instead they would gesture with their lips. Rouse, Irving (1963), "The Carib" in *Bulletin of Bureau of American Ethnology Smithsonian Institution*, Vol 143. Some of this delicacy may persist to this day. A modern guide to St. Vincent notes that "it is a serious breach of etiquette to call someone's name in public".
16 Seton letter, January 1789. CO260/9
17 Davidson (1787), pp17-18
18 Coke, Thomas (1808-11), *A History of the West Indies*, p265. Alexandre Moreau de Jonnès claimed that in the Second Carib War, the Caribs "ranks were swelled … by their women and girls transformed into bellicose warriors". No other witness to the war noticed these amazons. Moreau de Jonnès, Alexandre (1858),

Aventures de guerre au temps de la république et du consulat, 2 Vols., 2: 318, 1:177

19 Davidson (1787), pp17-18

20 Percin letter, 21 November 1787. CAOM F3/58: 188

21 Seton letter, January 1789. CO260/9

22 Seton letter, January 1789. CO260/9. Alexander Anderson, however, believed that the Carib chiefs spoke English equally as well as French but would only use the latter with the British. Anderson (1983), p57

23 Letter to John Wesley, in Hulme and Whitehead (1992), p187

24 Coke (1808-11), p260

25 Coke (1808-11), p262. Presumably this was Rabacca. Alexander Anderson described Rabacca as "by far the most extensive and beautiful quarter of what was denominated the Carib Territory". Anderson (1983), p20. It was the area in which Lieutenant Renton was killed.

26 Anderson (1983), pp57-8

27 Moreau de Jonnès (1858), 1: 127

28 ibid.

29 Seton letter, January 1789. CO260/9

30 Davidson (1787), pp7-8

31 Anderson (1983), p61

32 Anderson MS615, MS616, Seton letter, January 1789. CO260/9. Governor Robert Melvill, who set up the St. Vincent Botanical Garden, wrote to its first curator on 23 September 1766, advising him: "even old Carribs & Slaves, who have dealt in cures, might be worth taking notice of …". Anderson MS605

33 Percin letter, 21 November 1787. CAOM F3/58: 188

34 See pp12-13

35 Seton letter, January 1789. CO260/9

36 Anderson (1983), p98

37 Davidson (1787), p10

38 Coke (1808-11), p266

39 ibid., p267

40 Lincoln letter, 2 May 1784. CO260/7

41 Lincoln to Lord Sydney, 2 May 1784. CO260/7

42 Lafleur, Gérard (1993), "The Passing of a Nation: the Carib Indians in the Lesser Antilles" in *Amerindians Africans Americans*, pp38-9

43 Lincoln to General Mathew, 7 February 1784. CO260/7

44 Lincoln to Lord North, 6 April 1783. CO260/3

45 Lincoln to Sydney, June 1784. CO260/7

46 Anderson (1983), p58. Lincoln later softened his view: "Whilst the Charaibs (who are numerous) that reside by sufferance within our Boundary behave peaceably, I cannot help thinking them of Benefit rather than disservice to the new settlers; their removal could not probably be accomplished without some bloodshed, and therefore Humanity As well as good Policy induces me to wink at it whilst without injury to the King's Service it may be done." Lincoln to Sydney, 28 July 1786. CO260/7. London endorsed this view. Sydney to Lincoln, 6 January 1787, CO260/8

47 Lincoln to Lord Sydney, 8 March 1784. CO260/7

48 Chester letter, June 1784. CO260/7

49 Anderson, James [sic] (1903), "An Account of Morne Garou ..." *Philosophical Transactions, The Royal Society*, Vol 200, Part I

50 Anderson (1983), p8

51 Anderson (1903)

52 Young letter, 28 July 1772. CO71/3

53 Kirby, IAE and Martin, CI (2004), *The Rise and Fall of the Black Caribs (Garifuna)* 4th ed., p29

54 Young cited the lack of whip marks on the backs of slaves in St. Vincent as evidence of their benign treatment. However, Bryan Edwards, in whose history Young's remarks are contained, felt obliged to point out that unlike floggings in the Royal Navy slaves on the island were whipped on the buttocks. Edwards (1818-19), p249n

55 Young, Sir William, "A Tour through the several islands of Barbadoes, St. Vincent, Antigua, Tobago and Grenada in the years 1791, and 1792", in Edwards (1818-19), p255

56 Young (1971), pp256-7

57 Anderson wrote that Black Caribs wore only a loincloth, "chiefs excepted". Anderson (1983), p64

58 Young (1971), p262

59 Seton, January 1789. CO260/9

60 Coke (1808-11), pp262-3

61 This could be the same incident reported by Seton above.

62 Seton letter, January 1789. CO260/9

63 Leyborne to Dalrymple, 10 May 1773. CO101/17: 149-153

64 Leyborne to Dalrymple, 10 May 1773. CO101/17: 149-153

65 CO260/17

66 Young (1971), p284. Chatoyer's brother is here named as Dufond but this appears to be a mistake.

67 Coke (1808-11), pp262-3

68 Young (1971), p262

69 ibid., p283

70 Seton letter, January 1789. CO260/9

71 Lincoln to Sydney, 28 July 1786. CO260/7

72 Seton, January 1789. CO260/9

73 Drewry Ottley to Lord Sydney, 13 January 1791. CO260/11

74 General Matthews, 19 March 1789. C101/28

75 Census, December 1787. CO260/8

76 Seton to Lord Grenville, 26 May 1791. CO260/11

77 Resolution of council and assembly, 7 June 1792. CO260/11

78 Seton to Dundas, 2 April 1793. CO260/12

79 Chisholm, C (1801), *An Essay on the Malignant Pestilential Fever, introduced into the West Indian Islands from Boullam, on the coast of Guinea, as it appeared in 1793, 1794, 1795, and 1796* ... 2nd edition, etc., pp150-1

80 Shephard (1997), p53

6. The Cry of Liberty

1 Commissaires de la Convention au général Chatouillé, 23 Ventôse, Année 3, CAOM C10D2

2 "He was a man of undaunted courage, with great conduct and presence of mind, determined and steady in all his resolutions. He was more obeyed from fear than from love." Anderson (1983), p82

3 In 1802, by now in French Guiana, Hugues enforced the Napoleonic decree reintroducing slavery.

4 Hugues to Cn Touraille, CAOM C10D2. The British also recognized Chatoyer as the leader: "the Charaib Chief Chatoié has been acknowledged as the General and Commander of all the Forces who have made this unnatural war against us." Council minutes, 19 March 1795, CO260/14

5 Chatoyer was one of the Carib chiefs who had described Louis XVI as the "young hero who has demonstrated so much wisdom, experience and virtue". Carib chiefs' letter, 1781. CAOM C10D2. His proclamation of 12 March 1795 was dated using the pre-revolutionary calendar.

6 The document was said to have been found in one of the houses on Dorsetshire Hill after Chatoyer's death there on 15 March 1795. The phrase "*egorgerons leur femmes et leur Enfants*" echoes, or rather inverts, "*Egorger vos fils et vos compagnes*" of *La Marseillaise*, written in 1792 and adopted as France's national anthem four months after Chatoyer's death. CO260/13: 16

7 Rt Hon Henry Dundas letter, September 1794. WO1/82

8 Minutes of Privy Council, St. Vincent, 6 March 1795. CO260/14

9 Moreau de Jonnès (1858),1:127. Moreau de Jonnès also suggests a much higher figure for the number of Yellow Caribs—6,500—which contradicts all other sources. Moreau de Jonnès was just nineteen at the time but only published his account when he was an old man of eighty. His memoirs, *Aventures de guerre au temps de la république et du consulat*, read like a novel. Most of the section concerning St. Vincent is taken up with tales of beautiful Indian princesses, buried treasure, disguises and a daring escape through an underground passage. As the introduction to the English edition, written by Sir John Fortescue, observes: "His narrative during this period is a curious study. He gives with much detail a harrowing story of the ill-treatment of a Carib princess by an English naval captain, of her escape, and of the death of the said captain when his ship was wrecked by a hurricane. Now there was no hurricane in the Windward Islands in 1795, and the naval officer in question died of yellow fever in the West Indies in 1805. But there was a hurricane in 1806, which de Jonnès must have seen; and the details which he gives of other English officers in the West Indies in 1795 are so correct and were known to so few that he can only have gathered them on the spot. He must, therefore, have mixed up his reminiscences a little, though in the main they are accurate." Moreau de Jonnès (1929), *Adventures in the Revolution and Under the Consulate*, trans. C Hammond; Intro by the Hon Sir John Fortescue

10 Hulme (2006), p31

11 Seton to Portland, 16 March 1795. CO260/13

12 Shephard (1997), p61

13 Minutes of Privy Council, St. Vincent, 8 March 1795. CO260/14. The Caribs were identified as Dolbert, Canique, Destan, Boucar Lui and Elexer. Chatoyer and Du Vallée were named as the leaders of the insurrection.

14 Anderson MS615. "The stumbling block at this time for the planters was the want of confidence in their slaves from the mistaken Idea that by putting arms in their hands they would turn them against them by joining the Enemy." Anderson believed: "there is little doubt if that measure had been adopted, a speedy check would have been given to their progress, & greater part of the Island preserved from the subsequent devastation & horrors."

15 Shephard (1997), p62

16 Anderson (1983), p19

17 Commissaires de la convention to Chatouillé, 23 Ventôse, Année 3. CAOM C10D2

18 Shephard (1997), p67

19 "Two negroes from the same country out of the same cargo, the one bought by an Englishman and the other by a Frenchman, each adopting the manners of his master, in the course of eight or ten years are totally dissimilar in their habits, dress and modes of living and their prejudices generally as strong to one another as that of their masters." Anderson (1983), pp73-4

20 Young (1971), p119, Shephard (1997), p69. Governor Seton's contemporary account (CO260/13:13) does not name Chatoyer as the killer. Young gives as his source "a Negroe present".

21 CO260/13: 66

22 Report on cost of fortifications. CO260/7

23 "[T]he apparent superiority of the enemy began to shake the fidelity of the Negroes." Shephard (1997), p71

24 Seton to Portland, 16 March 1795. CO260/13

25 Anderson (1983), p27

26 Shephard (1997), p74. Young writes that Chatoyer "fell by the bayonet of the brave Major Leith". Young (1971), p116.

27 Anderson, John (2001), *Between Slavery and Freedom. Special Magistrate John Anderson's Journal of St. Vincent during the Apprenticeship.* Roderick A McDonald ed., p128

28 Joseph (1838), p96

29 Hulme (2006), p32

30 Hugues to General Du Vallée, 28 ventôse. CAOM C10D2. Hugues addressed Du Vallée as *chef d'une nation libre.*

31 Hugues to Souhallet, 3 Floréal 3 année. WO1/82: 419

32 Shephard (1997), p75. Shephard writes: "the fate of Chatoyer was severely felt by every individual among them".

33 Hugues to Cn Duvalay, Dufon, Durand, Samboula et Jn Pre de Rabacca chefs d'une nation libre 1 florial, année 3. CAOM C10D2

34 Proclamation, 31 March 1795. CO101/34

35 Proclamation, 20 March 1795. C260/13
36 Seton to Portland, 30 March 1795. CO260/13
37 Seton to Sir John Vaughan, 22 March 1795. WO1/83
38 Shephard (1997), p75
39 Southey (1827), p84
40 Shephard (1997), p84
41 Seton to Portland, 22 April 1795, CO260/13
42 Hugues to Audibert, 12 prairial année 3. CAOM C10D2.
43 Hugues au Commandant de Caraïbes, 23 prairial année 3. CAOM C10D2
44 It should, in fairness, be noted that Governor Seton, had also claimed that the Black Caribs were "extremely fond of money". Seton letter, January 1789. CO260/9
45 Alexander Anderson wrote: "In the last warfare their allies complained much of their cowardice, as they never stood the brunt of an engagement, always abandoned them at the first onset, but they always proved a dangerous enemy to an advancing or retreating opponent." Anderson (1983), p68
46 Seton to Portland, 22 April 1795. CO260/13. Moreau de Jonnès wrote that in addition to teaching the Caribs how to handle muskets, his artillerymen also taught them to "manoeuvre like our light troops". Moreau de Jonnès (1858), 2: 313
47 Coke (1808-11), p220
48 Seton to Portland, 23 June 1795. CO260/13
49 Shephard (1997), p104
50 Moreau de Jonnès (1858), 2: 364. Alexander Anderson wrote approvingly: "They [the black rangers] were the only people that could be a match for them for such a desultory warfare in bushes and through forests, to attack them in their recesses or fight them on an equal footing." Anderson (1983), p74
51 Memorial of Sir William Young, 9 May 1795. CO260/13
52 Sir William Young (1795), *An Account of the Black Charaibs of St. Vincent*
53 Shephard reports that on 23 July a schooner landed 100 men, 10 women, plus a mortar and marmizette from Guadeloupe. Shephard (1997)
54 Bisset letter, CO260/13
55 Shephard (1997), pp114-115
56 Seton to Portland, 7 August 1795. CO260/13
57 Joseph (1838), pp90-1
58 Buckley, Roger N (1975), *The Early History of the West India Regiments* 1795-1815, pp192-3
59 Seton to Irving, 5 September 1795. WO1/84
60 Myers letter, 10 September 1795. WO1/84
61 Myers to Irving, 18 September 1795. WO1/84
62 Ritchie to Myers, 25 September 1795. WO1/84
63 WO1/84: 423
64 Committee of planters to Irving, 6 Oct 1795. WO1/84
65 Shephard (1997), p136
66 Hugues to Audibert, 18 Brumaire 3 Année. CAOM C10D2

67 Hugues to Audibert, 12 Ventôse 4 Année. CAOM C10D2
68 Myers to Grey, 2 November 1795. Sir John William Fortescue, *A History of the British Army*, Vol 4, Part 1
69 Chisholm, C (1801), pp153-4
70 Rev F Owens letter, 22 January 1796. CO101/34
71 Abercromby letter, September 1796. WO1/82

7. Calvary of the Caribs

1 Abercromby to Dundas, 22 June 1796. WO1/85: 224
2 Abercomby letter. WO1/82: 583
3 Abercromby to Dundas, 22 June 1796. WO1/85: 224
4 Shephard (1997), p159
5 ibid.
6 Letter from Robert Bisset, commissary general, 27 July 1796. CO260/13
7 Hunter letter, 7 July 1796. CO260/14
8 CO260/13: 250
9 Robert Bisset letter, 27 July 1796. CO260/13
10 ibid.
11 Joseph Maria Chacon letter, 27 June 1796. SVG AA 5.1.4
12 Shephard (1997), pp166-7
13 Graham to Dundas, 19 September 1796. WO1/85
14 Graham to Dundas, 16 October 1796. WO1/86
15 Shephard (1997), p170
16 Young (1807), *The West India Commonplace Book*, p215
17 Anderson (1983), p74
18 According to Alexander Anderson, he was "a brave, fiery and daring fellow endowed with not a little of military skill and conduct." ibid., p92 He was shipped off to St Lucia on 10 November. ADM51/1226
19 WO1/82
20 Graham to Dundas, 16 October 1796. WO1/86
21 Hunter to Graham, 18 October 1796. WO1/86
22 J French to James Hartley president of Council, 7 November 1796. CO260/14
23 Dundas to Abercromby, 28 October 1796. WO1/85
24 CO260/14
25 The inhabitants agreed to supply such water as was necessary but called upon the military commander-in-chief to provide a weekly ration for each Carib of either three pounds of salt fish or 12 herrings or three pounds of beef, or two of pork, plus seven pints of manioc (cassava) flour or seven pints of black-eyed peas or seven pints of cornmeal or seven pints of rice, although it is not clear what provisions were actually received. Baliceaux had been used to grow a small amount of cotton: in 1784 it produced 4,500 pounds.
26 "Nor can there be any hesitation in ascribing the death of so many of them to the overabundance of food during their stay on Baliceaux." Anderson (1983), p95
27 Seton letter, January 1789. CO260/9
28 WO1/82. Shephard gives a figure of 5,080 Carib men, women and children

who surrendered as of 26 October. This figure probably includes some French "Brigands", 725 of whom were said to have surrendered, as well, perhaps, as some slaves and Yellow Caribs. The figure of 4,776 (4,633 of them Black Caribs), though, is not without its problems. The total is included in a document in the British archives which contains a detailed breakdown of the numbers shipped to Baliceaux (WO1/82). However, there appear to be several arithmetical or transcription errors in the tally and one reading of the document would indicate that only 4,338 men, women and children were transported to Baliceaux (see Appendix 2). The total of 4,633 was, however, used in other official documents. An archaeological site on Baliceaux was excavated in the 1910s by JW Fewkes. He found European-stye walls, pottery, skeletons and a midden. He concluded that "excavations verify the historical and legendary account that Balliceaux was inhabited by aborigines and that the Black Carib probably lived at Banana Bay after the Carib war in St. Vincent". Excavations by Ripley and Adelaide Bullen in the 1970s cast doubt on these findings, concluding that a shell used as dating evidence was much older than the eighteenth century and that the site had in fact been abandoned around 1420. The Bullens believed that only a small percentage of the Black Caribs had ever been confined on Baliceaux. The documentary evidence, however, clearly contradicts this view. *Annual Report of the Board of Regents of the Smithsonian Institution*, 1914; Ripley P and Adelaide K Bullen (1972). A rough calculation based on the numbers recorded as shipped to Baliceaux and the numbers who died month by month suggests that no more than about 3,600 Caribs were alive on the island at any one time.

29 WO1/86: 583

30 Dickinson, N. "History of the Causes of a Malignant Pestilential Disease, introduced into the island of Baliseau, by the Black Charaibs from Saint Vincent." WO1/769

31 Anderson (1983), p95

32 Abercromby to Dundas, 16 January 1797. WO1/86

33 Gonzalez (1988), p22

34 Chisholm (1801), pp145-6. Clark, James (1797), in *A Treatise on the Yellow Fever as it appeared in the Island of Dominica in the years 1793-4-5-6*, described the later stages of the disease: "About the close of the febrile stage, there was often a violent haemorrhage from the nose, which was a bad sign; as was a delirium first coming on at that time. In the space of twelve hours after the yellowness of the neck, breast, and eyes came on, and the pulse became slow, and the heat of the body natural, the black vomit made its appearance ..." p11

35 Anderson (1983), p96

36 According to Dickinson's figures, which appear to be rounded, 2,212 Caribs died of disease on Baliceaux by the end of 1796.

37 Roughly the distance, for example, from London to Ankara or from Chicago to Mexico City.

8. Aftermath

1 Nancie Gonzalez, who extensively researched the deportation, lists the ships as *Experiment, Sovereign (or Severn), Boyton (or Boyston or Boston), Topaze, Ganges, Fortitude, Prince William Henry, John and Mary, Sea Nymph and Britannia*, plus an American brig impressed en route to Roatán. Gonzalez (1998), p36n

2 ADM51/1226

3 A total of 722 men, 806 women and 720 children had embarked for Roatán.

4 Anderson believed the figure to be about 9,000. Anderson (1983), p96

5 Gonzalez (1988), p33. Their names are recorded in Spanish records as Dubale, Satulle, Sambula and Duran. Three Juan Baptistes are also listed and any of them could be or be related to the Jean Baptiste who was described as Chatoyer's "prime minister" in the First Carib War. Du Vallée's son, Regis, also went into exile on Roatán.

6 "During the battle [the Second Carib War] the head chief was slain, and the chieftainship then devolved on Samboler's father, who bravely led on his men, but was likewise slain; the present Colonel Samboler, then a boy of ten years old, became the chief, and was, with many of his people, taken prisoners, and conveyed by the British to the island of Roatan." Young, Thomas (1842), *A Residence on the Mosquito Shore*, p130

7 WO1/82: 723

8 WO1/82. The full list is reproduced in Gonzalez (1988).

9 John Wilson letter to Treasury, 10 June 1802. CO260/17. Wilson petitioned for a grant of land for himself in the former Carib territory.

10 Barrett letter, 7 July 1797. WO1/690: 102-105. The master of the *Experiment*, Richard Cox, on 2 May wrote of "leaving the Prince Wm. Henry with the Charibs hoisted in the Boats". ADM52/2976. Captain Barrett wrote a different version in his log on 2 May: "Saw a Stranger Sail to the Southward, brought her too and Boarded her, took out the Master and people and left Charibees on board her." ADM51/1226

11 Gonzalez (1988), p41

12 Wilson letter, 21 August 1797. WO1/799

13 WO1/82: 743-6

14 CO260/17

15 Gaceta de Guatemala, 26 June 1797, quoted in Gonzalez, p48. The same source suggests the British had appointed two "captains" as overall leaders: "Those who command, in the name of Great Britain, are two Black Carib brothers named 'Jack'." Quoted in Gonzalez (1988), p49n

16 The British archives contain a letter from the Spanish province of Guatemala dated 3 July 1797 which states: "when the English captured the small Island of Roaten, they landed there about 2000 Caribbee Negroes, and left them to themselves. These negroes applied to this Government to receive them under its Dominion, which we have done." WO1/692

17 González, Nancie L (1983), "New evidence on the origins of the Black Carib, with thoughts on the meaning of tradition" in *New West Indian Guide/ Nieuwe*

West-Indische Gids 57, no: 3/4, Leiden, p165n. Gonzalez notes that incorrect addition made the figure for Caribs in Trujillo 1,490 in the document itself. A Garifuna settlement exists at Punta Gorda on Roatán's north coast but this may date from later.

18 Defoe, D, (2000) *Robinson Crusoe*, p235
19 Governor Seton to Lord Portland, 16 November 1796. WO1/82
20 Council and assembly to Seton. CO260/14
21 Seton, 1 October 1797. CO260/14
22 Portland to Seton, 19 January 1798. CO260/15. A small population of Caribs remained in Dominica in a "reserve" on the windward side of the island. They still exist, although they are now much mixed with the surrounding black population and have long since lost their language.
23 Seton to Portland, 5 August 1797. CO260/14
24 Bentinck to Portland, 22 December 1798. CO260/16
25 Bentinck to Portland, 8 April 1798. CO260/15
26 Bentinck to Portland, 17 July 1798. CO260/15
27 Captain W Ottley to Lieutenant Colonel Fairbairn, 15 July 1798. CO260/16
28 Council to assembly, 21 January 1799. CO260/16
20 Drewry Ottley to Portland, 28 August 1800. CO260/16. What became of the Yellow Caribs who were to be housed beneath Fort Charlotte in 1797 is unclear.
30 Ottley to Portland, 3 August 1801. CO260/17
31 *St. Vincent Gazette* 13 July 1805. CO260/19
32 In 1804 Du Vallée's former land produced its first sugar crop under its new owners: 78,400 pounds of sugar and 1,977 gallons of molasses. CO260/21
33 Council minutes, 1 March 1805. CO260/19: 15
34 "This Colony was not exempt from the Dregs of a Charaib War, upon my arrival; these people, however reduced in numbers, wandered in the Mountains, with their Women and Children, and with Arms of various descriptions, fought desperately and not without success, when parties were sent against them". Beckwith letter, 14 May 1805. CO260/19
35 Beckwith to Camden, 10 June 1805. CO260/19
36 Captain JC Eddington letter, 10 Dec 1806. CO260/22
37 Browne, who had established a settlement at August, Georgia, before the American war, "was also superintendant of the different tribes of Indians attached to the English army". Shephard (1997), pp180-1
38 They were: Grand Sable, Mount Bentinck, Langley Park, Rabacca, Lot 14, Waterloo, Orange Hill and Tourama. Adams, Edgar (2002), *People on the Move*, p77
39 Shephard (1997), p189
40 Description of the eruption of the SOUFFRIER MOUNTAIN, on Thursday Night the 30th April, 1812, in the Island of SAINT VINCENT. CO26/0/29: 35
41 CO260/29: 56, 82. The governor of Trinidad referred to the Yellow Caribs as refugees from Morne Ronde. This could be a mistaken conflation of different groups on his part, or that Yellow Caribs had joined Black Caribs at Morne Ronde, or that distinctions between the two groups had become blurred. Given that the acting governor of St. Vincent carefully distinguished between Black and

Yellow Caribs, the first explanation is the most likely. CO260/29: 84

42 Spinelli, Joseph (1973) *Land Use and Population in St. Vincent, 1763-1960*, pp76-7

43 ibid., pp72-3

44 The play is often cited as the first full-length African American drama. However, no copy has survived.

45 Bayley, FWN (1830), *Four Years' Residence in the West Indies*, pp285-8

46 FO15/19: 169

47 Arrivillaga Cortés, Alfonso, "Marcos Sánchez Díaz: from hero to *híuraha* – two hundred years of Garifuna settlement in Central America", in Palacio (2006), pp74-5. Tata Marco was supposedly an unlikely 132 years old at the time.

48 Kerns, Virginia (1983), *Women and the Ancestors: Black Carib Kinship and Ritual*, p36

49 García Granados, Miguel (1952), *Memorias*, p388

50 Young, Thomas (1842), *A Residence on the Mosquito Shore*, p130

51 ibid., pp132-3

52 Quoted in Gonzalez (1988), p59

53 Fowler, Henry (1879), *A Narrative of a Journey Across the Unexplored Portion of British Honduras*, p52

54 Anderson, Mark (2009), *Black and Indigenous: Garifuna Activism and Consumer Culture in Honduras,* University of Minnesota Press, pp86-7. A further 88 employees of the Truxillo Railroad Company were described as being from British Honduras and may have been Caribs.

55 As early as 1839, Thomas Young reported that participants in a *dügü* in Honduras had come from as far afield as Belize. Cited in Kerns (1983), p35

56 In the 1980s the following Carib population figures were estimated: Sandy Bay – c. 900 Caribs; Petit Bordel – c. 350; Rose Bank – 250 Owia – 300; Fancy – 175; Greiggs – 200. Gullick, CJMR (1985), *Myths of a Minority, the Changing Traditions of the Vincentian Caribs.*

57 Palacio, Joseph O (2006), "Reconstructing Garifuna oral history – techniques and methods in the story of a Caribbean people" in Palacio. The Gulisi narrative states, inter alia, that six tribes of Black Caribs existed on St. Vincent each with its own distinct characteristics and marriage rules: the Awawaruguna, Oreyuna, Masiragana, Sawaina, Habaruguna and Arawaga. It should be noted, however, that several details of this oral history, recorded 200 years after the deportation, do not tally with aspects of the historical record.

Further Reading and Bibliography

A good starting point, and my own, is Sir William Young's *An Account of the Charaibs of the Island of St. Vincent's*, first published in 1795 while the Second Carib War was still raging. Young knew the island and the principal people involved well and his narrative draws on the papers of his father of the same name, who was responsible for the sale of lands in St. Vincent following the start of British rule there in 1763. Charles Shephard's *An historical account of the Island of Saint Vincent* covers the Second Carib War, in particular, in some detail. Both these contemporary or near-contemporary accounts are openly hostile to the Black Caribs ("the cruel and perfidious Charaib" – Young; "these perfidious and deceitful people" – Shephard).

Wild Majesty is an invaluable compilation of European accounts of Caribs from the time of Columbus to the twentieth century, edited by Peter Hulme and Neil Whitehead, and includes a number of selections devoted to the Black Caribs of St. Vincent. Philip Boucher's *Cannibal Encounters* chronicles European-Carib relations up to 1763 with emphasis on the European literary imagination. For readers of French, Gérard Lafleur's *Les Caraïbes des Petites Antilles* covers Carib history across the region up to the Black Caribs' defeat in 1797, drawing extensively on the French archives.

Sojourners of the Caribbean by Nancie González is primarily an anthropological study of modern-day Garifuna customs in Central America but also contains important chapters on the deportation from St. Vincent and the early Garifuna settlement along the Central American coast. *The Garifuna: A Nation Across Borders* is a selection of essays, principally of social anthropology but also containing some historical contributions, edited by Joseph O Palacio. *St. Vincent in the History of the Carib Nation* by the Vincentian author Edgar Adams offers another telling of the story of the island's Caribs and reproduces a number of important original documents.

Research for this book was conducted in the archives of the United Kingdom, France and St. Vincent and the Grenadines, as well as in the British Library.

The National Archives in Kew, southwest London, contain numerous official government and military documents with a bearing on the Black Caribs. Of particular interest are those Colonial Office documents in the series CO101/13-18, covering the period when St. Vincent fell under the governorship of Grenada, and CO260 for the period when St. Vincent constituted its own government. (CO260/1 starts in 1776 and CO260/22, for example, features papers from 1807.) A number of War Office files are relevant, including WO1/82-86 covering the Second Carib War and its aftermath. The Treasury and the Admiralty also preserve relevant material (T1/500, for example, contains Sir William Young's claim for expenses as a land commissioner and ADM51/1226 is the log of HMS *Experiment* which carried the Caribs to Roatán).

The Centre des Archives d'Outre-Mer in Aix-en-Provence contains archives relative to France's colonial empire. Of particular interest is the sub-series F3/58 compiled by Moreau de Saint-Méry as well as the series C10 D2, both of which contain documents relative to the periods of French rule in St. Vincent.

The National Archives in Kingstown, St. Vincent, lack original documents from the eighteenth-century colonial period but have photocopies of a few relevant historical papers in addition to some modern writings, including doctoral dissertations.

Translations from French and Spanish are my own except where the footnotes indicate an existing translation as the source. Proper names occur in a wide variety of spellings. I have generally used what I take to be the most commonly used forms.

Abercromby, James (1861), *Lieutenant-General Sir Ralph Abercromby KB, 1793-1801, A Memoir by his Son*, Edinburgh: Edmonston & Douglas

Adams, Edgar (2002), *People on the Move*, Kingstown

Adams, Edgar (2007), *Saint Vincent in the History of the Carib Nation 1625-1797*, Kingstown

Allaire, Louis (1980), "On the Historicity of Carib Migrations in the

Lesser Antilles" *American Antiquity* 45:238-45

Anderson, Alexander (1983), *Alexander Anderson's Geography and History of St. Vincent, West Indies*, London: Linnaean Society

Anderson, Alexander (n.d.), Manuscripts held by Linnaean Society, London

Anderson, James [sic] (1903), "An Account of Morne Garou…" *Philosophical Transactions*, The Royal Society, vol 200, part I

Anderson, Mark (2009), *Black and Indigenous: Garifuna Activism and Consumer Culture in Honduras*, Minneapolis: University of Minnesota Press

Arens, W (1979), *The Man-Eating Myth*, London: Oxford University Press

Authentic Papers relative to the Expedition against the Charibbs and the Sale of Lands in the Island of St. Vincent (1773), London: J Almon

Avila, Tomás Alberto, ed. (2009), *Black Caribs – Garifuna: Saint Vincent' Exiled People and the Origin of the Garifuna*, Providence, RI: Milenio Associates

Bateman, Rebecca, B. (1990), "Africans and Indians: A Comparative Study of the Black Carib and Black Seminole" in *Ethnohistory Vol 37*

Bayley, FWN (1830), *Four Years' Residence in the West Indies*, London: William Kidd

Beauçage, Pierre and Samson, Marcel, (1967), *Historia del Pueblo Garífuna y su Llegada a Honduras en 1796*, Tegucigalpa

Beckles, Hilary (1983), *European Settlement and Rivalry 1492-1792*, Kingston, Jamaica and London: Heinemann

Bertilson, Kathryn (1989), *Introducción al Idioma Garífuna*, Tegucigalpa: Cuerpo de Paz Honduras

Boucher, Philip P (1992), *Cannibal Encounters: European and Island Caribs 1492-1763*, Baltimore: Johns Hopkins University Press

Breen, Henry Hegart (1876), *Warrawarra, the Carib Chief. A Tale of 1770*, London: Tinsley Brothers

Breton, Raymond (1877), *Grammaire caraibe composée par le P. R. Breton, suivie du Catéchisme caraibe*, Paris: Leclerc

Breton, Raymond (1978), *Relation de l'ile de la Guadeloupe*, Basse-Terre: Société d'histoire de la Guadeloupe

Breton, Raymond (1999), *Dictionnaire Caraïbe-Français*, Paris: Karthala

Buckley, Roger N (1975), *The Early History of the West India Regiments 1795-1815*, McGill University

Bullen, Ripley P (1972), *Archaeological Investigations on St. Vincent and the Grenadines, West Indies*, Springfield, Vermont: William L Bryant Foundation

Byres, John (1777), *References to the Plan of the Island of St. Vincent, as surveyed from the year 1765 to 1773*, London

Calendar of State Papers, Colonial Series (44 vols) (1574-1720), London: Her Majesty's Stationery Office (1860-1969)

Caulfield, Col JEWS (1899), *One Hundred Years' History of the 2nd Batt West Indies Regiment from date of raising 1785 to 1898*, London: Forster Groom & Co

Cayetano, E Roy (2005), *The People's Garifuna Dictionary*, Belmopan: National Garifuna Council of Belize

Chisholm, C (1801), *An Essay on the Malignant Pestilential Fever, introduced into the West Indian Islands from Boullam, on the coast of Guinea, as it appeared in 1793, 1794, 1795, and 1796* ... Second edition, etc., London: J Mawman

Clark James (1797), *A Treatise on the Yellow Fever, as it appeared in the Island of Dominica in the years 1793-4-5-6*, London: J Murray & S Highley

Clodoré, Jean de (1671), *Relation de l'Amerique, by V.J.C.S.D*, Paris

Cobbett, William (1813), *Parliamentary History of England*, Vol 17 1771-74, London: Bagshaw

Coelho, Ruy Galvão de Andrade (1995), *Los Negros Caribes de Honduras* (2nd ed.), Tegucigalpa: Guaymuras

Cohen, JM, ed. (1969), *Christopher Columbus: The Four Voyages*, London: Penguin

Coke, Thomas (1787), *The Case of the Caribbs in St. Vincent's*, London

Coke, Thomas (1808-11), *A History of the West Indies*, Liverpool: Nuttall, Fisher & Dixon

Craton, Michael (1982), *Testing the Chains*, Ithaca and London: Cornell University Press,

Craton, Michael, in Okihiro, Gary Y, ed. (1986), *In Resistance*, London: University of Massachusetts Press

Craton, Michael (1996), "The Black Caribs of St. Vincent: A Re-evaluation" in Paquette, Robert L, and Engerman, Stanley L, *The Lesser Antilles in the Age of European Expansionism*, Gainesville: University Press of Florida

Crawford, MH (1984), "The Anthropological Genetics of the Black

Caribs (Garifuna) of Central America and the Caribbean" *Yearbook of Physical Anthropology 26*

Crouch, Nathaniel (1685), *The English Empire in America*, London

Davidson, George (1787), *The Copy of a Letter from a Gentleman in the Island of St. Vincent*, London

De Poyen, Colonel H (1896), *Les Guerres des Antilles de 1793 à 1815*, Paris, Nancy

Dickinson, N, *History of the Causes of a Malignant Pestilential Disease, introduced into the island of Baliseau, by the Black Charaibs from Saint Vincent*, 1797. National Archives, WO1/82

Duffy, Michael (1987), *Soldiers, Sugar, and Seapower: The British Expeditions to the West Indies and the War against Revolutionary France*, Oxford: Clarendon Press

Edwards, Bryan (1818-19), *The History, Civil and Commercial, of the British Colonies in the West Indies*, 3rd ed., London

England, Sarah (2006), *Afro Central Americans in New York City: Garifuna Tales of Transnational Movements in Racialized Space*, Gainesville: University Press of Florida

Fabel, Robin FA (2000), *Colonial Challenges, Britons, Native Americans, and Caribs 1759-1775*, Gainesville: University Press of Florida

Fergusson, DGN (1990), *The Historical Development of the Black Caribs of St. Vincent 1500C-1800*, Polytechnic of North London

Fergusson, DGN (1997), *Sir William Young and the Black Caribs of St. Vincent*, Polytechnic of North London

Fraser, Adrian (2002), Chatoyer (Chatawae), *First National Hero of St. Vincent and the Grenadines*, St. Vincent: Galaxy Print

Frederick, Hilary (1982), *The Caribs and their Colonizers*, London: EA-FORD

García Granados, Miguel (1952), *Memorias*, 4 vols, Guatemala: Ministerio de Educación Pública

Gearing, Margaret Jean (1988), *The Reproduction of Labor in a Migration Society: Gender, Kinship and Household in St. Vincent, West Indies*, University of Florida

González, Nancie L. (1983), "New evidence on the origins of the Black Carib, with thoughts on the meaning of tradition" in *New West Indian Guide/ Nieuwe West-Indische Gids 57*, no: 3/4, Leiden, pp143-172

González, Nancie L (1988), *Sojourners of the Caribbean: Ethnogenesis and Ethnohistory of the Garifuna*, Urbana and Chicago: University of Illinois Press

Grove, Richard H (1995), *Green Imperialism: Colonial Expansion, Tropical Island Edens and the Origins of Environmentalism*, 1600-1800, Cambridge: Cambridge University Press

Gullick, CJMR (1976), *Exiled from St. Vincent*, Malta

Gullick, CJMR (1978), "The Ecological Background to the Carib Wars" *Journal of Belizean Affairs* 6: 51-60

Gullick, CJMR (1979), "The Black Caribs in St. Vincent: The Carib War and Aftermath" *Actes du 42e Congrès International des Americanistes* 6: 451-59, Paris

Gullick, CJMR (1985), *Myths of a Minority, the Changing Traditions of the Vincentian Caribs*, Assen: Gorcum

Hamshere, Cyril (1972), *The British in the Caribbean*, London: Weidenfeld and Nicolson

Harburn, Dr. Todd E, and Durham, Rodger (2002), *"A Vindication of My Conduct" The General Court-Martial of Lieutenant Colonel George Etherington of the 60th or Royal American Regiment*, Maryland: Bowie

Hawtayne, GH (1886), "Remarks on the Caribs" *Journal of the Anthropological Institute of Great Britain and Ireland*, 16:196-98

Hulme, Peter (1986), *Colonial Encounters*, London: Methuen

Hulme, Peter, and Whitehead, Neil L, eds. (1992), *Wild Majesty, Encounters with Caribs from Columbus to the Present Day*, Oxford: Clarendon Press

Hulme, Peter (2003), "Black, Yellow, and White on St. Vincent: Moreau de Jonnès's Carib Ethnography" in *The Global Eighteenth Century*, ed. Felicity A. Nussbaum, Baltimore: Johns Hopkins University Press, pp182-194

Hulme, Peter (2006), "French Accounts of the Vincentian Caribs" in Palacio, Joseph O, ed., *The Garifuna A Nation Across Borders*, 2nd ed., Benque Viejo del Carmen, Belize: Cubola

Joseph, EL (1838), *Warner Arundell, the Adventures of a Creole*, London

Journal of the Commissioners for Trade and Plantations (14 vols) (1704-1782), Great Britain: Board of Trade

Kerns, Virginia (1983), *Women and the Ancestors: Black Carib Kinship and Ritual*, Urbana: University of Illinois Press

Kiple, Kenneth F, and Ornelas, Kriemhild C (1996), "After the Encounter: Disease and Demographics in the Lesser Antilles" in Paquette, Robert L, and Engerman, Stanley L, *The Lesser Antilles in the Age of European Expansionism*, Gainesville: University Press of Florida

Kirby, IAE and Martin, CI (2004), *The Rise and Fall of the Black Caribs (Garifuna)* 4th ed., Toronto: Cybercom

Labat, Jean-Baptiste (1931), *The Memoirs of Père Labat, 1693-1705*, London: Constable

Laborde, Sieur de (1712), *Voyage dans L'Amerique*, Paris

Lafleur, Gérard (1992), *Les Caraïbes des Petites Antilles*, Paris: Karthala ·

Lafleur, Gérard (1993), "The Passing of a Nation: the Carib Indians in the Lesser Antilles" in *Amerindians Africans Americans*, Mona, Jamaica: Department of History, University of West Indies

Le Breton, Adrien (1998), *Historic account of Saint Vincent, the Indian Youroumaÿn, the island of the Karaÿbes*, Mayreau: Mayreau Environmental Development Organization

Lee, William (1869), *Daniel Defoe, His Life and Newly Discovered Writings*, Vol II, London: JC Hotten

Marshall, Bernard (1973), "The Black Caribs - Native Resistance to British Penetration into the Windward Side of St. Vincent, 1763-1773", *Caribbean Quarterly* 19

Miller, David Lawrence (1979), *The European Impact on St. Vincent 1600-1763*, Milwaukee: University of Wisconsin

Montagu, John (1725), *A Relation of the late intended settlement of the Islands of St. Lucia and St. Vincent, in America*, London: J Peele

Moreau de Jonnès, Alexandre (1858), *Aventures de guerre au temps de la république et du consulat*, 2 Vols, Paris: Pagnerre

Moreau de Jonnès (1929), *Adventures in the Revolution and under the Consulate*, trans. C Hammond; Intro by the Hon Sir John Fortescue, London: Peter Davies

Morris, Valentine (1787), *A Narrative of the official conduct of V. Morris Esq*, London

Niddrie, DL (1966), "Eighteenth-century settlement in the British Caribbean" *Transactions of the Institute of British Geographers*, No 40

Oldmixon, John (1742), *The British Empire in America*, London: J Brotherton

Pagden, Anthony (1995), *Lords of all the World: Ideologies of Empire in Spain, Britain and France c.1500-c.1800*, New Haven and London: Yale University Press

Palacio, Joseph O, ed. (2006), *The Garifuna: A Nation Across Borders*, 2nd ed., Benque del Viejo, Belize: Cubola

Pelleprat, Pierre (1857), "Relation des missions des PP. de la Compagnie de Jesus dans les Isles, et dans la terre ferme de l'Amerique Meridionale. Avec une introduction à la langue des Galibis, sauvages de la terre ferme de l'Amerique" in *Jesuits, Voyages et Travaux des Missionnaires de la compagnie de Jésus*, Paris

Pitman, Frank Wesley (1967), *Development of the British West Indies 1700-1763*, London: Frank Cass

Pritchard, James (2004), *In Search of Empire: The French in the Americas 1670-1730*, Cambridge, New York: Cambridge University Press

Rennard, Abbé Joseph (1929), *Les Caraïbes de Guadeloupe (1635-1656), Histoire des vingt premières années de la Colonisation de la Guadeloupe d'après la relation du RP Breton*, Paris

Rennard, J (1935), *Baas, Blénac, ou les Antilles Françaises au XVII siecle*, Thonon-les-Bains

Rey, Nicolas (2005), *Quand la révolution, aux Amériques, était nègre...: Caraïbes noirs, negros franceses, et autres oubliés de l'histoire*. Paris: Karthala

Rochefort, Charles de (1666), *The History of the Caribby-Islands*, London

Ross, Charlesworth (1970), "Caribs and Arawaks" *Caribbean Quarterly,* 16(3): 52-59

Rouse, Irving (1963), "The Carib" in *Bulletin of Bureau of American Ethnology Smithsonian Institution,* Vol 143

Scott, Julius S. (1996), "Crisscrossing Empire: Ships, Sailors, and Resistance in the Lesser Antilles in the Eighteenth Century" in Robert L. Paquette and Stanley L. Engerman, ed., *The Lesser Antilles in the Age of European Expansion,* Gainesville: University Press of Florida, pp128-43.

Shephard, Charles (1997), *An historical account of the Island of Saint Vincent,* London: Frank Cass

Southey, Thomas (1827), *Chronological History of the West Indies,* London

Spinelli, Joseph (1973), *Land Use and Population in St. Vincent, 1763-1960,* University of Florida PhD

Taylor, Douglas (1951), *The Black Carib of British Honduras,* Viking Fund Publications in Anthropology, 17, New York: Wenner-Gren Foundation.

Taylor, Douglas M (1958), "Carib, Caliban, Cannibal" *International Journal of American Linguistics 24:* 156-7

Taylor, Douglas (1977), *Languages of the West Indies,* Baltimore and London: Johns Hopkins University Press

Taylor, Douglas M, and Berend J Hoff (1980), "The Linguistic Repertory of the Island Carib in the Seventeenth Century: The Men's Language – A Carib Pidgin?" *International Journal of American Linguistics 46(4)* 301-12

Thomas, J Paul (1983), "The Caribs of St. Vincent: A study in Imperial War Maladministration 1763-73" in *The Journal of Caribbean History Vol 18:2* pp60-73

Uring, Nathaniel (1725-27), *A history of the voyages and travels of Nathaniel Uring*, London

Vázquez de Espinosa, Antonio (1968), *Description of the Indies c.1620*, Washington: Smithsonian Institution Press

Warner, Robert Stewart Aucher (1933), *Sir Thomas Warner, Pioneer of the West Indies. A chronicle of his family*, etc., London and Frome: West India Committee

Williamson, James A (1926), *The Caribbee Islands under the proprietary patents*, London: Humphrey Milford

Young, Thomas (1842), *Narrative of a Residence on the Mosquito Shore*, London

Young, Sir William [senior] (1764), *Considerations Which May Tend to Promote the Settlement of Our New West-India Colonies by Encouraging Individuals to Embark in the Undertaking*, London: J Robson

Young, Sir William (1971), *An Account of the Black Charaibs in the Island of St. Vincent's*, London: Frank Cass

Young, Sir William (1807), *The West India Commonplace Book*, London

Index

THE BLACK CARIB WARS

1-8, 21-36, *200n*; appearance 4-5; arms 6-7, 36, 44; attachment to French 37-38, 201n; boats 7; cannibalism 23-24; cassava 5-6, 25; chiefs 4, 6, 32, 38; children 3, 4, 6; conflict with English 27, 32, 33, 34-35, 36-37; conflict with French 25-27, 29-30; diet 5-6; drinking 6; fishing 5; head deformation 5; houses 4; in modern St. Vincent 17; language vi, 17; longevity 4; music 5, 6; name vi; origins 7-8; political organization 3, 204n; provisions 5; raids 6, 7; religion 18, 28-31, *199n*; slaves 7, 11; spirit of independence 3; treaties 31-33, 35; warfare 6-7, 26-27, 36; weapons 6-7; women 4, 5, 6, 7, 8, 24 see also Yellow Caribs, Black Caribs

Caylus, Marquis de 46, 47, 50,

Chateaubelair 29, 46, 58, 65, 75, 79, 130, 133, 134, 138, 139, 145

Chatoyer iii, iv, vi, 59, 60-62, 63, 64, 66, 68-69, 75, 82, 87, 94, 95, 96, 97, 101, 102, 105, 107, 113, 114, 116, 118, 120, 121, 122, 123, 127, 129, 130, 131, 132, 133, 134, 135-136, 137, 139, 146, 170, 172, 173, 180, 181, *202n, 204n, 206n, 208n, 209n, 211n, 212n, 213n, 214n, 217n*; appearance 60-62; his children 120, 122, 123, 137, 155, 156, 157, 158, 166, 181

Coke, Thomas 112, 113-114, 122-123, 143

Colonarie 78, 81, 97, 100, 118, 124, 125, 156, 157

Columbus, Christopher vi, 11, 23

Commission for the Sale of Lands in the Ceded Islands 51, 52, 53, 54, 55-57, 58-59, 62-63, 64, 65, 68, 69-70, 71, 102, 103, 105, *202n, 203n*

cotton 5, 12, 43, 46, 95, 124, *216n*

Coubamarou 65, 81, 186

Crowe, Governor Mitford 37, 38

Cuba v, 23, 51

Dalrymple, General William 71, 74, 75, 76-77, 78, 81, 82, 83, 93, 185, *205n*

Davidson, George 110-114, 195

Defoe, Daniel vi, 23, 39, 119, 168

disease (see also yellow fever) v, 10, 15-16, 17, 23, 27, 76, 82, 149, 159-163, 165, 216-*217n*

Dominica 3, 4, 11, 12, 14, 25, 26, 27, 30, Dorsetshire Hill iii, 101, 119, 127, 133, 134, 136, 137, 138, 142, 147, 151, 180, *212n*

Dumontet (governor) 103, 104, 105

Duplessis (governor) 105-107

Durumain, Chevalier 101-102

Dutch 9, 22, 25, 26, 32, 34

Du Tertre, Jean Baptiste 3, 12, 31, *197n, 198n*

Dutton, Governor Sir Richard 32, 36

Du Vallée 107, 116, 122, 123-124, 129, 131, 133, 136-137, 139, 140, 141, 146, 153, 158, 166, 170, 172, *204n, 213n, 214n, 217n, 218n*

English (see also Caribs, conflict with English) 11, 23, 25-26, 31-32

Ennery, Count d' 63, 65-66, 76

Esnambuc, Belain d' 25

Estaing, Count d' 97, 99

Etherington, Lieutenant-Colonel George 79, 93-94, 100, 101, 102, 168, *206n, 207n, 208n*

Fancy 180, *219n*

Fénélon, Marquis de 54

First Carib War 71-83

Fitzmaurice, Lieutenant Governor Ulysses 66, 194

French *passim* (see also Black Caribs, attachment to French, conflict with French; Caribs, attachment to French, conflict with French; Yellow Caribs, relations with French) language 45, 113, 124, 155, *210n*; rule in St Vincent (1779-1783) 103-108, 115; seizure of St Vincent (1779) 95-97, 98-102

Galibis 7

Garifuna (people) 3-4, 16-17, 168, 178-180; language iii, iv, 8, 179, 180, *198n*

Georgetown 172

Graham, General 157

Grand Baleine 61, 123

Grand Sable 58, 59, 61, 62, 63, 69, 75, 78, 79, 83, 96, 98, 99, 100, 114, 121, 122, 123, 131, 132, 144, 156, 157, 169, 172, 186, *204n, 218n*

Greiggs 180, *219n*

Grenada 3, 26, 29, 34, 35, 51, 52, 55, 66, 67, 68, 77, 87, 107, 117, 131, 134, 138, 144, 148, 151, 165, 193; governor of 46, 70, 71

Grenadines 1, 8, 9, 46, 69, 117, 159, 180

Guadeloupe 3, 9, 24, 26, 27, 33, 35, 51, 129, 131, 141, 142, *214n*